Infrastructure Financing

Infrastructure Financing
Trends, Challenges and Experiences

Edited by
Garimella G K Murthy

2010

Icfai Books
The Icfai University Press

INFRASTRUCTURE FINANCING – TRENDS, CHALLENGES AND EXPERIENCES

Editor: Garimella G K Murthy

First Edition: 2010
Printed in India

Published by

The Icfai University Press
52, Nagarjuna Hills, Punjagutta
Hyderabad, India – 500 082
Phone: (+91) (040) 23430–368, 369, 370, 372, 373, 374
Fax: (+91) (040) 23352521, 23435386
E-mail: info@icfaibooks.com, icfaibooks@icfai.org, ssd@icfai.org

ISBN: 9788131408094

Editorial Team: Usha N Raghunandan and Sreedar S
Quality Support: V Sandhya Srikanth and J K Vadana

Contents

Section II

A Sectoral Overview

Section III

Experiences

Overview

Development of infrastructure provides vital support to the productive sector and improves the overall standard of an economy. Creation of such an infrastructure and its development require a huge investment and also call for a proper financing system for effective implementation of the projects. Infrastructure financing is regarded as the lifeline of a nation in view of its significance in economic growth and sophistication of a country. With the upswing of economic reforms process and globalisation effects, umpteen avenues are there for infrastructure financing not only from sources within the country, but from outside too. There are several dimensions of infrastructure financing and the dynamics of various avenues of financing infrastructure need critical appreciation and appraisal by examining various factors.

Large infrastructure projects are unique as they require huge capital investment, apart from taking long years for completion. Pooling up of such huge resources for any country is fraught with several constraints. The lack of long-term debt seems to be the core issue faced by the infrastructure sector. This is the main factor for India's trailing behind other developed nations all these years. Till 1990s, infrastructure portfolio was held in the public sector, and governments could not earmark adequate funds for this sector at the cost of other priority heads of expenditure. Hence, the progress of infrastructure projects remained tardy. It is only after the advent of economic reforms, infrastructure development is gaining momentum, for the reforms enabled sizeable inflow of investments into the sector by various modes. Nevertheless, the needed thrust in this regard is yet to come.

During the last one decade and odd, infrastructure in India is seeing several strides, with many projects having been undertaken with public private participation. While a very large amount of funds is locked up in the projects (which are either completed, or in the process of completion), new projects are also in the offing somewhere or the other. It is, in this context, essential that these huge projects need effective monitoring and control in terms of their performance. Such a measure, which is crucial for the financial structuring and inflow of funds, also boosts the confidence of investors. When investors acquire confidence about their investments, further flow of funds becomes easy.

As far as India is concerned, many infrastructure projects like private airports, water projects, power projects, telecom projects and transportation projects – are taken up on hand, which mostly revolve around creation of urban infrastructure. While economists always hold that India's economy is mostly rural-centric, the issue relating to Rural Infrastructure Development is yet to be addressed properly and effectively. Infrastructure projects are tangible assets to any nation. Several concepts like public private partnership in financing infrastructure have emerged and are getting established over the years, for the simple reason that governments are unable to take care of infrastructure funding needs due to budgetary constraints. Modern project finance and global project finance markets are in contrast with conventional corporate financing. Hence, financing of such large infrastructure projects entails different approaches in different countries. Financing infrastructure calls for many innovations also, considering these challenges.

This book "**Infrastructure Financing – Trends, Challenges and Experiences**" attempts to capture the contemporary issues and challenges of infrastructure financing in India and other countries. It further aims to present a critical view of the changing dynamics of infrastructure financing. This book comprises three sections. The first section consisting of 7 articles presents an overall picture of the challenges and trends of infrastructure financing. The second section comprising 6 articles presents a sectoral overview of financing of infrastructure, covering sectors like renewable energy, power, telecommunications, water, airports, transportation projects. This section amply discusses the current trend of financing infrastructure through public private partnership. The third section comprising 5 articles delves on Indian and global cases and experiences relating to infrastructure financing of a few select projects.

Section I: Challenges and Trends

Garimella G K Murthy in the first article titled "**Infrastructure Financing – Issues and Challenges**", furnishes an account of the issues in financing infrastructure in the context of the present Indian economy and an overview of the challenges associated with it. Infrastructure is highly vulnerable to the changes in social and macroeconomic environment, which can greatly impact the viability of the projects involved. Even though the flow of investments for infrastructure sector has greatly improved since a decade, there are many challenges that encounter infrastructure financing in the present system. Vulnerable among the challenges are tariff regulations posing special challenges for private investment, as also the various risks associated with infrastructure projects, which call for complex risk mitigation arrangements. Apart from these financial and managerial aspects and risks, there are other challenges which include issues of human rights violation, impact on environment and those related to culture, flora and fauna, which are more of a social nature than financial, but relevant to mega projects. The article concludes on the note that lack of a conducive regulatory system at present is also responsible for lack of proper financing for infrastructure in India and private investment in infrastructure not being able to fuel, stresses the need for a framework that would nurture a healthy investment climate for infrastructure.

The second article "**Public Private Partnership and Infrastructure Financing in India**" by *P Nair* and *Deepak Kumar*, explains various elements for financing, such as the systemic reduction of risk and optimal allocation of risk to each stakeholder, proper and reasonably secure ROI, development of the debt market, and the mobilization of public savings. Traditionally, the financing of infrastructure projects is the responsibility of the government. However, because of budgetary constraints and other priorities to be taken care of, governments have not been in a position to fund infrastructure development activities effectively. With the development of PPP projects in India, a new need has arisen for sophisticated financing models to suit various types of projects. This may eventually lead to a "clearing house for such projects" with standardized financial models. Ultimately, it has been understood that to bring the private sector in, and at the same time retain some control of the state, PPPs have to be accelerated. Accordingly, most financial instruments have to be tailor-made in order to suit the concept of Public-Private Partnerships. The article takes a short survey of PPP experiences in countries like Britain. Malaysia, China, etc. It also dwells upon the general criteria for infrastructure projects and other finance models like take-out finance, FDI and FII financing.

The third article "**Infrastructure Financing – Current Scenario**" by *Sanjeev Kumar*, discusses the current scenario of infrastructure financing in India, besides touching upon aspects like recent changes, investment requirements of infrastructure projects, pattern of investments, etc. Over the past few years, India has seen a tremendous development in the infrastructure. The change in the trend has resulted from reforms in various infrastructure sectors. In the budget proposal for the fiscal 2005-2006, the government has taken various steps to develop infrastructure. Rural telecommunications has been given a boost by the allocation of Rs.1,200 crores. The National Highway Development Program (NHDP) has been provided Rs.1,400 cr for Golden Quadrilateral in 2005-06 for the development of 4000 km of four-lane highway. The total outlay for National Highway Development has increased from Rs.6,514 cr in 2004-05 to Rs 9,320 cr in 2005-06. For electrification in rural areas, the government has made a provision of Rs.1,100 cr this year to cover 1.25 lakh villages in five years. Further, for Indira Awas Yojana, the allocation has been increased from Rs.2,500 cr in the current year to Rs.2,750 cr in Budget Estimate (BE) 2005-06. Besides these measures, the government has also recently come up with a scheme, known as the Scheme for Financial Support to Public Private Partnerships (PPPs) in Infrastructure, for providing financial support in order to boost the private-public participation in infrastructure.

Infrastructure assumed a commercial character and emerged as an income generating activity in the wake of globalisation, which also brought in market competitiveness. With the coming up of opportunities to finance the infrastructure projects, the private sector emerged as the champion in sourcing and pooling the means of finance, offering various financial products and services. The next article "**Models in Infrastructure Financing**" by *M Yunus,* attempts to provide insights in regard to various options of financing infrastructure and furnishes an overview of institutions involved in financing infrastructure. It furnishes a broad view of models like BOO, BOOT, BLT, BOT, relating to infrastructure financing and captures sources of funding of private sector infrastructure finance though domestics and external sources under 'Equity Finance' and 'Debt Finance' and the various players in this regard. Aspects relating to take-out financing, liquidity support, securitization, external debt financing export credit agencies, international commercial banks, international bond markets and multilateral institutions are also adequately covered in the article.

The fifth article "**Special Purpose Vehicle: Scope for Banks?**", by *Naveen Kumar,* discusses how special purpose vehicles can solve the problem of the huge demand for infrastructure finance in India, to a certain extent. It explains how banks and financial institutions can get good return at low risk by investing in SPV created by the government. If we look at any of the developed countries like America, England, Australia, Japan, Singapore and others, we find that they are essentially good at basic infrastructure and have done the basic spade work of building good roads, railways, ports, airports, power projects, communication networks etc., long back, which is the secret behind their advancement. The Special Purpose Vehicle (SPV) also called Special Purpose Entity is created for some well-defined, specific purpose whose scope is limited and focused. The Special Purpose Vehicle may be considered a corporation and is required to follow all rules and regulations laid in the Companies Act, like a company. The Special Purpose Vehicle raises funds from the market by issuing long-term debt financial instruments, say bonds, which are mostly subscribed by various banks and financial institutions, thereby playing a key role in the infrastructure development of the country, by indirectly lending to infrastructure projects by subscribing to the bonds and debentures issued by Special Purpose Vehicles. The article concludes that it promises to be an ideal mechanism to channel money to finance infrastructure projects.

While the urban infrastructure development has been pursued with great vigor, lack of such developments in the rural and semi-urban areas has been a cause for serious concern among policy makers. Accordingly, the authorities have been looking for effective measures to develop rural infrastructure, without which, the rapid growth of the rural economy would not be possible. The sixth article titled "**Rural Infrastructure Development Fund – Empowering Projects**" by *Deepak Kumar,* talks about how the rural infrastructure sector has been taken care of by the Rural Infrastructure Development Fund (RIDF). This is one of the financing models that have been successful in India, as in this case, the projects are appraised, monitored and implemented by NABARD in consultation with the state governments. The Rural Infrastructure Development Fund is like a Special Purpose Vehicle (SPV) for creating and strengthening rural infrastructure, whose major aim is developing rural infrastructure, generating additional employment opportunities and improving the quality of life of the rural people. The objectives of the RIDF are multidimensional and it focuses on how to accelerate the overall growth rate of the Indian economy by taking care of building rural infrastructure and providing better amenities. The main aim of RIDF is to finance rural infrastructure projects, such as rural roads, water harvesting systems, forest development, plantation and horticulture, developing market yards, drainage system, rural educational institutes, village knowledge centers, soil conservation, protection from flood, etc.

The seventh article "**The Community Led Infrastructure Finance Facility (CLIFF)**" by *Ian Morris* and *Malcolm Jack,* discusses in detail CLIFF, how it operates, its financial products, its sources of funding, its achievements and the significance of community capacity. Poverty is becoming increasingly 'urbanised' – between 2000 and 2030, the urban areas of the less developed regions will absorb 95 per cent of the world's population growth. At least 900 million people live in slums, and the UN estimates that as many as 55% of the world's poor currently live in urban areas. Effective urban development strategies can contribute to reducing the global incidence of poverty and to achieving the Millennium Development Goals and it has been identified that "funding to finance community-based slum upgrading" is a 'Quick-Win' solution to the situation. The Community Led Infrastructure Finance Facility (CLIFF) is distinctly different from the Municipal Development Fund mechanisms as it provides venture capital and other financial products directly to organisations of the urban poor, rather than to the government, to support community-led slum upgrading schemes conceived in partnership with city authorities. Community involvement is vital if slum development is to be locally appropriate, effective and sustainable, in addition to the human rights argument for doing so and going by the achievements of CLIFF till date, it could well assume a much greater importance in community infrastructure financing in the days to come.

Section II: A Sectoral Overview

The first article in this section **"Financing of Renewable Energies"** is by *Usha N Raghunandan* describes how renewable energies are different in comparison to the conventional energy projects and their impact on their financing needs and ability to attract finance. It also discusses various types of financing instruments used for financing renewable energy, while highlighting the barriers and financing gaps that make funding difficult. The role of Renewable Energy (RE) is of utmost importance towards alleviating adverse global climate change, addressing the regional and local environmental concerns, reducing poverty and increasing energy security. To enable renewable energies achieve their true market potential, financial instruments and policy frameworks that can assure the financiers and provide incentives to shift investments away from carbon-emitting conventional technologies to large-scale investment in clean energy systems are essential. This current momentum of renewable energy development, together with the geographic advantage of availability of resources, can provide a strategic advantage in developing renewable energy, provided India gears up for the challenge by making available more instruments for financing the renewable energy. It also provides useful insights into the role of Ministry of Environment and Forests, India and its guidelines in respect of renewable energy in India; financing support provided by IREDA towards promoting renewable energy in India besides discussing aspects like Clean Development Mechanism, Carbon Credits and Kyoto protocol, in brief.

The ninth article **"Financing of Power Projects"** is by *Dr. M V S Birinchi.* It provides insights into the various dimensions of financing power projects with a broader focus. It covers the various issues, challenges, perspectives relating to financing power projects in contemporary times, with particular reference to the Indian context. The article, at the outset, unveils the Power Scenario of India touching on the critical aspect of peak power shortage in the existing (10th Plan) and the 11th plan period and resultant picture of energy deficit. The article discusses certain important features of National Power

Policy and E-Act 2003 provisions related to delicensing of generation of power, proposed capacity additions—fuel based projections, which help in paving way for greater thrust in financing power projects. The article discusses adequately the parameters and tools like debt equity ratios in the context of financing power projects, the scenario in respect of institutional funding, debt market, All India Financial Institutions (AIFIs), External Commercial Borrowings (ECB) market and equity participation. The article suggests that the current scenario in regard to power projects call for new initiatives altogether. One such initiative could be that dividend during construction can be capitalised towards equity, with a view to augmenting the capital for the project. The article concludes on a note that the future of power sector financing depends greatly on the ability to rope in retail investors in equity and debt markets to meet the growing needs of power generation in the country.

Telecom sector has gained importance in recent years with rapid developments in information technology. The government has realised the need to encourage private investment by providing a competitive environment. The share of communications in central plan outlay has risen from 5.1% in 1999-2000 to 7.2% in 2004-05. This throws open a big opportunity for investments in this sector. Presently, the major domestic private players are Bharti Televentures, Reliance and TATA group. The Universal Service Obligation (USO) fund – imposes 5% of adjusted gross revenues of telecom companies. BSNL plans to invest Rs.2000 cr for its broadband infrastructure. Bharti, Airtel and BSNL are planning to invest in the telecom sector from their surplus revenues. Reliance plans to raise $ 1 bn. through FCCBs. The ceiling on foreign direct investment in the telecom sector has been hiked from 49% to 74%. DoT has retained authority to restrict licenses in sensitive areas in view of security concerns. The share of FDIs in telecommunication sector has risen from 4.39% in 2003-04 to 12.28% in 2005-06. The investment opportunity amounting to $22 billion is across many sectors – Telecom services and internet software, broadband and DTH services telecom software etc. This growing potential has attracted leading European banks to commit over Rs.2000 cr for infrastructure development in telecom sector. The tenth article "**Infrastructure Investment in Indian Telecom Sector**" by *Kalyani Rampilla* presents an overview of trends of investments in telecom sector.

The next article "**The Financing of Water Projects: An Overview**" is by *Deepak Kumar.* It discusses a few water projects drawn from India and overseas. These could have never been successful without involving the private sector and, of course, the role of different international agencies like USAID, the World Bank, UNDP and the World Economic Forum. The article also covers aspects like types of financing water projects and furnishes handful of examples of water projects financed in India. Financing water projects had always been a Herculean task till the private sector came into the picture. The need to have private participation arises from the need to leverage limited government funding, while taking advantage of the efficiencies of the private sector management. Involving private sector in water projects is not an easy task, in view of the risks associated therewith, such as regulation, stability of economy, growth prospects and developmental risks. As far as operational risk is concerned, the main risk is how to get the tariffs, as the private sector is very much concerned of this. The tariff must be transparent and should protect commercial interests of private investors. This paper concludes that the record of stakeholders in the water sector has not been particularly satisfactory as on date, due to the tendency to put the developed country methodologies into practice in developing countries and thus, need an integrated coordination among themselves.

The twelfth article "**Airport Privatization and Financing: Experiences from Countries and Lessons for India**", is by *Padmalatha Suresh.* It discusses the airport infrastructure privatization and financing, which is promising to be a global mega trend. It discusses the financial structure of the privatized airports, illustrating the financial structure of the privatized airports around the world. It says that the listed airports were financed by a combination of debt, equity (private investors) and government stake in the proportion of 33:50:17. The unlisted airports appeared to take on more financial risk than their listed counterparts, as evidenced by their leverage ratios, substantially higher than the average for listed airports. With the opening up of the civil aviation sector in India, the financial markets and banking sector in particular, should gear up to assess risks unique to airport projects and finance the projects through innovative instruments. Growth in 'high risk-high return' financing has to be supported by a strong and well-structured securitisation framework. The article furnishes a general illustration that the participation of the private sector in funding airport infrastructure has increased the economy substantially. Examples of privatization of the British Airport Authority, Sydney's Kingsford Smith Airport, Auckland International Airport of New Zealand, provide insights into the pattern of financing of the airport infrastructure with private participation.

The thirteenth article "**Private Sector Participation in Transport Infrastructure Development**" by *Pradeepta Kumar Samanta,* highlights the increasing role of private players in financing the development of transport sector in the global arena and the scope for its participation in the port sector in India. Transport system is considered the artery and the nerve, which connect the entire economy of the country. An efficient transport system is the prerequisite for attaining higher level of economic growth. The growing manufacturing sector in India is highly dependent on the transport sector for attracting FDI as well as global market players. The article further brings to light that, development of new infrastructure assets through private rather than public financing for a country, including benefits, such as preserving the government's borrowing capacity is expected to result in lower costs and higher operating efficiency, flowing from the stronger commercial disciplines operating in private firms. In most of the developing countries, where the public sector infrastructure providers have a poor track-record in operating efficiency, participation of private sector in infrastructure can help improve the existing situation to a great extent.

Section III: Experiences

This case **"The Road from Mumbai to Pune"** by *Jyoti Ahluwalia* and *Swapna Gopalan,* evokes thoughts of how the users and the government have to perceive the operational success of infrastructure projects, so as to assure uninterrupted inflows of revenues to meet the committed financial obligations of the project. The Mumbai-Pune Expressway is the country's first expressway project, with massive investment connecting two vibrant commercial hubs—Mumbai and Pune—covering 94 km, and built according to global standards. The Rs.1630 cr Expressway project was planned with a 60:40 debt equity ratio; but after the change of government in 1998, the new government withheld the equity contribution forcing MSRDC to finance the project with debt alone. In January 1998, MSRDC issued Rs.500 cr bonds with a proposal to raise a similar amount through the green-shoe option and successfully raised Rs.1,300 cr through private placements. MSRDC offered 14% for taxable bonds and 11.5% for tax-free bonds for seven-year resources. However, after the Expressway was fully operational, the revenue generated from the tolls was not sufficient to pay off the debt. The idea of paying tolls did not go down too well with the Indian public, especially the truck drivers, who continued to use the parallel non-tolled NH4. In such a worsening financial situation, MSRDC decided to sell the entire stretch of 95 kms of the Mumbai-Pune Expressway. To make the project viable for the private operator, it added the Mumbai-Pune section of NH4 to the offer. This case thus illustrates how significant is the financial arrangements for infrastructure projects and how unforeseen risks, in this case, political risks, can affect the successful operation of the projects after completion. It also points out the fact that the government requires a paradigm shift in the perceptions towards 'the user pays concept' for providing funds for infrastructure.

It is vital for the European transport sector to decide the suitable user charges for transport sectors so that it can provide new and consistent ways of financing, not only for maintaining the existing infrastructure but also for building new infrastructure so as to promote its economic growth. This case "**Fair Payment for Infrastructure Use: A Phased Approach to a Common Transport Infrastructure Charging Framework in the EU**", by *Deepak Kumar,* discusses how the user charges can influence the flow of investments from the private investors for infrastructure development taking the example of transport sector in the European Union. It also explains how user charges can be developed as a means of raising funds to finance new projects, apart from the maintenance of the existing projects. The case points out that direct charging of the traffic may be the best means of promoting PPPs, as this encourages private parties to invest more in the infrastructure projects. It also explains in brief the concept of 'Community Approach to infrastructure charging, whose main aim is to take exact user charges for infrastructure usage, which would provide greater efficiency in financing for development and maintenance of infrastructure'.

The article titled "**Renewing Australia's Infrastructure**" by *Lindsay Tanner M P,* discusses the impediments for infrastructure development and funding in Australia, its infrastructure investment climate, besides referring to some of the avenues of infrastructure finance in Australia. Planning and funding infrastructure has always been a difficult task, owing to its dependence on forecasting future use, and often involves very large financial commitments. The overall picture of the physical state of Australia's infrastructure is mixed, suggesting that there is no immediate crisis, but there is a fairly urgent need to act so as to ensure that no future crisis eventuates. Australia has had a lengthy history of inappropriate infrastructure investment, driven by short-term political considerations. Although this is, perhaps, less of a problem than it was in the past, there are still instances of poorly directed investment, more designed to build political support than economic development. Though the emergence of specific purpose vehicles like PPPs has changed infrastructure investment in Australia, the need for government borrowing is still substantial, for the recent cycle of fiscal consolidation has reached a point where refusal to borrow for infrastructure investment is economically counter-productive.

Sustained, rapid population growth and a variety of fiscal constraints have challenged the ability of California's state and local governments to provide and maintain adequate levels of civil infrastructure that necessitated Governor's proposing a ten-year program to revitalize the state's infrastructure. The next case titled **"Funding Innovations for California Infrastructure: Promises and Pitfalls"** is by *Ellen Hanak* and *Kim Rueben.* It examines the infrastructure challenges facing California, the current state of infrastructure spending and the extent to which new public and private sources can be mobilized to build for the future. With a focus on two main areas of public infrastructure needs – transportation and water resources the authors point out the pitfalls of relying too heavily on additional bond financing or general-source revenues and focus on the potential for strategies, that align the benefits of new infrastructure with the costs of provision. Innovations that can raise funds while aligning the incentives of infrastructure customers with efficient use of the system should be encouraged. The article concludes on the note that by aligning costs and benefits, California can help satisfy its current and future infrastructure needs, while protecting the ability of future generations to make their own spending choices.

"Financing Strategy of the Urban Wastewater Sector in Selected Municipalities of the Sichuan Province in China" by *Sadhu Ramakrishna,* narrates the experience of china in the context of wastewater management projects. The wastewater management in most of Chinese cities was neglected until 1980s, which gave rise to a significant risk to human health and environment. During 1980-1990, it was also found that the newly built wastewater treatment plants were not being used efficiently, and there was a shortage of funds for regular operations and maintenance of these plants. This case describes the steps taken by the OECD (Organization for Economic and Cooperative Development) and the Chinese government for treatment and usage of wastewater in the urban areas of China and the issues involved in financing these projects. It also discusses the environmental condition of the Sichuan province in

China and presents an overview of various financial strategies to improve the wastewater treatment, sewage facilities and water supply networks. An analysis of various strategies brought to surface issues, like affordability that were likely to occur at some point in their execution process. Therefore, it was suggested that for the above strategies to be both socially and politically feasible, it was important to allocate some social protection budgets, in order to compensate the poor families and households for the payments they made towards water and sanitation bills.

A study of the various challenges attendant on infrastructure finance in India, as presented above, thus brings into focus the gap in the micro level dynamics of infrastructure financing. This book has attempted to capture all the relevant and contemporary aspects of infrastructure financing in India, citing examples of similar initiatives in other parts of the globe. It is hoped that this book would be able to provide insights into the dynamics of infrastructure financing in the present context of globalised economy.

SECTION I

CHALLENGES AND TRENDS

1

Infrastructure Financing – Issues and Challenges

Garimella G K Murthy

Infrastructure projects entail long gestation periods. Even though the flow of investments for infrastructure sector has greatly improved since a decade, there are many challenges that encounter the infrastructure financing in the present system. This article attempts to capture aspects like regulated tariffs, competitive bidding, public acceptance of tariffs, etc. It also provides insights into risks like market risk, payment risk, operational risk, foreign exchange risks, and regulatory and political risks and the risk mitigation measures useful to tackle these challenges. It concludes on a note that lack of a conducive regulatory system at present is also responsible for lack of proper financing for infrastructure in India and private investment in infrastructure not being able to fuel. There needs to be in place, a framework that would nurture a healthy investment climate for infrastructure.

Introduction

Infrastructure can be described as the physical framework of facilities that enables the reach of goods and services to the people in a country. It can be broadly categorized as 'Public utilities', 'Public works' and 'Other transport'. Facilities like power, telecommunications, piped water supply, sanitation and drainage fall under the category of 'Public utilities' where as the roads, major irrigation projects and canal works come under 'Public works'. Items such as urban and inter city rail systems, urban transport, ports and waterways; and roads are categorized as other transport infrastructure. Infrastructure is the key to the economic growth and a powerful tool in providing vital support to the productive sector. The general perception, that was held till a few years back, was that the government is the only institution for the allocation of non-market resources for such highly capital intensive activities. Over the years, infrastructure development in the country has been sluggish, because of the budgetary constraints of the governments and inefficiencies in handling the projects at various levels.

Financing Infrastructure

The system of managing and financing infrastructural facilities has been undergoing several changes since the mid-eighties. Public agencies are sought to be accountable for the financial viability of the projects taken up with the State support. Also, the State level organisations, responsible for providing infrastructural services in the metropolitan and other urban areas, were expected to make capital investments on their own, besides covering the operational costs for their infrastructural services. Due to the bureaucratic procedures and approaches, there have been several loose ends in the entire process, whereby the costs of borrowing have gone up significantly for all these agencies over a period. Gradually, these factors, discouraged the agencies in taking up the schemes that are socially desirable but financially unremunerative.

Infrastructure is highly vulnerable to the changes in the social and the macroeconomic environment, which can greatly impact the viability of the projects involved. Further, infrastructure projects entail long gestation periods. Financing of the infrastructure projects is fraught with heavy risks due to several factors. The regulatory compliance norms concerning the capital adequacy deters banks and financial institutions, to lock their resources in unduly long maturity ventures are prone to high degree of risks. For these reasons, banks and the financial institutions could not play a significant role in financing the infrastructure sector all these years. With a change in the approach of the banks and financial institutions in the recent times, and launch of Special Purpose Vehicles by Government, things however look up.

The Challenges

India is the fourth largest economy, in terms of Purchasing Power Parity (PPP) with a GDP growth of more than 7%. An attractive investment climate coupled with good corporate governance is central to growth and poverty reduction in an emerging economy like ours. A vibrant private sector creates jobs; provides goods and services needed to improve living standards, and contributes taxes necessary for public investment in basic amenities such as health, education, and other services. Even though the flow of investments for the infrastructure sector has greatly improved since a decade, there are many challenges that encounter the infrastructure financing in the present system. The challenges associated with the infrastructure projects are manifold, making the whole issue complex. Vulnerable among them are tariff regulations, posing special challenges for private investment, as also the various risks associated with infrastructure projects, which call for complex risk mitigation arrangements. A critical appreciation of these challenges is considered necessary to understand the dynamics of infrastructure finance.

Tariffs

Tariffs on all infrastructure projects are regulated and private operators are not free to fix or adjust tariffs at will. The tariff is fixed in advance and is adjustable over time, only in accordance with the predetermined contractual terms. Private investment can be attracted into a tariff-regulated sector, only if the investors are convinced that tariffs will be set and periodically adjusted in a manner that ensures an adequate rate of return. Equally important, the public utility character of infrastructure projects requires that the tariff to be perceived as "fair" to the consumers. This balance is not always easy to strike, and disputes over tariffs can delay the project implementation. Some of the alternative ways of fixing remunerative tariffs and the problems associated with them are discussed in the subsequent sections.

Tariffs and Competitive Bidding

Competitive bidding is an alternative approach for fixing tariffs. In this approach, technical and production characteristics relevant to the project are specified in advance, and qualified bidders are required to bid in terms of the lowest tariff for undertaking the project. These tariffs, however, need to be adjusted over time to reflect inflation, just as in the case of cost-based tariffs. The willing bidder has to specify the manner in which this will be adjusted. Transparency of bidding requires that the minimum technical requirements of the project are to be fully specified, calling for considerable homework before bids are solicited. This is the limitation so far as the competitive bidding approach is concerned.

Regulated Tariffs with Competitive Bidding

Many a time, tariffs are not determined under competitive bidding and are fixed by a regulatory or by some other specific authority. Competition, in such cases, plays the key role in selecting the private investor, whose bid is expected to be competitive in terms of the license fee, during the contract period. It can be in terms of an arrangement for sharing the revenues. Such an approach is well suited to projects in which the independent producer can directly deal with the final consumer, and where the demand forecasts enable profitable operation. This approach is ideally applicable to sectors like telecommunication and port development.

Public Acceptance of Tariffs

While any of the aforementioned methods can be used to fix tariffs to ensure adequate returns to the investors, the only difficulty is to ensure that the resulting tariffs pass through the test of public acceptance. The typical factor operating in this regard is that the private sector often expects higher tariffs over the public sector, for the simple reason that the public sector operating in roads urban services, or even power, tend to be heavily under priced due to subsidy. A shift from under priced public sector services to fully priced private sector services tend to be expensive and therefore attracts consumer resistance. To over come this challenge, the private sector can provide an additional higher quality supply source, where consumers retain a choice for continuing with the lower-quality public sector service already in existence.

Risk Involved in Infrastructure Financing

Risks associated with the projects pose another serious challenge in financing infrastructure projects and their final implementation such as market risk, operational risk, interest rate risk, payment risk, foreign exchange risk and construction risk having a direct bearing on financing infrastructure. The other risks are related to political and regulatory system. Let us take a close look at these risks, how they influence the projects, and how best these could be tackled.

Market risk concerns uncertainty in market conditions that are assumed in determining the viability of any project. An obvious example of market risk is non-fulfillment of demand projections. Investors expect that the monopoly purchaser should guarantee a minimum level of purchase, to eliminate market risk for the investor. This generally happens where an independent power producer is to sell power to one monopoly distributor. This can also be true when a water supply project has to sell water in bulk to a monopoly urban water-distributing firm. But, this is not so in the telecommunications, ports and roads where the private producer directly deals with the individual users who face competing options and the market risk is borne by the investor himself. To minimize market risks, investors are well advised to study the markets and satisfy themselves by which adequate profitability can be derived from market demand projections at feasible levels of tariffs.

Operational risk is related to the technical performance of the project during its operational phase. The performance often falls below the projected levels for a variety of reasons. Operational risk is comparatively low for infrastructure projects such as roads and power, which rely on a tested technology unlike those sectors like telecommunications, where the technology is fast changing and is untried. Operational risks can be overcome by entrusting the project to the experienced contractors and by inclusion of suitable clauses for liquidated damages, while entering into the project contracts. Another way of risk mitigation in operations is to insure against such risks, which now a days, are insurable by many insurance companies.

Interest rate risk arises because of the varying interest rates during the life of the project. Interest rate risk is crucial in infrastructure projects because of their high capital investments and long payback periods. Interest rate risk can be handled effectively by passing it on to the consumers under pass through tariffs. Alternatively, the investor himself can bear the risk by hedging the same through devices like interest caps and collars. The cost of hedging will be loaded into the project and can reflect in the tariff. But it may be noted that the feasibility to hedge interest rate risks is dependent on how sophisticated these financial markets are in this regard and also the availability of suitable hedging instruments.

Foreign exchange risks are of two types, one relating to exchange convertibility, and the other relating to the exchange rate. Exchange convertibility is an assurance for converting the revenues generated in foreign exchange in the country to make payments in any other country. Foreign exchange convertibility risk needs to be borne by the government through suitable convertibility guarantees. Exchange rate risk is caused by the fluctuations in the exchange rates resulting in large decrease in the domestic currency costs of payments denominated in foreign currency. Foreign Exchange risk is more pertinent in case of infrastructure projects, which have to heavily rely on foreign financing while their tariffs are fixed in domestic currency. It is, therefore, advisable to restrict the external financing as a measure of reducing the foreign exchange risk. But again, this depends on a healthy domestic capital market being in place in a country, which can provide adequate domestic finance for infrastructures.

Payment risk arises when investors in infrastructure would not be paid for services delivered. This however varies from sector to sector. Due to the weak financial condition of public sector utilities in developing countries, investors are concerned about payment risk. This type of risk is more common in power or water sector, rather than in sectors like telephone, road or port. Improving the financial standing and creditworthiness of the utilities seems to be the long-term solution to this problem.

Construction risk arises when any unexpected event takes place during the construction stage, resulting in cost and time overruns or performance parameters of the completed project fall short of the expectations. It is an established fact that the projects are prone to delays resulting in cost overruns due to high capital intensity and a relatively long construction period. In this way, construction risk is generally higher in sectors like power and roads than telecommunications and urban services sectors. It is to be understood that construction risk cannot be totally eliminated, but a portion of it can only be mitigated. Project sponsors can diversify the construction risk by shifting a portion of it to the contractor. This is possible through construction, engineering and procurement contracts, which contain provisions for turnkey responsibility, involving penalties for delays and shortfalls in the performance parameters.

Regulatory risk arises as all the infrastructure projects have to interface with one regulatory authority or another. Often, the tariff formulae proposed at the start of the projects assuring remunerative pricing, are declined by regulatory authorities, on the grounds that the tariff is too high. Stringent environmental restrictions on a project, during its life are also another form of regulatory risk. It is quite natural for private investors to expect firm assurances that cost increases imposed on account of regulatory action, will be offset by a corresponding adjustment in the tariff. Regulatory risk can best be handled by establishing strong and independent regulatory authority. The operations and procedures of such an authority should be transparent to the optimum within a legal framework, capable of providing investors with an effective recourse against any arbitrary action.

Political risk is the outcome of any political action upsetting the settled commercial terms of an infrastructure project. Such an event, in extreme cases, can also result in cancellation of the licenses, leading to nationalization. Political risks can partially be overcome by obtaining political risk insurance cover from multilateral organizations. These risks can also be factored into the project agreements by means of suitable clauses for compensation against arbitrary actions, and wherever justified, can refer to international arbitration. The World Bank's new partial risk guarantee instrument can be a good example in this context. This instrument covers debt service payments in case the projects are interrupted by the nonperformance of specific government obligations.

Risk Mitigation and Private Financing

All investment projects involve some risk, but infrastructure projects in developing countries are perceived as unusually vulnerable to risks, which constrains financing. Risks are perceived as high, partly because projects are undertaken not by established utility companies with strong fundamentals, but by special purpose companies executing individual projects on a build-operate-transfer or build-own-operate basis. Project financing is on a non-recourse basis (that is, lenders do not have recourse to the sponsor company, but look solely to the revenue stream of the project to meet debt service obligations). The risks associated with the revenue stream are therefore subject to scrutiny. Equity investors may be willing to accept higher levels of risk in return for higher expected returns on their equity, but lenders typically have a lower tolerance for risk and a greater need for risk mitigation mechanisms. Although governments conduct project negotiations with the sponsors, it is the lenders behind the scenes who set risk mitigation standards and determine whether projects are financeable.

Risk Mitigation Costs

Many of the risks that are associated with the private sector are equally true for the public sector projects. Often, questions are raised about private sector project costs while analyzing risk mitigation costs. In fact, such risk mitigation costs do not render them more costly against the overall economy. It is also important to appreciate that the same costs, whether explicitly mentioned or not, are incurred in respect of the public sector projects also. An improved way of managing risk lies in the explicit assignment of risk to agents, which would reduce costs. If such measures are available, banks can handle those complex measures as part of their risk management system. Banks can adopt some simplistic approaches like risk-based pricing mechanism as a parallel measure to the traditional approach, so that the difference can be compared. Such an approach by banks would be aimed at better risk sensitivity with a definite analysis for pricing the loan.

Sources and Methods of Financing

Once suitable tariff fixing mechanisms and risk mitigation structures are in place, private sector projects become financeable. At this stage, project implementation depends on the ability to develop a financing package with a mix of finance, suitable for the project. This mix varies across sectors. Telecommunication projects, which face relatively high market risks, may require a relatively low debt component, with debt to equity ratios close to 1:1. Power projects with assured power purchase arrangements may be financeable with debt to equity ratios of 2.5:1 or even 3:1. The maturity requirements of debt would also vary across sectors. Power and roads, which have longer payoff periods, require long maturities, while telecommunications projects can manage with shorter maturities. There are limitations and constraints associated with each source of debt and equity financing, which should be kept in mind when devising financing packages for individual projects.

Risk-based Pricing

Another critical area of functioning in a bank's operation is pricing of a loan. Loan pricing decision can have a direct impact on factors like earnings and on the capital adequacy, which in turn can affect the safety and soundness of banks. Pricing of a loan envisages that apart from covering cost of funds, profit margin, administrative costs and overheads, it should also cover the risks associated with the particular exposure for the bank. Loan pricing under traditional system, at best, can take care of the tangible aspects and would not be able to take care of the risk factor. To bridge this gap, few proactive measures are suggested under Basel II norms, with regard to pricing of loans, with a view to completely address the risk factor of an exposure. Banks have formulated a credit risk assessment system based on these suggestions, which provides for quantification of risks like exposure at default, loss given default and a probability of default. An appropriate risk-based pricing mechanism on similar lines can be adopted for infrastructure loans for managing the credit risk efficiently.

Measuring and Monitoring Performance

Another challenge of infrastructure financing pertains to measurement and monitoring the performance of a project after financing. This is a crucial function to gauze the efficiency of the project implementation against cost and time overruns so that bank's funds are not locked up in the project for longer period than expected. Metric deployment, for this purpose, can help establishing the results to be achieved by a project in a specified period. The metrics are project specific, which are developed in relation to the size of a project and the complexities involved therein. Project metrics approach is basically a management tool for the infrastructure company, in evaluating and monitoring the performance of a project. The financing banks can also use this as a supporting tool for their monitoring of infrastructure loans.

Social Cost Benefit Analysis (SCBA)

In financing and implementing infrastructure projects, social cost benefit analysis has assumed a new dimension, crossing the boundaries of intellectual speculation. In the wake of huge public investment in various sectors of the economy, the need for a practical method of aiming social cost benefit analysis has acquired great significance and urgency, calling for an exclusive policy in this regard. The philosophy of an extended social cost benefit analysis is important not only for the public sector, but equally relevant to the private corporations, who should have moral responsibility to undertake socially desirable projects. The Planning Commission has decided that in future, the feasibility studies for public sector projects will have to include an analysis of social rate of return which speaks how important and relevant this is for infrastructure. While analyzing the alternatives of capital expenditure, a private corporation is supposed to keep in view the aspect of social contribution the envisaged project can make. The purpose of social cost benefit analysis technique is not to replace the existing techniques of financial analysis, but only to supplement and strengthen them. Cost benefit analysis components are usually valued at "opportunity cost" or shadow prices to judge the real impact of their burden as costs to society.

Need for the Social Cost Benefit Analysis:

(1) Market prices that are used to measure costs and benefits in project analysis do not represent social values.

(2) The external effects can be positive like development of infrastructure or negative like pollution and imbalance in environment. Monetary cost benefit analysis fails to consider these externalities or external effects implied in a project.

(3) Taxes and subsidies are monetary costs and gains, but these are only transfer payments from social point of view, and therefore irrelevant.

(4) The SCBA is essential for measuring the redistribution effect of benefits of a project, as benefits need to go to the poorer sections rather than affluent sections.

(5) Projects manufacturing liquor and cigarettes would need to be distinguished from those generating electricity or producing necessities of life. Thus, appraisal of social relevance assumes priority over other considerations.

Considering these factors, social cost benefit analysis is a significant benchmark in the evaluation of the infrastructure projects.

Other Challenges

Apart from the financial and managerial aspects and risks associated with the infrastructure financing, there are challenges, which cannot be exactly estimated or predicted. At the same time, such issues, when encountered, can drag the fate of a project and its implementation to uncertainty, as managements of the infrastructure companies or the financing agencies have little or no control in solving them completely. These include issues of human rights violation, environmental and those related to culture, flora and fauna.

Human Rights

Execution of mega projects necessarily involve displacement of people settled in that area. These people must be living there since many generations and their livelihoods include traditional farming practices and hunting, etc. When these people are required to move out or relocate, it is fraught with serious consequences of their forgoing the very livelihood, as they cannot accustom again to a new environment or new livelihood. It is also true that tribal communities have an emotional attachments for the places they live and they refuse to leave that place come what may. This results in conflicts between the inhabitants and the authorities and attracts the attention of the international media casting a shadow on the prospects of the project. It becomes an issue involving human rights infringement and the fate of the project hangs in uncertainty. Hence, when infrastructure finance proposals are to be appraised by any financial intermediary, scrutiny of human rights issues is a must before committing to the project finance. Even projects undertaken by government are not to be exempt from this scrutiny. The Sardar Sarovar project of India, Amazon road project of Brazil, Shell in Nigeria are some examples where infrastructure projects got entangled in the human rights issues, which could not be satisfactorily resolved for years together.

Environmental Issues

Another issue most commonly encountered by infrastructure projects is the impact of a project on environment or environmental sensitivity of the project. One dimension of this issue is to obtain environmental clearances extensively before starting the project, while the other dimension is that such clearances would always be subject to challenges in a court through a public interest litigation petition by NGOs or direct action by the environmental activists. Thus environmental issues are also resulting in delay in the construction or even disruption of operations. An example of this nature is Dabhol Power Project in Maharashtra. To assess the impact of a project on the environment, it should be evaluated right from the construction stage. For all the road and rail projects, the impact on the natural environment needs to be investigated at the project design stage. An assessment of the impact at the operational stage can also bring to surface, those sections, which require new protection measures and would stress upon the usefulness of long-term monitoring.

Estimates of Internal and Economic Rates of Return

Analysis of economic rate of return is considered necessary so as to estimate the positive as well as the negative externalities concerning a project. But, in practice, these are found to be inadequate in many cases. To assess the full impact of an infrastructure project, its impact should not only be estimated in terms of income, but also against dimensions like basic service, collective activities representing the well being. Again, it is necessary to compute the impact on the population at large and not confining only to the direct users of such infrastructure services. Decisions on the infrastructure projects, whether by government or private promoters, should stretch beyond the evaluation of the economic rate of return and such practices are found to be common. Conventional cost-benefit analysis is often prone to the elusive effects of the potential benefits of infrastructure. Hence, in case of infrastructure like roads and electric power-generation, it is strongly recommended to assess the social rates of return. This can be done by evaluating the effect of the project on the aggregate output and thereafter comparing it with the costs of construction.

For example, economic rate of return when calculated in a traditional way as applicable to transport sector (say, evaluation of time saving) involves comparison of the benefits with the capital and operating costs. Other non-quantifiable benefits such as reduction in the number of accidents, may increase the rate of return. At the appraisal stage, the economic rate of return in road sector may be above 10%

and may be 25% in some cases. For projects with a negative internal rate of return, the economic rate of return may be around 3%. The economic rate of return for a sector like 'rail', where the volume of traffic is lesser may also be lesser than the road sector. In effect, it would be important to see that the economic and internal rates of return would be higher than the rates of borrowing.

Conclusion

With the policy makers in India laying more emphasis on the growth of infrastructure such as airports, seaports, roads, infrastructure development attracts special attention. Government is facilitating private investments in infrastructure through modes like Special Purpose Vehicle (SPV). Despite all the measures, inclusive of regulatory reforms, banks have not shed their inhibitions yet, towards taking up the infrastructure finance extensively. As far as banks are concerned, this could be a new avenue for gearing up their fund-based lending activities. One thing is true that, with the increasing exposure to infrastructure, banks and financial institutions need to be careful and alert regarding the inherent credit risks and long gestation periods associated with infrastructure financing. Infrastructure projects have a correlation with factors like GDP growth rate, which are macro economic in nature, capable of influencing income generation and timely recovery of the credit extended. Financing agencies should always be on their guard against these challenges.

Lack of a conducive regulatory system, at present, is also responsible for lack of proper financing for the infrastructure in India. Private investment in infrastructure has not been able to fuel due to many reasons discussed above. Raising private investments for infrastructure is not a big problem in the present environment, but there is a need for developing a healthy debt market. Further, there needs to be in place, a frame work with other sources, and objective tax structure that would nurture a healthy investment climate for infrastructure. In both the public sector and in the private sector, the need to commercialize infrastructure sector is imminent.

With a positive outlook, one can see that efforts in the right direction are already underway, though at a slower pace. Still, more clarity is expected in policy and candid efforts by governments, which can automatically create congenial climate for attracting private investments in infrastructure. These favorable experiences help in improving the expectations of the investors and in reducing the risk perception. This process is hoped to accelerate the pace of the infrastructure development and that is feasible through proactive responses from all the stakeholders involved.

(G G K Murthy, Consulting Editor, Icfai Books. He can be reached at murthy_ggk@yahoo.com).

Reference

1. Planning Commission of India.

Mega Infrastructure Projects in India

Metro Rail Project in Bangalore: Ground-level preparations for the ambitious metro rail project in Bangalore are being made with the State Government freezing development activity in 247 premises and buildings it had tentatively identified for this purpose. The government has asked the Bangalore City Corporation, BDA and other civic bodies to seek a no-objection certificate (NoC) from the BMRTL before it approves any construction activity. Bangalore Metro will have a standard gauge and will take cover under the 100-year old Mysore Tramways Act, which will require some amendments by the state government to suit the present day needs. With this, BMRTL can avoid going to the railway ministry for all sanctions. The total cost of the project is estimated to be around Rs.6207 crore which would be financed in the following manner:

- State: Rs.1807 cr
- Centre/Federal: Rs.1447 cr
- Financial Institutions: Rs.2953 cr

Source: http://www.karnataka.com/watch/blr-metro/

The Navi Mumbai International Airport Project

The Navi Mumbai International Airport would be one of the world's few "Greenfield" international state-of-art airports offering world-class facilities for passengers, cargo, aircrafts and airlines. The airport will support the rapidly growing air travel needs of the Mumbai Metropolitan Region. It is expected to absorb annually 4.5 million passengers in its first operational year, doubling to 8.2 million by 2010 to 13.7 million by 2020 and 30 million by 2030 according to developer CIDCO. The site of the airport in Panvel, to be developed through a public-partnership model, is located in an area of 950 hectares. CIDCO plans to sell 470 hectares in the periphery of the airport for development of hotels, malls, multiplexes and other aviation related facilities.

Source: http://www.inrnews.com/

Simhadri Power Plant

The Rs.4,000-crore Simhadri expansion project unlike the existing 1,000 MW plant near Visakhapatnam (which is supplying power only to Andhra Pradesh), will offer power to other States as well. Power sector major NTPC Ltd, is set to commence work on the 2x500 MW power plant at Simhadri in Andhra Pradesh, with coal linkage from Western Coal Fields. It is now eyeing overseas coal mining projects through strategic partners. The 1000-MW Simhadri project had created new benchmarks with aggressive pricing of Rs.3.6 crore per MW and the current expansion would cost about Rs.4-4.2 crore per MW. While the first phase of Simhadri 1000 MW plant was totally dedicated to the State, NTPC considered the option of selling part of the power to eastern grid. However, with the State keen on garnering all the power generated from the 1000-MW expansion, the entire power could now be available for the State.

Source: http://www.blonnet.com/

Tirupur Water and Wastewater Treatment Project, India

The recently completed Tirupur water system is the first public-private partnership project in the history of India's water sector, which gained a distinction in the industrial category of the Global Water Awards, being highly commended by the judges. The project involved the construction of two new treatment works, ultimately providing the area with a daily supply of 185 million litres of potable water and the capacity to treat 30 million litres of domestic sewage. In addition to the plants, the scheme also required the construction of an intake structure downstream of the Bhavani-Cauvery river confluence, 55km of transmission pipeline, a system of 25 reservoirs, a master balancing reservoir and a distribution and sewer network.

Project funding was a mixture of debt and equity, an approach, which involved a number of sources including public money, various commercial interests, financial institutions and international funding agencies. Assistance came from the Infrastructure Leasing and Financial Services (IL&FS) and from the US Agency for International Development (USAID) with loan guarantees over 30 years for $25 million (US). The project came in on its $220 million budget.

Source: http://www.water-technology.net/

2

Public Private Partnership and Infrastructure Financing in India

P Nair and Deepak Kumar

Traditionally, the financing of infrastructure projects is the responsibility of the government. However, because of budgetary constraints and other priorities to be taken care of, governments have not been in a position to fund infrastructure development activities effectively. Earlier, urban local bodies were not encouraged to raise money by themselves. They were subject to a tight central and regional control. The article discusses the experience of Britain, which has made a significant progress in the management of enterprises through private finance initiatives. Since the late 1980s, it is often argued that the Private Finance Institutions (PFIs) provide additional investment to the public sector and enable projects to proceed that are not otherwise possible, since in this case, the investment may be made directly or indirectly. China has also made effective use of partial guarantees and other such instruments to attract substantial FDIs. Their forte has been joint ventures and successful pilot projects. All of these provide effective models for them to follow. The article also explains various elements

Source: The Icfai Journal of Infrastructure, March 2006.

for financing such as the systemic reduction of risk and optimal allocation of risk to each stakeholder; proper and reasonably secure ROI; importance of inexcessive user charges; certain sweeteners that are required from the state to make the project commercially viable; the development of the debt market; and the mobilization of public savings.

"We have reserves of over $140 bn. I would think we should be able to use up at least $5 bn a year in the next two-three years. That is equal to about an extra Rs.23,000 cr every year."

– Dr. Montek Singh Ahluwalia,
Deputy Chairman, Planning Commission of India.

Introduction

Financing infrastructure in India is a story of gradual movement from pure public sector projects to various forms of Public Private Partnership (PPP) with an increasing role for the private sector. This is vital for the sustained economic growth of the country. The financing of infrastructure projects has been, traditionally, the responsibility of the government. However, owing to the 'budgetary constraints' and other priorities, successive governments were not in a position to fund the infrastructure development activities effectively. As a result, the much needed development has lost its momentum. One of the options that most of the developing countries prefer is Foreign Direct Investment (FDI). However, attracting FDI is easier said than done. It flows according to trend and market conditions. Therefore, alternative methods of financing are to be found out, since a huge investment in Infrastructure is needed (Table 1).

It may be pointed out that funding is not just the financing of the capital assets. Financing of the revenue expenses such as manpower, raw material, fuel etc is also very important. If the state could somehow take care of this aspect, it could divert such funds into creating hard capital assets. It is also not that difficult to get the private sector in O&M (Operation and Maintenance) activities. It depends upon the structuring of contracts and laying out of a clearly defined

Table 1: CII Projections – Investments in Infrastructure

	2003-04	2004-05	2005-06
Real GDP Growth (%)	8	9	9
Inflation (%)	6	6	6
Savings as % of GDP	27.5	30	31
Investments as % of GDP	30.5	32.5	33.5
Savings—Investments gap	2.50	2.5	2.5
Investments in Infrastructure	7	8	8.5
Investments in Infrastructure (in cr.)	2,09,504	2,75,348	3,36,441

Source: CII.

role for the private sector based upon those contracts. Here we have a synthesis of tenders and contracting with financing.

The 'appropriate use of the foreign exchange reserve' has also been an issue of much debate. If at least 10% of these reserves could somehow be converted into long-term sources of funding for infrastructure, year after year, the country could perhaps receive its most stable source of funding.

This is the core of the problems which affects the financing of infrastructure. The funds required are long-term—"hot money will not do". The nation has a substantial amount of money in terms of foreign exchange reserves, and savings in the public domain such as the public provident fund. The latter is genuine long-term money but it involves an issue of touching public savings. However, since tax money is limited and the economy is growing at a rapid pace, the need for infrastructure has become paramount. Therefore, it is clear that this money has to be utilized in some form, if not totally. This presents the classic moral dilemma for the state: To touch or not to touch the savings in the public domain for the socially desirable cause of creating modern infrastructure assets for the state. Much of this will be discussed in the article.

With the development of PPP projects in India, a new need has arisen for sophisticated financing models to suit the various types of projects. This may eventually lead to a "clearing house for such projects" with standardized financial models.

History and Background: The Indian Context

Infrastructure has been the last bastion to get privatized. Whilst Agriculture and Industry as well as the services sector, always had some degree of privatization and autonomy and private sector operation, in the case of Infrastructure, there was never any question about the same—it belonged to the state-period! The reason for this absolute certainty is that the assets so created were perceived to be "socially relevant assets". They could not be handed over to the private sector. They could not be charged at commercial rates (a strategy that almost certainly would dry up commercial funding). Control of these assets would lead to monopoly and oligarchy and harm the society. Therefore, the private sector was out-period!

The approach leads to an almost complete dependence on budgetary financing. This was bearable in the pre-liberalization era (i.e., prior to 1990), where the growth rate generally veered around 3-4%, there was a monopoly on goods and services and delays and inefficiencies were generally tolerated. In the liberalization era, India has taken several steps forward in the development of Infrastructure, particularly telecom. The distribution side was privatized for the first time by creating several STD booths, thus breaking the monopoly of the nation's post offices, which virtually used to dominate since Independence. All these naturally brought in new financing into the system—the first hesitant steps towards privatization of infrastructure. However, the government continued to handle the rest of the operations. The only role of the private sector was to construct the assets themselves and even this was done through dubious tenders which were awarded to political and bureaucratic favorites.

Earlier, urban local bodies were also not encouraged to raise money by themselves. They were subjected to tight central and regional control. The 46th amendment was a step in the right direction, since it is for the first time, enabled the urban local bodies to raise money on their own. But the whole atmosphere was one of tight government control and the municipalities continued to be staffed by people who were essentially paper-pushers for the state. People with these skills were hardly the ones to raise independent finances.

The recent rapid development of the urban sector and the capacity to pay have really changed the urban scenario. A number of the major metros have been allowed to raise bonds, under adherence to certain parameters and under the monitoring of the Ministry of Urban Development and Poverty Alleviation. At the same time, the rapid growth of urbanization in the recent past has escalated the need for infrastructure upgradation and development.

Funding has been done against specified projects only which are clearly designed and delineated from the projects funded by the municipality, in order to ensure proper utilization of the fund. The repayment options are also set out clearly and the model for repayment methodology is given. The model agreements for funding urban infrastructure projects show that (at least of late) the authorities are very well versed with the requirements of attracting citizens funding for urban infrastructure projects, particularly through the mechanism of tax-free bonds.

The city of Ahmedabad came up with the first tax-free bond issue, which was a roaring success. Many other issues were introduced in Mumbai, Hyderabad, Bangalore and Pune. All of them were successful. Repayments were usually through the escrow of end user charges with a few grants and subsidies from government thrown in. The repayment mechanisms were usually in the hands of responsible nationalized banks who earmarked a particular set of municipal charges (such as Octroi or property tax) and worked out a mechanism to pay the lender from a designated account before returning the general pool to the municipality.

Tax-free bonds ensured that the lender/subscriber got a 35% return over and above the stipulated coupon rates. For this reason, a number of corporates and financial Institutions applied.

The increase of end user charges and the general culture of payment ensure that many other municipalities would be able to tap a substantial number of private funds to aid their development.

Evolution of the PPP Model

Ultimately, it has been understood that to bring the private sector in, and at the same time retain some control of the state, PPPs have to be accelarated. Therefore, most financial instruments would have to be increasingly tailor-made in order to suit the concept of Public-Private Partnerships. Different instruments would have

Figure 1: Project Finance Global Lending by Sector

in billions of US$

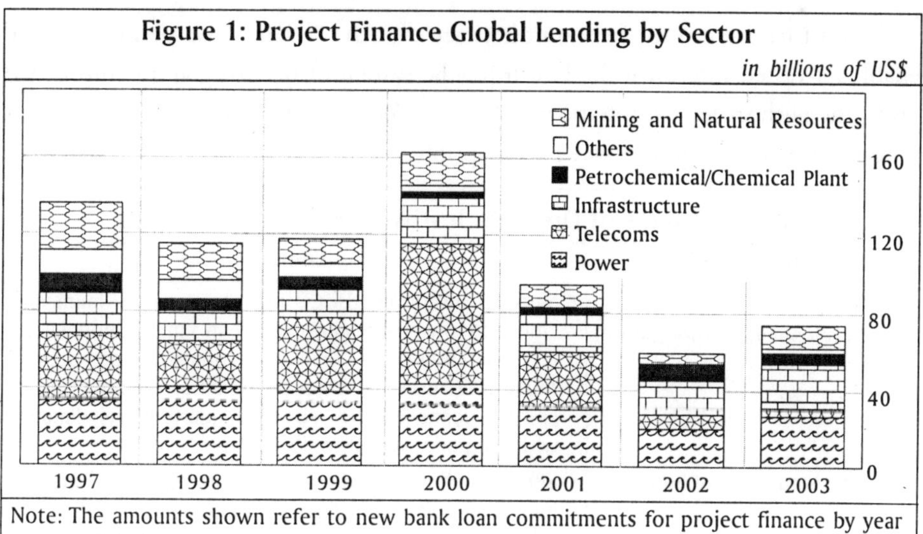

Note: The amounts shown refer to new bank loan commitments for project finance by year and sector.

Source: Dealogic ProjectWare database.

to be made to suit various PPP models such as Design-Build-Operate, Build-Operate-Transfer etc. These would give rise to a whole new market for financial instruments.

However, the key issue is that these PPP projects need to be economically viable, prior to being put up for bid to the private sector. For this, following things must evolve on a continuous basis:

- The regulatory framework must be in place to enable the private entrepreneur to operate properly and in a commercially viable manner.
- End user charges must be commensurate with the cost of the projects run by such entrepreneurs.
- Investment and backups of a suitable tenor should be available. Infrastructure projects require long tenor debt and equity investments which are prepared to sit out a long gestation period.

None of these events were forthcoming in the earlier years which meant that private investment in Infrastructure was moving at a relatively slow pace.

It must be mentioned here quite openly that the "licence and permit raj" had enabled a vested interest to be built up. The system of licensing and controls had given the authorities sizeable power. No one gives up power easily unless there is a need, and Infrastructure was no exception.

Table 2: Effects of Different Institutions to Deliver Funds

	Institutions	Efforts
1.	Housing and Urban Development Corporation Limited (HUDCO)	• Since its inception HUDCO provides loans to municipal cities and towns which have less than a million population at a lower interest rate than other commercial banks. Even today, it finances the major public infrastructure projects and the loans can be repaid in quarterly installments within a period of 10 to 15 years.
2.	The State Bank of India (SBI)	• SBI, through its subsidiaries, have attempted to fund the long-term aspects of infrastructure projects as well as the working capital required to run and maintain the project. Their "structured finance" and "pooled finance" schemes have worked very well in terms of escrowing receivables, and many new projects, especially energy and power projects have been financed in this way.
3.	The Infrastructure Leasing and Financial Services (ILFS)	• Established in 1989, ILFS has come up as an important financial institution in the recent years. It is a private sector financial intermediary in which the Government of India owns a small equity share. Its activities have more or less remained confined to the development of industrial-townships, roads and highways where risks are comparatively less.
4.	Financial Institutions Reform and Expansion (FIRE) Program	• Launched under the auspices of the USAID, whose basic objective is to enhance resource availability for commercially viable infrastructure projects through the development of a domestic debt market.
5.	Infrastructure Development Finance Company (IDFC)	• 50% of the project cost is financed from funds raised in the US capital market under the Housing Guaranty fund for a period of 30 years at an interest rate of 6%. • The USAID and DFID have essentially worked on structuring the projects, so that they would appear viable and attractive to international investors. • It is a specialized financial intermediary for infrastructure. IDFC, as on March 31, 2005, on a cumulative basis, has approved financial assistance to 198 projects aggregating over Rs.2,45,936 mn.

Compiled from the respective websites of the institutions discussed here.

One of the areas which could attract financing quite easily was the housing and township sector. Here, one has a clear and identifiable asset which is owned by someone and which earns some revenue. If these were households, there was a salary or income to pay the "end user charges".

The institutions (Table 2) have made an active effort to deliver long-term funds for Infrastructure purposes in India and the project finance global lending over the years sector-wise are given in Figure 1.

The US Experience

The US is the master of pooled finance. Their bond markets, being mature and dynamic have a lot of depth and tradability for long-term finance. The US treasury rate usually acts as the true arbiter for the same. A number of municipalities have raised pool finance in bonds, through participation certificates, since the 1980s. Their experience is therefore worth looking at, as the arbiter of pooled finance in India.

In the USA, the private initiatives started in 1960s. Since then, laws have been passed in almost every area to allow the private sector to participate. Even so, there was a substantial resistance in the '60s and '70s until budgetary realities forced a sizeable change, as far as roads, healthcare, power and educational institutions were concerned. Privatization went to the extent where even trading in power was encouraged. Many varied instruments came up to take care of the financing aspects. The stock markets freely quoted utility companies and so equity financing was not an issue. Pooled finance against certificates of participation came up in many urban centers. These certificates were traded and retraded many times. Institutional loans were not an issue, as end user charges were freely available. Therefore, federal grants were kept to a minimum. Privatization has penetrated into the smallest places in the USA and they really do not have a serious financing problem. But whether or not this model is relevant to that of a developing country remains an important point. This elaboration serves as a model as to how it works in the most developed country.

Private sector participation in infrastructure, both in the development of new projects and in the acquisition of privatized public sector monopolies, offers many potential benefits. Competition generally improves the supply and quality of infrastructure service, thus boosting local standards of living. In addition, the participation of the private sector in infrastructure allows governments to devote more of their public funds to pressing social problems or to the development of projects that are unattractive to private investors.

Asia and Latin America have a considerable potential for future private sector participation in infrastructure sector. However, the issue of end user charges will continue to plague the promoters of PPP projects and restrict their abilities to raise finances.

PFI Initiatives in Britain

Britain has made significant progress in the management of enterprises through private finance initiatives (Table 3). Since late 1980s, it is often argued that the PFI provides additional investment for the public sector and enables projects to proceed which would not otherwise have been possible. In this case, the investment may be done directly or indirectly.

Essential features of PFI (As given by Malcolm Sawyer):

- Capital investment projects (for the public sector) are financed as well as constructed by a private company, and then leased back to the public sector over a predetermined period (generally 25 to 30 years), and that generally the private company provides a range of services associated with the capital project (e.g., maintenance).
- PFI involves not only alternative sources of finance for public investment but also services related to the capital.
- The PFI appeared to be a way of drawing on alternative sources of finance in such a manner which would not increase the (reported) budget deficit.
- Under the PFI, the concerned company borrows at a higher rate of interest which is reflected in the price it charges to the government, but the company bears the risks associated with the operation and maintenance of the investment project.

Table 3: Private Finance Initiative – Estimated Capital Spending by the Private Sector (Signed Deals) Projects in £ million			
	2004-05	2005-06	2006-07
Educations and Skills	471	0	0
Health	460	412	292
Transport	1858	1704	1380
Office of Deputy Prime Minister	34	23	78
Home Office	82	6	0
Constitutional Affairs	13	13	4
Defence	778	453	286
Foreign and Commonwealth Office	6	5	5
Trade and Industry	5	3	4
Environment, Food and Rural Affairs	56	39	23
Work and Pensions	38	40	31
Scotland	148	17	0
Wales	39	9	0
Northern Ireland Executive	13	41	16
Chancellor's Departments	46	37	34
Cabinet Office	6	1	0
Culture, Media and Sports	13	5	0
Total	4066	2808	2153

Notes: PFI activity in local authority projects is included under the sponsoring central government department.

Source: HM Treasury. Budget Report 2004. Table C17.

Malaysian Example: Investors also want to Keep the Asset

Malaysia initially followed the traditional methods of financing, i.e., through the government grant and international loans, supported by government guarantee etc. However, in the '90s, particularly with the advent of Dr. Mahathir Mohammed, the Malaysian Government drew up an ambitious plan for expansion of the private sector. In the 16 years, i.e., from 1983-1999, more than 200 projects came up which had a reasonable degree of privatization. Most of these projects either made break even or profit. This attracted the interest of the world, and Malaysia bacame a model for the developing countries. The Malaysian Government also encouraged the ingress and egress of their senior staff to go to the private sector on three and five year deputations. These staff members often came back with massive experience on how to structure a commercially viable deal. This highlights a very important issue—the relative lack of know-how of senior state officials on how to make a deal commercially viable. This is due to a lack of understanding from the investors' point of view that can be rectified with real work experience of the sector. This issue cannot be underestimated in spite of the mass of technical reasons that is given for the relative failure of the private sector in infrastructure.

In addition to this, the Malaysian Government made very effective use of guarantees and funding as "last mile coverage". In short, when all the structuring was done and a little "juice" was required to sweeten the deal, the state often came forward with the sweetener. This approach made the best use of limited government funds.

There is no doubt that this helped to develop a number of projects which would otherwise have languished. The sweetener could be in the form of state guarantees—full or partial, bank guarantees, part funding, or any other form of comfort to get the private investor and international community to pump in the funds.

The Malaysian methods have been copied either fully or partially by many other developing countries. China has also made very effective use of the partial guarantees to attract substantial FDI. Their forte has been joint ventures and successful pilot projects. All of these provide effective models for them to follow.

China

China has some well-established principles for attracting funds for infrastructure, which have stood the test of time. For example:

- They generally raise debt in the local market through the banking system, varying around 17% on average.
- Equity is raised by means of joint ventures and international issues. Joint venture tends to have 51% government participation. Foreigners seem to be generally happy with 49% which allows them significant say in the management of the company.
- Any new and innovative idea is readily accepted and first tried on a small scale, which is implemented quickly and readily. If it works, then it is

expanded on a large scale. This is where India could learn from China. India, being a democratic country, tends to take a lot of time implementing a project. If the project could first be tried on a small scale (say in select municipalities and panchayats where the decision-making is absolutely from the ground level), then this would encourage the shareholders and stakeholders that something was indeed happening. Offices would be set up and the commitment starts. Any errors/problems could be quickly rectified so that the large projects would not suffer from major operational deficiencies. All this is absolutely essential to get the right stakeholder/ financier inland to see the actual color of his money.

Some General Criteria for Financing Infrastructure Projects

Figure 2 points out six general criteria for financing infrastructure projects:

The Systemic Reduction of Risk

It is ensured that the financed amount will be paid in time without delay, thus it depends on:

- Overall financial viability of the project—at least it should break even.
- Guarantees and escrows.
- Clear identifiable streams of revenue.
- Ability to control the assets through pledge/hypothecation etc.

Figure 2: General Criteria for Financing Infrastructure Projects

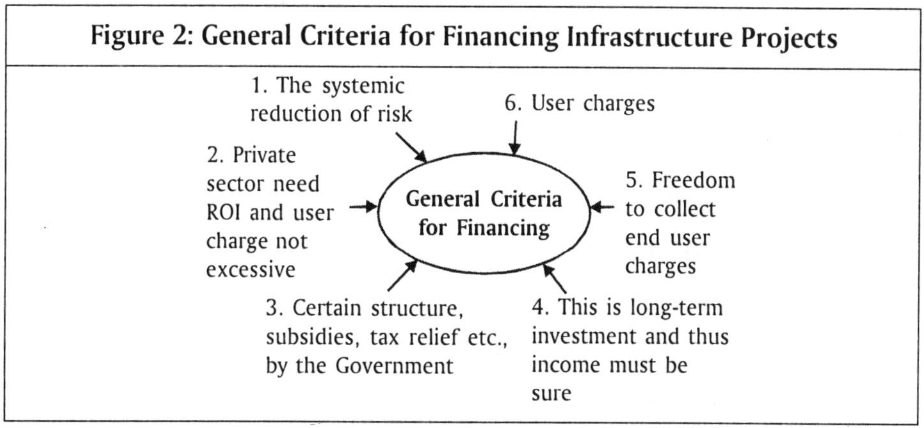

- Professional operation of the assets under consideration through O&M etc.
- Proper insurance of the assets, especially the coverage of political and legal risks.

ROI and User Charges

The private sector invests for a longer period and it expects a desired ROI. While receiving ROI (desired return on investment), the private sector cannot impose heavy tolls which may be violated by the general people. Thus, private sector is very sensitive in selecting the viable projects. In case of roads, the private sector expects that estimated traffic flow and other government supports. Unnecessary delays in clearance of projects create problems and investors lose the confidence in such projects. In case of international investors, it is very important to take care of approval process, government support and an assurance of return of the investment.

Thus, when we build up the confidence of investors, we cannot ignore the users and impose heavy traffic charges/user charges on beneficiaries for availing the infrastructure use.

Sweeteners by the State

In reality, no matter how skillful the structuring is, the state will have to step in at some stage. This could be by way of:

- Guarantees.
- Part or full subsidy.
- Tax incentives.
- Providing the land for the project at reduced cost, or costing it as equity.
- Taking their returns after the private party has recovered his investment.
- Any other method which adds comfort to the proposal and, thereby, allows the investment to come in.

Procedural formalities could also be smoothened out through clear and transparent policies, a single window clearance system, time bound approval process etc. Once word gets around, the money would start coming in.

The Formalized Rating

Of these projects, by accredited rating agencies would also help the investors to understand the real risks involved in these projects. Unfortunately, the concept is yet to really take off in India, and really good models which encapsulate all the socioeconomic risks in a systematic way have not yet been developed. A lot of international expertise needs to be borrowed for this, particularly from the UK and USA.

Freedom to Collect End User Charges

Despite all the structuring and effective use of state and lender money, the idea that the asset should ultimately pay for itself is widely gaining ground. In many cases, the end users are willing and able to pay for better infrastructure, but there is no effective mechanism in place that would assure them of better service. This is the case of Bangalore at present. There are long traffic delays and the infrastructure is totally clogged due to tremendous economic expansion. The users have plenty of money but to translate that money into effective infrastructure requires effective and transparent models. Political issues are there, but one feels that a systemic development of expertise should ultimately overcome all these problems.

Some of the effective strategies that have been employed by countries with a similar ethos are:

- Adding tolls to property taxes in the city.
- Charging vehicles a one time tax.
- Adding a few decimal points to gas tax, supermarket tax and any other tax on revenue and other business related items. As the sale and purchase of goods get more electronic, it should always be possible to add very little money to each transaction, without the customer even bothering about it. This money is collected "electronically" and transferred to a dedicated fund, which is then used to pay the revenues to the private operator/owner or other infrastructure development.
- Partial government subsidy which is a very effective method, when combined with other methods, to get the Internal Rate of Return (IRR) up to a minimum acceptable level.

- Indirect earning is one of the most important (and yet not exploited fully) avenues for making an infrastructure project viable. The concept consists of putting the asset to other uses. A highway, for example, could have motels, signboards, advertising on sides, shops and multiplexes etc., at suitable places. A special fee could be charged for the same. A flyover could have pizza stalls, hawker stands etc. who pay rent for the same. Mumbai is a city which really utilizes these avenues fully.

Other Financial Instruments

1. Take-out Finance

This is an instrument, designed to increase the tenor of an instrument in a market which does not have depth in 12-15 year financing. The idea is to share the risk between two Institutions. The first institution will take on the debt for, say, seven years and depending upon the performance of the asset, would "sell" the debt to the second institution at a discounted or appreciated price. In this way, the second institution takes out the finance, but as far as the operator is concerned, the project continues to enjoy the benefits of 15 year finance. It is a concept worth exploring in India, which as of now does not have the required depth in its debt market for long-term debt instruments, unlike the USA where pooled finance instruments get traded frequently, or Hong Kong where water companies get traded on the stock market.

Figure 3: Other Financial Instruments in Infrastructure

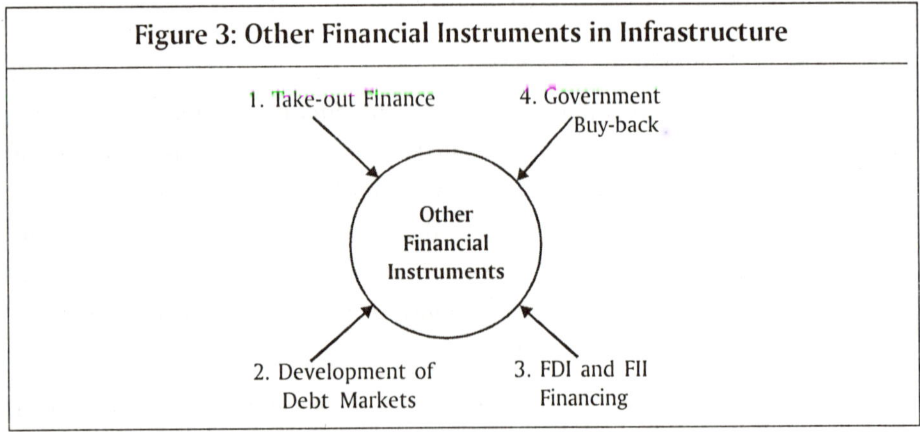

2. Development of Debt Markets

The single most important factor to develop financing for infrastructure is to build the debt markets. Take-out finance and the like can at best be one off arrangements. But a full-fledged debt market gives the investor the confidence that such instruments can be traded freely and there is always an exit option available at some sort of market price. With the number of bonds appearing in the market, it is clear that the debt market would evolve over time like the equities market. But in order to expedite infrastructure financing, perhaps it has to be helped in a manner such that the state regulates the market for gilt-edged securities, and acts as both buyer and seller at specified rates. At the inception, these securities could be discounted at artificially cheaper rates on both sides.

Local governments seek to finance projects through loans or by issuing bonds for several reasons. First, some projects are too large to allocate the required amount in one year. Moreover, setting aside funds from annual budget surpluses over several years to finance a future project would result in substantial amount of funds being unutilized. Again, project financing accelerates infrastructure development, creates jobs, and improves the quality of life of a region. By spreading the costs of a project over 10 to 30 years the costs of infrastructure improvements are distributed more equitably among project beneficiaries.

The success of these issues demonstrates that local governments can access the capital market for resources for delivery of urban infrastructure. The ability of municipalities to take advantage of these opportunities, however, depends on their presenting themselves as viable financial entities. ULBs must demonstrate creditworthiness and obtain an investment grade credit rating. This forces them to improve their revenue base by introducing reforms, including improved cost recovery and financial management, and better management of urban services. Another prerequisite for issuing municipal bonds is the development of Commercially Viable Infrastructure Projects (CVIPs), i.e., projects that can recover full costs including the cost of debt service.

3. FDI and FII Financing

The most desirable form of financing is definitely FDI financing. It is usually in the form of equity though there may be some quasi-equity or convertibles at times. All options should be open regarding FDI and new instruments should be designed which could make the FDI particularly suitable for infrastructure purposes (Table 4). Some of the innovations could be:

- Pushing convertibles with a long lock-in period.
- Regular coupons on debentures which could get converted later.
- Options.

If India expects pure equity to be invested for a 12-year period, we are likely to be disappointed. The private fund manager/investor has to show some results in his account. With the gestation period for these projects being long, it is imperative that there be suitable "running incentives" to keep the principal locked in.

Table 4: FDI Inflows into India and China

(in Million US$)

Year	FDI in India	FDI in China
1992-93	279.5	10723
1993-94	369	27086
1994-95	872.1	33088
1995-96	1418	36930
1996-97	1091.6	41470
1997-98	2955	44901
1998-99	2000	45463
1999-00	1581	40319
2000-01	1910	40715
2001-02	2988	46878
2002-03	4,269*	52743
2003-04	5,335*	53510

*(*UN Conference on Trade and Development (Unctad)).*

Source: www.adb.org

FII money is the other end of the spectrum and constitutes a sizeable amount of the foreign exchange reserves. But through the ingress and egress of funds, there remains a minimum constant factor. Given the fairly healthy state of the finances, there is no reason why the country should not try to utilize at least 5-10% of this base level of FII funds. If anything goes wrong, and then the country has the resources to pay the FII investor. Once the debt markets develop, then FII money would automatically get locked into bonds with varying coupon rates and tenors. But till then, innovative methods would have to be found.

This money could be held in a special fund and used as the sweeteners. In this manner, it could be used to catalyze external funds, rather than be a source of direct funding. Possibly three to four times the funding may come in, if the instruments are structured right.

4. Government Buy-back

The state has been looking for ways in which to make the last mile pitch and have finally come out with an SPV. The presence of the state in many projects, does give the investors confidence, provided the stakes are not too high. In this case, the project appears to be "state approved" and may well attract national and international money. The presence of an SPV with a transparently professional operation and evaluation system would also help greatly.

Another way in which the government can support the whole process, is by subordinating their returns to that of the investor. The state is really not interested in profit—it is interested in developing the project for the welfare of the society. Therefore, if the private sector is able to obtain clearly defined returns, after which the state starts receiving its share of the profits, the risks would dramatically decrease and money would start flowing in. That optimum point, where the risk-return portfolios of all the parties concerned are finely balanced, needs to be found again and again if there is to be any dramatic increase in external funding, both in debt and equity. This type of skill is quite different for Infrastructure and other socioeconomic projects and the purely Industrial projects. The risks are different and the returns are different. Direct wealth creation is not the object of an infrastructure project. It is indirect wealth creation through the boosting of Agriculture, Industry and Services sectors of the economy, which is the ultimate objective. The Infrastructure asset is often for the direct benefit of the society, and often has a political tag loaded on, at least in democratic societies such as India. An analyst without this mindset, will struggle and that is why this set of skills has to be developed separately through training, technical assistance and suitable recruitment from overseas, if needed.

The Way Forward

There is one clear cut way forward, i.e., develop the depth and strength of the debt markets. This is one sure shot method of ensuring a continuous flow of funds towards fulfilling the needs of infrastructure projects. The reason is (as mentioned earlier) that there is a satisfactory exit option for the investor, should he want to drop the project from his portfolio. The way forward seems to be the active participation of the state, possibly using some portion of the insurance, pension and foreign exchange reserves. This buffer would ensure that there would always be a buyer and seller in the debt market, at a specified price. It is in the pricing of projects that the real skill comes in and it is here that the state really needs to create a "clearing house" of some kind, manned by skilled staff, along the lines of the National Stock Exchange. Over a period of time, this separation could possibly be done away with, but it needs to be there at the start to define the market clearly, and allow the investors to understand what they are really getting into.

Another issue is to provide sweeteners to develop the equities market, although this is less important than the urgent need to develop the long-term debt market. The necessary funds can be obtained through taking a call on FII funds, pension and provident funds and the like. This is a huge source of money. Some of it needs to be used for the public good. Infrastructure is for the public good. Ideally, the Indian Parliament should draft an Act, specifically authorizing the same. At the inception, perhaps 1-2% of these funds could be taken, and the performance monitored over 3-5 years, by the leading public financial institutions in collaboration with the finance ministry.

All things considered, the future looks pretty rosy. The trick is to put in place the policies that give a fair but not excessive deal to the investor to keep the money rolling in, at a fair clip on a long-term basis.

(P Nair, Senior Consultant, The Icfai University, Hyderabad; and Consulting Editor, The Icfai Journal of Infrastructure. E-mail: paddynair@icfai.org

Deepak Kumar, Former Associate Consultant, The Icfai University Press, Hyderabad. He can be reached at bornwaldeepak_11@rediffmail.com).

References

1. www.ciionline.org
2. www.idfc.com
3. www.usaid.gov/in
4. www.3inetwork.org
5. www.adb.org
6. www.saag.org
7. www.findarticles.com
8. www.indiansinireland.com
9. *HM Treasury*. Budget Report 2004.
10. *BIS Quarterly Review*.

3

Infrastructure Financing – Current Scenario

Sanjeev Kumar

Infrastructure plays a key role in economic growth; it provides vital support to the productive sector and improves overall standard of an economy. Since infrastructure development requires huge investment, the proper financing system is required for effective implementation of these projects. This article provides a primer on various options available for infrastructure finance in India and issues pertaining to them.

"A good investment climate is central to growth and poverty reduction. A vibrant private sector creates jobs, provides the goods and services needed to improve living standards, and contributes taxes necessary for public investment in health, education, and other services. But too often governments stunt the size of those contributions by creating unjustified risks, costs, and barriers to competition."

– François Bourguignon
Senior Vice-President and
Chief Economist, The World Bank.

Source: Treasury Management, December 2005. This article was originally published as "Infrastructure Financing".

Finance Minister P Chidambaram in a press conference on October 6, 2005 announced a Special Purpose Vehicle (SPV) with the objective of disbursing about Rs.10,000 cr for various projects this year. The main objective for SPV was to finance infrastructure projects. Apart from them, the Finance Minister also finalized a note on the procedure for public-private partnership in road projects. The initiative for setting up of an SPV had been proposed by the Finance Minister in the current fiscal budget. Clearly, the government has taken aggressive steps to meet the financing requirements of various infrastructure projects. The issue of finance is a key part for any infrastructure project. So what kind of financing instruments should be considered and who will be the major financier is a crucial question for any infrastructure project. This article provides a primer on various options available for project financing.

Reserve Bank of India defines the word "infrastructure" as, power, roads, highways, bridges, ports, airports, rail system, water supply, irrigation, sanitation and sewerage system, telecommunication, housing, industrial park or any other public facility of a similar nature as may be notified by the CBDT in the Gazette from time to time.

Undoubtedly, infrastructure development is an integral part of economic development; Quality infrastructure not only determines the standard of living but is also a key factor to sustained growth of any economy. For industries and agriculture performing to their maximum extent, they have to be supported by an efficient and cost effective infrastructure. For example, poor transportation system increases the cost of inputs for industries in terms of high transportation cost, high transit time, and risk of accident. Similarly, shortage of power can be the cause of high operating cycle, high labor cost etc. The entire factor indirectly could lead to increase in the cost of production for industry as well as agricultural sector. Poor infrastructure not only affects the GDP growth of the country but also discourages foreign investment in the country. In fact, foreign investors view infrastructure development as a key parameter and giving it priority over other parameters (viz., wages, regulation etc.) in assessing the investment potential in developing countries. A number of research studies have also found a nexus between the infrastructure and economic development.[1] Though these researches have

[1] CMIE (1995), CII (1995), GOI (1996) and Nayak (1999).

established the fact that a strong correlation exists between per capita GDP and availability of infrastructure, but whether increased infrastructure causes growth or growth causes increased infrastructure is yet to be fully established.

Historically, the problem concerning infrastructure in India has been acute especially in the area of road, power and telecom. But post reforms, India emerged as a big economy for foreign players and the future for Indian economy looks bright. The growing per capita income, consumer choice, healthy forex reserves, a $70 bn export market and leadership in the IT sector are the most impressive changes that Indian economy has seen in the past few years. At present, India is the fourth largest economy in terms of Purchasing Power Parity (PPP) with a GDP growth of more than 7%. But the biggest question that arises is: Can India sustain 8% plus annual growth? If there is any uncertainty about sustaining the growth rate; it seems to be emanating from the poor infrastructure of the country. In other words, India requires a world-class infrastructure to sustain the economic growth. But in a relatively short span of time it's a big challenge as the country requires a massive investment, proper planning and a stringent regulatory system. Let us discuss some of the issues pertaining to the above-mentioned scenario.

Recent Changes

In the budget proposal for the fiscal 2005-2006, the government has taken various steps to develop infrastructure. The Rural Infrastructure Development Fund which was revived in July this year has proposed to provide a corpus of Rs.8,000 cr in 2005-06 also. Rural telecommunication has been given a boost by the allocation of Rs.1,200 cr. The National Highway Development Program (NHDP) has been provided Rs.1,400 cr for Golden Quadrilateral in 2005-06 for the development of 4000 km of four-lane highway. The total outlay for National Highway Development has increased from Rs.6,514 cr in 2004-05 to Rs.9,320 cr in 2005-06. For electrification in rural area, the government has made a provision of Rs.1,100 cr this year to cover 1.25 lakh villages in five years. Further, for Indira Awas Yojana the allocation has been increased from Rs.2,500 cr in the current year to Rs.2,750 cr in Budge Estimate (BE) 2005-06.

Apart from taking above-mentioned measures, the government has also announced a Special Purpose Vehicle (SPV) with borrowing limit of Rs.10,000 cr for financing large infrastructure projects. In the budget speech Prime minister Dr. Manmohan Singh proposed to draw foreign exchange resources for financing necessary imports. The Prime Minister also proposed to establish an SPV to finance infrastructure projects in specified sectors like roads, ports, airports and tourism.

Infrastructure Investment Requirements

Despite the various steps taken by the government, there is a huge requirement of investment in infrastructure. An investment of $13 bn is required for developing 13,146 km of roads. In Telecommunications, the tele-density continues to be less than 10 and this sector also requires an investment of $20 bn in order to reach the tele-density level of 25. Apart from these, an investment target of one billion dollars has been set for modernization of airports and an estimated $22 bn investment is required for the marine sector. Announcing the India Economic Summit, the Finance Minister P Chidambaram also indicated that development of infrastructure will require US$150 bn in the next 10-15 years. He also announced setting up of commission to attract domestic and foreign investment for infrastructure sector.

Pattern of Infrastructure Investment

Over the past few years, India has seen tremendous development in the infrastructure. Sectoral Analysis of investment reveals that major development has taken place in telecom, cargo and the port sector. (Refer Table 1) Growth in new telephone connections has increased from 27.2% in 2001 to 40.1% in 2004; similarly growth in cargo handled at major ports has increased for 3.4% in 2001 to 9.9% in 2004.

Table 1: Investment by Sector

	(% Growth Rate Fiscal Year)			
	2001	**2002**	**2003**	**2004**
Electricity generated through thermal utilities	7.4	2.5	6.2	3.5
Electricity generated through hydel utilities	(7.6)	(0.7)	(13.7)	15.6
Cargo handled a major ports	3.4	2.3	9.0	9.9
Passengers handled at international airport terminals	4.6	(5.0)	4.8	6.5
Passengers handled at domestic airport terminals	7.7	(5.7)	9.6	13.1
New telephone connections	27.2	23.9	21.5	40.1

Source: Economic Survey 2004-05

The change in the trend has resulted from reforms in various infrastructure sectors. Further, major financiers in infrastructure were the public sector units. In pre-reform period public sector investment in infrastructure was more than 75% of the total investment. As per the ISR report, during the 10 year period from 1980 to 1990, the total infrastructure investment ranged from 4.5 to 5.5% of GDP, out of which public sector investment was 3.5 to 4.3% of GDP. But the trend has changed after liberalization. Investment in infrastructure by private sector has increased significantly in the past 15 years. The reforms started with the public-private partnership but finally independent private players were also allowed to participate in the sector. Total project investment made by public sector and private sector in the past five years is summarized (Table 2).

Table 2: Project Investment (2000-2005)

Rs. in cr

	2000	2001	2002	2003	2004	2005*
Project investments by central government	14,80,095	16,91,760	18,43,278	19,07,217	20,31,756	18,47,472
Project investments by state government	11,88,252	13,47,024	14,97,639	15,56,477	16,15,085	13,73,536
Project investments by government local bodies	43,881	43,775	52,086	57,206	70,702	78,573
Project investments by Indian private sector	16,63,665	18,96,425	20,08,233	18,60,061	22,33,506	23,36,857
Project investments by foreign private sector	9,38,689	9,18,840	6,04,536	2,93,207	3,88,286	4,66,056

* For nine month period March-September

Source: CMIE

Public-private Participation

Infrastructure projects have long gestation periods and require huge investment; financial viability of project is also difficult to estimate. Taking these points into consideration it is very difficult to meet all fund requirements from the budgetary resources of the countries alone. The demand to allow private players increased particularly in 1996-97, when the requirement for infrastructure development was on peak and also India was experiencing fiscal deficit. Though the trend of PPP started in 1990, it picked up only after 1996-97. In fact the trend of PPP started in

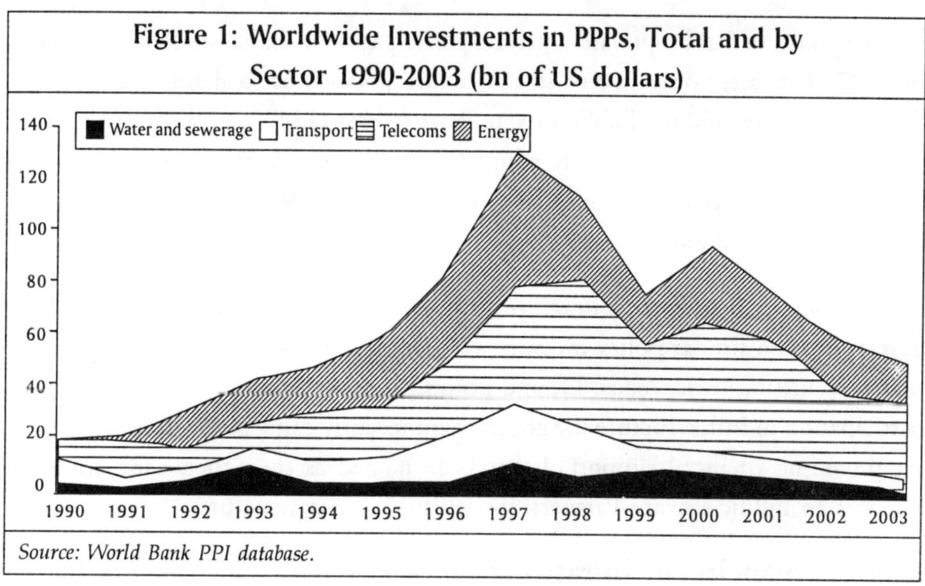

Figure 1: Worldwide Investments in PPPs, Total and by Sector 1990-2003 (bn of US dollars)

Source: World Bank PPI database.

various developing countries during this period only. The trend tuned southward after 1997 because most of the developing countries started opening up this sector for FII and other private players. Despite the negative trend worldwide, India was among the top 10 players of investing using PPP (Table 3).

Table 3: Top 10 Countries for PPPs, 1990-2003

		(in %)
Brazil	1,57,098	19.7
Argentina	72,858	9.1
China	61,170	7.7
Mexico	59,753	7.5
Malaysia	36,695	4.6
India	33,108	4.2
Philippines	31,017	3.9
Indonesia	29,210	3.7
Thailand	23,662	3.0
Chile	22,003	2.8

Source: World Bank PPI database

The policy of Public-private—private participation in India was first announced in 1997. The basic objective of infrastructure policy was to define a framework for operationally suitable Public-Private Partnerships (PPP) and the process under which government would largely adopt for leveraging private finance initiatives. IDFC, the first private-public NBFC was set up in 1997 with an objective to explore private capital.

In order to further encourage private sector participation in infrastructure development, a similar policy measure was started in various infrastructure sectors such as tourism, ports, roads, IT, and power. In order to boost the private-public participation in infrastructure the government recently came out with some scheme for providing financial support. It has been named as the Scheme for Financial Support to Public-Private Partnerships (PPPs) in Infrastructure.

Private Financing of Infrastructure

Despite the policy pertaining to the participation of private sector, participation didn't take place with greater pace. At present private sector participation is only in few sectors like telecom, power and roads. On the other hand, demand for massive investment in infrastructure is growing at much faster rate. In the present economic scenario there is a universal trend of massive investment in infrastructure and most of the trend can be seen from the developing countries; hence creating compulsion on the government to increase the investment in infrastructure at a faster rate in the coming future is the need of the year. Therefore the investment requirement to meet infrastructure demand would be unmanageable on the part of the public authorities and the ultimate solution is to rely on private players for infrastructure investment.

According to the World Bank Report, 2005, the private sector contribution to global infrastructure development accounted for approximately 20% of the total annual infrastructure investment in developing countries. Further, the investment levels have been increasing significantly in several countries, such as Bulgaria, India, and Vietnam.

Private capital is basically funded either by privatization of existing utilities or through construction of new projects on a Build-Operate-Transfer (BOT) basis.

Under BOT basis, the contractor is initially allowed to build the project and then a fixed share of revenue in the project is normally kept for the contractor.

Sources of Finance

Source of finance for infrastructure: The source of private finance for infrastructure can be equity market, loan from commercial banks and bond market (Table 4). But in India, loans from commercial banks are very limited. The biggest reason is the long gestation period for infrastructure and the risk associated with them. Risk assessment is also the key part of project evaluation for banking or financing institution because most of the projects are taken by the special purpose companies which may not have strong balance sheet. And further, financing on non-recourse basis, where the lenders have to solely depend on the revenue stream of the project is uncertain. Bond market is also underdeveloped in India due to various reasons. Ultimately the source of most of the private finance is capital market, but the investor may be willing to take higher risk for higher expected return. Clearly equity investor may have higher risk tolerance than the lender.

External borrowing is also a popular source of finance but it can be financed within a reasonable limit because of one additional risk called foreign exchange risk.

Table 4: Financing Sources for Private Sector Infrastructure

Domestic Sources	External Sources
Equity Domestic developers (independently or in collaboration with international developers) Public utilities (taking minority holdings) Other institutional investors (likely to be very limited)	International developers (independently or in collaboration with domestic developers Equipment suppliers (in collaboration with domestic or international developers) Dedicated infrastructure funds Other international equity investors Multilateral agencies (International Finance Corporation, Asian Development Bank)
Debt Domestic commercial banks (3-5 years) Domestic term lending institutions (7-10 years) Domestic bond markets (7-10 years) Specialized infrastructure financing institutions	International commercial banks (7-10 years) Export credit agencies (7-10 years) International bond markets (10-30 years) Multilateral agencies (15-20 years) Bilateral aid agencies

Source: planningcommission.nic.in (speech by Montek S Ahluwalia)

Emerging Instruments

Some of the innovative financing instruments that attract domestic financing are also popular now-a-days. Mezzanine debt, subordinated debt, convertible debt, debt with stock warrants, and debt with an additional interest payment are some of them. Mezzanine debt is a type of hybrid instrument that lies somewhere between debt and equity. These instruments are attracting investors seeking for higher returns than debt for limited risk. There are various financial institutions like ICICI, IDFC, and Shrei International which have issued these instruments in the recent past in India.

Box 1: Infrastructure Development Finance Company

The Infrastructure Development Finance Company (IDFC) was incorporated in January 1997 with 300,000 equity share of Rs.10 each by the GOI and the equal amount subscribed by IFCI, HDFC, RBI, UTI, and ICICI. Further, IDBI also signed the memorandum of association with an equity corpus of 200,000 at Rs.10 each. On March 30, 1998 the GOI, RBI and other financial institutions like IFCI, HDFC, UTI-I, ICICI, IDBI further allotted with share capital for subsequent cash contribution. In the same year foreign investor institutions like IPL, CDCFS, DB, FOFEA, SLAC and BNL also contributed in cash and allotted 278,000,000 equity share of Rs.10 each.

The basic objective of IDFC is to finance viable projects in power, telecommunications, roads, ports, and urban services. Apart from them, IDFC also encouraged innovative financing to help other institutions. IDFC's service includes direct lending, take-out financing, purchase of loans, and co-financing; standby finance, and refinancing of longer maturities. Apart from them IDFC also provides partial credit guarantees and other forms of credit enhancement for infrastructure projects; securitization of infrastructure loans and market making for these loans; and mezzanine finance.

Source: The Icfai Research Center

Specialized Financial Institutions

In most of the countries there are some specialized financing institutions that cater to infrastructure financing. Infrastructure Development Finance Corporation (IDFC) in India, Pakistan Private Sector Energy Development Fund, established in 1988, and Jamaica Private Sector Energy Fund, established in 1992, are some examples from Asian countries. A similar type of organization has been set up in Colombia also.

These Institutions are not only involved in direct financing, but they also encourage other financial institutions, through innovative services like, take-out financing, liquidity support, securitization etc.

Take-out financing is an arrangement under which projects can be financed initially from shorter-term debt and then can be refinanced later with the longer-term debt. Under liquidity support system bond issuance by infrastructure sector is encouraged by providing facilities in the form of put option prior to maturity or in the form of market making.

Securitization is one of the emerging instruments used to clean up balance sheet by sale of certain specific assets to a Special Purpose Vehicle (SPV). The SPV in turn issues securities that can be in the form of certificates or debt papers that could be effectively marketed to both domestic and international institutional investors.

Conclusion

Despite active participation of the government, the pace of infrastructure investment remains stable. The basic reason is the lack of proper financing and regulatory system that India is required to sustain for future growth. Private investment is still not fuelled due to various constraints. Risks associated with infrastructure projects are also a major problem in project implementation. Apart from market risk, there are operational risk, foreign exchange risk. There is a great need to handle other risks related to political and regulatory system. Raising money through equity markets is not a problem in current situation but, there is a need to develop a healthy debt market too. Apart from them, government should work for other sources of finance, tax strutting etc. that could provide a healthy environment for development of infrastructure projects. Overall, there is a need to commercialize infrastructure projects whether in the public or private sector. In other words, infrastructure projects should involve competent service providers, well-defined budgets and managerial and financial autonomy, while at the same time, holding them accountable for their performance.

(Sanjeev Kumar, Faculty Member, Academic Wing, The Icfai University.)

4

Models in Infrastructure Financing

M Yunus

Infrastructure assumed a commercial character and emerged as an income generating activity in the wake of globalaisation, which brought in market competitiveness. This article attempts to provide insights with regard to various options of financing infrastructure and furnishes an overview of institutions involved in financing infrastructure. It discusses few models of infrastructure financing like BOO, BOOT, BLT, BOT etc. The article also captures the sources of funding of private sector infrastructure finance though domestics and external sources under 'Equity Finance' and 'Debt Finance' and various players in this regard besides touching upon take-out financing, liquidity support, securitization, external debt financing export credit agencies international commercial banks, international bond markets and multilateral institutions. It also furnishes an account of innovative instruments of debt financing such as mezzanine debt, convertible debt, debt with stock warrants, simple subordinated debt and debt, etc.

Introduction

Infrastructure development involves huge capital investment in any country. Constraints of governments due to budget deficits, liabilities on account of excessive borrowings and low capacities of financing agencies, often result in neglect of the infrastructure projects. This has led to privatization of the infrastructure sector, in the aftermath of globalization and reforms initiatives by several governments world over. International capital markets induced by the high profit potential of this sector, started encashing on the emerging opportunities to finance the infrastructure projects in a big way. Globalization brought in market competitiveness in the infrastructure financing activities both in terms of value and time by leveraging between the huge infrastructure costs and time over-runs. Private sector, in this climate, emerged as the champion in sourcing and pooling the means of finance, offering various financial products and services, in the form of innovative and diversified financial instruments.

This article seeks to present an overview of the models that are commonly in vogue in the context of financing infrastructure. These models also are widely in use in other parts of the world where infrastructure projects are being developed and grounded. These are very relevant where infrastructure projects are undertaken and completed by private participants to determine the rights over the infrastructure assets after completion. A broad coverage is also being furnished in the later part of the article as regards some of the external sources for financing infrastructure.

Private Financing of Infrastructure

Global capital markets explosion and expansion of private capital flows to emerging market economies associated therewith, opened up new opportunities in financing infrastructure projects in these countries, subject, of course, to the projects being commercially viable. Many international companies with experience and expertise at their command started showing interest for investing in infrastructure development in Asia. For this, the overall investment climate should be perceived, as lucrative and domestic entrepreneurs in several countries of the region are keen to gain entry into these sectors. The underpinning of all markets and private sector participation in them is an administrative system with enforceable property rights, that can be transferred through the contract and that includes the means to resolve disputes over liability, when performance is not accepted by one of the parties.

In this light, the following models have been developed to clearly specify the rights on the infrastructure assets, after the respective projects have been commissioned. These models are well-recognized and practiced world over. By the very name, it would be possible to identify the nature of the project, how it was financed, and who would be the ultimate owner of the assets.

1) BOO (Build-Own-Operate) Model

Under this model, an infrastructure project is financed, constructed, owned and operated by a private sector entity and the government does not have any rights on the assets. That means the project is wholly undertaken and completed by private individuals or firms by obtaining institutional finances on their own. The terms of this model BOO would enable the firm to have exclusive ownership rights on such assets. But in India, these kinds of models are rare.

2) BOOT (Build-Own-Operate-Transfer) Model

Under this model, an infrastructure project is financed, constructed, owned and operated by a private entity. However, the right of the private party is only for a specified period as laid down in the contract and at the expiry of the contract period, the assets are to be transferred. To amplify, under this model the construction contract is awarded in favour of the private entity that is capable of undertaking the construction of it by making its own arrangements for financing the project. As a consideration of this, government permits the construction firm to have ownership of the asset for a limited period decided by a mutually agreed contract, till such time the firm recovers its costs and agreed portion of profits. Thereafter, the terms of BOOT require that the firms should transfer the rights on the assets to the government.

3) BT (Build-Transfer) Model

Under this model, the infrastructure project is financed by the government and is constructed by the private sector entity. The ownership of the assets is transferred soon on completion of the construction of the project. This means the construction firm is awarded the contract only for the purpose of construction as per agreed specifications and standards. The cost of construction with the margin of profit is agreed upon between the government and the construction firm. Upon completion of the project, the government becomes the absolute owner of the assets and the contractor is required to transfer rights on the asset in favour of the government, under the terms of BT Model.

4) BLT (Build-Lease-Transfer) Model

Under this model, the private sector entity finances, constructs the infrastructure project. Upon completion of construction, the asset is leased by Government to the private party for a specified period and upon expiry of the lease term, government becomes the owner of the asset. This model operates when the cost of the project is very huge or when the government cannot make suitable allocations for the project for any reason. In such cases, the construction of the project is assigned to a private construction contractor under due process. The contractor is supposed to make his own arrangements for financing the project on his own efforts and government would not involve in the matter. However, after completion of the project, as an incentive, the government enters into a lease agreement with the contractor for specified period, enables the firm to recover costs and profit by collecting user charges or cess or toll on the assets from the public. At the end of the contracted period, the asset gets transferred in government's favour.

5) BOT (Build-Operate-Transfer) Model

Under this model, the infrastructure project is financed by the government and constructed by the private sector entity. After completion of the project, the private entity is authorised to operate facility, on-behalf of the government. To amplify, the private construction company and the government would enter into an understanding or agreement whereby the assets is to be transferred in government's favour upon completion of the project. But the government also would permit the construction company to operate the asset as an agent of the Government. That is to say, the ownership lies with the government, but the firm can be allowed to operate the asset on behalf of the government.

These are the five major models for financing and operating the infrastructure projects. It is a common knowledge that the award of construction contracts to private companies by governments entails detailed and lengthy process, procedures and formalities, which would be superfluous to discuss here. The rights to retain the ownership on the infrastructure assets or to have rights to operate the assets, would be decided by so many factors relating to the project outlay, sources of financing, arrangements for financing, risks involved in the projects, the lead time involved in grounding the projects, etc. and are documented in the form of agreements between the parties concerned.

Other Sources for Financing Infrastructure

I would like to delve about few other aspects relating to the sources of financing infrastructure projects, other than debt and equity financing which would have been covered in other articles elsewhere in this book. In this context, I shall speak about the external sources of financing, take-out financing, about liquidity support, securitization, apart from external debt financing modes like export credit agencies, international commercial banks, international bond markets and multilateral institutions.

External sources for infrastructure finance comprise international developers either independently or having collaboration with domestic developers, equipment suppliers in collaboration with domestic or international developers, dedicated infrastructure funds, other international equity investors multilateral agencies such as International Finance Corporation, Asian Development Bank. International commercial banks lend for long periods ranging 7 to10 years, Export credit agencies that also lend for periods ranging from 7 to 10 years, International bond markets provide finance for more higher terms ranging from 10 to 30 years, multilateral agencies financing for a term of 15 to 20 years. Foreign sponsors, generally look for collaborative arrangements with domestic investors at this with view to obtain shield from political risks. By virtue of their tendency to evaluate risk less conservatively than foreign investors, their involvement often is considered helpful in improving the perceptions of foreign investors.

Take-out Financing

Infrastructure financing arrangements involve short-term debts initially, for example supplier's credit for purchase of equipment, which can be refinanced later by long-term debt at a later stage. A specialized institution could help guarantee. Such refinancing would be guaranteed by a specialized institution at a financing cost determined in advance. This arrangement is referred to as 'take-out financing', which provides an assurance to the project promoters that in case refinancing is not available when needed, the institutional would either provide direct finance or the differential of the predetermined financing cost and the cost at which funds can be raised from other market sources could be reimbursed for implementation of the project. Take-out finance entails commercial fee for the services rendered.

Liquidity Support

Under this mode, Issuance of Bonds for infrastructure finance are encouraged providing liquidity support for such bonds in the form of a put option prior to maturity or in the form of market sourcing.

Securitization

Another form of providing infrastructure finance is 'Securitisation'. Under this mode, a specialized financing institution would securitize the cash flows out of loans in a pool, successfully operating in a wider market for such assets. This is aimed at reducing risk through diversification and creating a high-quality asset, which can be effectively marketed to domestic as well as international institutional investors.

External Debt Financing

Well-structured private sector infrastructure projects with reasonable credit ratings are often the target for several external debt financing agencies across the countries. These agencies include export credit agencies, international commercial banks, international bond markets, multilateral institutions.

Export Credit Agencies

Export credit agencies have been a dominant source of international capital to finance infrastructure projects.. They provide direct finance and also guarantee the commercial bank credit. Traditionally, these export credit agencies are used to fund public sector projects that are backed by sovereign guarantees, but of late show inclination to finance against commercial bank guarantees also, to stay in the business in a competitive era.

International Commercial Banks

International Commercial Banks are the universal source for financing private infrastructure development in many developing countries. These banks lend on the basis of a detailed project risk appraisal. But the important point to be mentioned here is that due to the limited number of international banks actively involved in project financing in developed countries, these banks are constrained by exposure and country-wise limitations to take up financing of infrastructure, often leading to Syndication Mode which again is subject to cumbersome procedures. These international banks normally seek loan maturities between seven years to ten years, against the real maturities of fifteen to twenty years involved in infrastructure projects. This mismatch operates as the barrier for obtaining loans from these international commercial banks. The possible solution to tide over these limitations would be to lengthen the maturities of commercial bank loans through multilateral guarantee support. The crux of the issue is reliance on bank financing for infrastructure should either be part of a mix involving other long-term lending sources or it must be backed by suitable refinancing arrangements.

International Bond Markets

Ideally, bond financing is the suitable source of financing infrastructure, in many ways. This mode, though costlier than the syndicated loans, offers typically longer maturities ranging from ten to thirty years or more for creditworthy issuers. Due to the ease of long maturity, bond financing has emerged as the fastest growing source of infrastructure finance in the developing countries during the recent years. With more and more private sector infrastructure projects being successfully implemented in the developing countries and the companies gaining financial recognition and developing track records of successful implementation, bond markets are becoming increasingly popular and important over the years. As regards newly established infrastructure firms who may find it difficult to access bond markets during initial stage, they may be able to tap this resource, during the post-construction stage, when risk perceptions diminish and projects start generating steady revenue streams. Bond financing could thus be used for refinancing the initial shorter-term loans taken at the construction stage.

Multilateral Institutions

The Asian Development Bank and World Bank importantly rank under multilateral financing institutions, which are very much known for their traditional funding of public sector infrastructure projects. While in the changed environment of globalization, even though these agencies are willing to support private sector projects, their role should be mentioned as limited. The reason for this is there are many competing claims on the scarce resources of these two multilateral agencies and diversion of resources for funding private sector projects may not be gainful for the economy. However, these agencies could play a catalytic role in a significant way during the early stages of attracting the private sector into infrastructure. To elaborate, the transparency of their project evaluation procedures and also their ability in benchmarking individual private sector projects in a particular country against international experience of similar projects, could be emulated by domestic financial agencies to avoid controversies that may otherwise arise about private sector projects. Given their active involvement as lenders for a project, the risk perception on the part of other investors can be reduced. The only problem is that these institutions follow cumbersome procedures, which would not be accepted by the private sector investors often.

Innovative Instruments of Debt Financing

Use of innovative financing instruments like mezzanine debt, can facilitate by attracting domestic finance for infrastructure projects. Mezzanine debt is a hybrid instrument placed in between debt and equity as far its features are concerned. In other words it is subordinated to secured debt but is superior to equity in the hierarchy of creditors. Similar innovative instruments are plenty, some of which are—convertible debt, debt with stock warrants, simple subordinated debt and debt with an additional interest payment above the coupon rate contingent to financial performance. These instruments are more appealing to investors looking for higher returns than secured debt. Mezzanine debt, when introduced at a given level of equity in project financing, is considered helpful in improving the quality of the superior debt and hence its marketability.

Emergence of dedicated mezzanine debt funds, for example, the Asian Infrastructure Mezzanine Capital Fund, sponsored by the Prudential Capital

Insurance Company, reflects the demand for mezzanine debt. A combination of lower-cost superior debt and higher-cost mezzanine debt, if adopted as mixed strategy to rely upon, would widen the pool of investors those can be tapped and helps lowering the overall financing cost of the project.

Conclusion

The common feature in most developing countries is that despite active state of private infrastructure investment and the growing number of success tales, the pace of investment flows remains slower than what was initially expected. The reasons for this are the preconditions for private financing of infrastructure, which are difficult to establish. Another factor is inadequate preparatory work leading to unanticipated problems and delays in seeing private sector infrastructure projects through.

Infrastructure projects require long debt maturities, corresponding to the long payback period. In the absence of long-term debt, they need reasonable assurance of refinancing or take-out financing. Availability of domestic finance in adequate doses perhaps seems to be the most serious constraint on infrastructure financing. Infrastructure projects cannot exclusively be financed or even primarily through external capital, for the simple reason that tariffs are usually fixed in domestic currency and a large scale international financing only implies a correspondingly higher foreign exchange risk. Therefore, it is desirable that a substantial share of project costs are financed through domestic means. Effective measures for developing domestic debt markets are crucial to support private sector infrastructure projects.

The development of domestic debt markets also depends upon an environment of fiscal prudence. This means that fiscal deficits are moderate and do not put pressure on domestic interest rates. Apart, development of an efficient and liquid market for government debt is essential to provide foundation for development of a broader market for corporate debt. Ultimately, the climate should usher development of institutions engaged in mobilizing long-term savings, particularly the insurance and pension funds, which have a potential to provide high-quality, long-term debt.

(MYunus, Banking Consultant, Advisor and Trainer (Formerly Assistant General Manager, SBI.)).

5

Special Purpose Vehicle: Scope for Banks?

Naveen Kumar

There is a huge demand for infrastructure in India. According to one estimate, more than Rupees one lakh crore is required for electricity, roads and railways. Special purpose vehicles can solve the problem to some extent. Banks and financial institutions by investing in SPV created by government can get good return at low risk.

Need for Infrastructure

If we look at any of the developed countries like America, England, Australia, France, New Zealand, Japan, Singapore and others, we find that they are essentially good at basic infrastructure. They have done the basic spade work of building good roads, railways, ports, airports, power projects (Thermal Power and Hydro Electric), communication networks (like telephone, telegraph, internet, satellite network etc.) long back. This is the secret behind the advancement of the developed countries. If India wants other nations to regard it as a developed country and not a developing country, it has to concentrate seriously on its infrastructure.

Source: Professional Banker, October 2005.

Present Scenario

Having recognized the importance of infrastructure for the development of the country, we will see what are the areas in which we are strong and the areas where there is the need for investment in infrastructure and the reasons for failure in improving in some critical areas.

Information technology and Biotechnology are the two areas where we can compare ourselves to world leaders. We are in a position where we are able to launch our own satellites like Polar Satellite Launch Vehicle (PSLV), Geo Synchronous Satellite Launch Vehicle (GSLV), which help us in transmitting information and in detecting weather conditions. The Indian Space Research Organization (ISRO) is also looking at for launching of satellites commercially viable so that we can launch these vehicles for other small nations, that lack the capability and the technical know-how. We have also achieved desired progress in telecommunications and Internet infrastructure. The cost of communication through basic telephones, mobile telephones and Internet is lowest in the world. Now the broadband speed prices have come down to such a level where a common man can easily afford them. Technology in the communication sector can match the best in the world.

Basic physical infrastructure is neglected to a great extent and we will take many years before we match ourselves with the world standards. We have started moving in the right direction by taking up golden quadrilateral project whereby the National Highways Authority of India (NHAI) is constructing 5,850 km of roadways to connect all four metros of India at an estimated cost of Rs.2500 cr. We require many such projects for the development of India. Manufacturing sector in India is severely affected due to lack of basic infrastructure facilities like power, water, roads, ports and cost effective transportation modes. "The sad state of infrastructure is adding anywhere from 20-40% extra cost to Indian products. The result of this is increased cost of production to manufacturing sector, rendering our products internationally uncompetitive."

This is making us lose to products manufactured by other countries like China. Traffic problems are faced in almost all major cities and towns because of constricted and congested roads. Power is again a major problem in all cities. We all face power cuts and water shortages every summer. Many manufacturers have shut their shops because of power shortages and high fluctuations in power. Recently, information technology companies of Bangalore went on one-day strike to protest against the condition of bad roads. This is something which should be taken seriously as multinational companies would not like to operate in a country where basic infrastructure facilities are in pathetic condition.

Need for Investment in Infrastructure

To improve the infrastructure facilities, we need to improve our roadways by constructing more golden quadrilaterals, more national highways, more flyovers etc. To improve railways we need to have high speed trains with zero accident rates which require efficient signaling system. There is a need for constructing Mass Rapid Transport Systems, Multi-Model Transport Systems as in developed countries like Singapore, England, France, America and other developed countries. Underground railways and Sky Bus facilities etc., are needed. We need to construct more Thermal Power Plants for more generation of power and also construct more dams across rivers for generation of Hydro Electric Power. We need to concentrate more on Hydro Electric Power Projects than on Thermal Power Projects as the electricity generated from Hydro Electric Power Projects is cheaper than that generated by Thermal Power Plants. India is having a peculiar problem, i.e. there is an uneven distribution of rainfall throughout the country during rainy season. While some states receive excess rainfall, other states receive scanty rainfall. Some states experience floods during rainy season, while some states are affected by famine and drought. There is need for linking of rivers to supply water uniformly to all the states. This will not only quench the parched throats but also bring hundreds of uncultivated lands under cultivation, which will result in increased contribution from agriculture sector towards Gross Domestic Product (GDP). There is need to construct more international airports like Changi airport in Singapore. We need to construct more ports and international airports of world standards to increase trade volumes and attract foreign direct investment. This will also result in increasing the exports.

India's investment in infrastructure was a mere 6% of Gross Domestic Product (GDP) in 2002 equivalent to $31 bn whereas China's was 20% of GDP, i.e., around $260 bn. "In a recent meeting of CEOs in New York, Prime Minister

Dr. Manmohan Singh mentioned that India would need around $150 bn of foreign investment in infrastructure over the next decade. According to a number of sources, the total investment needed should range from $600 to $800 bn. Indian government does not have the required finances for infrastructure investment."

Way Out Suggested

In the current Budget, Finance Minister P Chidambaram has proposed to set up a Rs.10,000 cr Financial Special Purpose Vehicle to fund projects in the infrastructure sector.

What is a Special Purpose Vehicle?

The Special Purpose Vehicle (SPV) can also be called Special Purpose Entity. The SPV is created for some specific purpose. The scope of SPV is limited and focused. We can say that the name SPV is given to an entity, which is formed for a distinct, well-defined, and specific purpose. For any lawful purpose, Special Purpose Vehicles can be created. For any unlawful purpose or for undertaking activities which are contrary to the provisions of law or public policy, SPVs cannot be formed.

The Special Purpose Vehicle is like a corporation. It has to follow all rules and regulations laid in the companies act. Like a company, Special Purpose Vehicle is an artificial person. It has all the characteristics of a legal person. It is independent of members subscribing to its shares. The Special Purpose Vehicle has an existence of its own in the eyes of law. It can sue and be sued in its name. The Special Purpose Vehicle can do all things, which are mentioned in the memorandum of association or permitted by the Companies Act, but its scope of operation is limited and specific. The objective of keeping the scope of Special Purpose Vehicle limited is to reassure lenders who are worried about their investment. The Special Purpose Vehicle will have promoter or sponsor like a company. The sponsoring company hives off assets from the rest of the company into a Special Purpose Vehicle. The assets are separated from the parent company; hence the performance of the new entity will not be affected by the ups and downs of the originating entity, which results in Special Purpose Vehicle having fewer risks. This separation of Special Purpose Vehicle from its sponsoring company makes it identity different from the subsidiary company.

Role of Banks and Financial Institutions

The Special Purpose Vehicle will raise funds from the market by issuing long-term debt financial instruments say bonds, which are mostly subscribed by various banks and financial institutions. Banks and financial institutions are playing a key role in the infrastructure development of the country, i.e., they are indirectly lending to infrastructure projects by subscribing to the bonds and debentures issued by Special Purpose Vehicle. Later on, this fund is lent directly to either public or private sector companies, which take up projects in infrastructure at an interest rate far below the prime lending rates to make this project more attractive and viable to both public and private sector. Institutions like Infrastructure Development Finance Company (IDFC), Power Finance Corporation (PFC), Indian Rail Finance Corporation (IRFC) etc., can now use the funds raised by Special Purpose Vehicle. The central government will offer a counter-guarantee to bonds issued by the Special Purpose Vehicle. The Special Purpose Vehicle will become an intermediatory for channelizing funds for infrastructure projects. Indirectly, Special Purpose Vehicle is playing the role of supple mentor of loans already issued by banks and financial institutions for infrastructure projects. In simple terms, Special Purpose Vehicle will act as a unique platform that will facilitate consortium lending to infrastructure projects by banks and financial institutions. The Special Purpose Vehicle will play a role of facilitator. Apart from subscribing to the bonds issued by Special Purpose Vehicle, banks and financial institutions play a major role of appraising an infrastructure project and project's viability. The Special Purpose Vehicle on its own does not have the capability of vetting the projects.

Banks and Financial Institutions can also be partners in the formation of Special Purpose Vehicle.

In an interview to *Business Standard* newspaper, Planning Commission Deputy Chairperson Montek Singh Ahluwalia says, "The existing public sector system is so used to getting money from the budget, they cannot prepare a good project for scrutiny by financial institutions." The Special Purpose Vehicle will play the role of arbitrator in resolving various policy and regulatory issues concerning these infrastructure projects as the finance ministry administers it.

What Planning Commission Deputy Chairperson Says

In an interview to the same newspaper, Ahluwalia points out "If the country is deluged with people wanting to pick up financial assets from the country, there are a number of ways of handling it."

One option will be to let the money flow in and not sterilize it. If people do not want to use forex, the rupee can be allowed to appreciate. But this idea is likely to be opposed.

Another option is not to sterilize the inflows, protect the impact on the exchange rate, cut customs duty and encourage imports. This has been done to an extent in the budget. Of course, you would also remove controls on capital outflows. These options are sensible, but they will have to be done gradually. The alternative is to invest in infrastructure that can be pushed up steeply. In my view, the inflows should go into infrastructure. The ideal way will be to sterilize the inflow, build reserves and push liquidity into system. The country needs a lot of infrastructure. The Special Purpose Vehicle is a mechanism to channel money to finance 'infrastructure projects'.

SPV for Infrastructure May not Create Fiscal Deficit

Many Asian countries, which have high Forex reserves, are planning to use these reserves to develop their own infrastructure instead of using them to lend to other countries. In the past, USA and China did successfully use Forex reserves for developing their physical infrastructure.

International Monetary Fund (IMF) Managing Director Rodrigo de Rato recently said, "We think the Special Purpose Vehicle that the Government of India is proposing is a positive step forward. It is certainly within the limits of the budgetary provisions of the Indian government."

Asked whether the Special Purpose Vehicle was a "hidden fiscal deficit" as the government will offer a counter-guarantee to it, de Rato said it will not impact government finances as it was "within the limits" of fiscal provisions of the budget.

The Planning Commission welcomed the move, but felt it may have an indirect effect on fiscal deficit. The Plan panel had earlier suggested that a small portion of the burgeoning forex reserves, now touching $140 bn, could be utilized for infrastructure development. When asked whether it was feasible to use forex reserves for funding infrastructure, Rodrigo de Rato said: "We are of opinion that forex reserves should be used by the central bank (Reserve Bank of India) for desired purposes and should not be monetized."

Conclusion

We should not worry about the fiscal deficit but worry about the most important deficit that India has, i.e., infrastructure deficit. The only way to reckon India as super power is to become fundamentally strong by investing in infrastructure.

(Naveen Kumar is a Faculty Member at The Icfai School of Financial Studies, Hyderabad.)

Flipside of SPVs

Post Enron, there was a substantial controversy about special purpose vehicles and their possible misuse. Special purpose vehicles were publicly seen as a device to dodge tax and accounting scrutiny. A special purpose vehicle is like a secret bank locker: its owner or beneficiary cannot be established on a primary appearance, and it is still safe since it is a hived-off bundle of assets with only specific assets or activities. Since the voting capital in special purpose entities is abysmally low (and would typically be declared for public charity, or otherwise widely dispersed), such entities could not come for consolidation based on their voting capital.

Therefore, US standard setters set on a who-dunnit kind of a mission to spot the real beneficiary of special purpose entities. The result was an interpretation called FIN 46, which deals with consolidation of certain entities on a basis other than voting control. Thus, FIN 46 is an exception to the usual consolidation rules in Accounting Research Bulletin (ARB) 51. A new term was coined for this purpose: Variable Interest Entites to which the new consolidation rule would be applicable. A variable interest entity (VIE) is essentially nothing but an accounting jargon for the commercial world phrase "special purpose entity". The Interpretation identifies two key indicias of an SPE: inadequacy of at-risk capital, and exercise of absentee control by the *de facto* owner of the entity and not the front-running equity holders who are mere nominalities. If a company is deemed to be the primary beneficiary of a variable interest entity, they will be required to consolidate the variable interest entity within their financial statements. The required consolidation will affect the financial statements of the company and should be addressed proactively with bankers and bonding agents as it can be significant based upon the size of the variable interest entities which are required to be consolidated.

Impact to Construction and Real Estate Companies

Common situations that may cause a construction or real estate company to be impacted by FIN 46(R) include:

- Construction contractors often establish separate legal entities to acquire and hold equipment that is then rented to the contractor. Often, such entities are created for tax and estate-planning purposes.
- Construction contractors may establish a separate legal entity to acquire and hold an office building and equipment yard for their company use.
- Construction companies may form joint ventures with other companies to build a project due to the requirements and the expertise needed to complete the project.
- Real estate developers frequently form separate legal entities to own the property, which is to be developed. The purpose of the separate legal entity is to isolate the developer's exposure if the project is unsuccessful.

In each of these circumstances, the separate legal entities may meet the criteria in FIN 46(R) to be considered a variable interest entity.

Compiled from www.vinodkothari.com/fin46vk.htm and www.mossadams.com

6

Rural Infrastructure Development Fund – Empowering Projects

Deepak Kumar

The article talks about how the rural infrastructure sector has been taken care of by the Rural Infrastructure Development Fund (RIDF). This is one of the financing models that have been successful in India, as in this case the projects are appraised, monitored and implemented by NABARD with consultation of the state governments. The projects are prioritized to create employment and improve the quality of life.

"Inadequacy of public investment in agriculture is, today, a matter of general concern. This is an area which is the responsibility of the states. But many states have neglected investment in infrastructure for agriculture. There are many rural infrastructure projects which have been started but are lying incomplete for want of resources. They represent a major loss of potential income and employment to the rural population."

– Union Budget Speech 1995-96,
by the Indian Finance Minister

The Indian economy bears no resemblance to what it was 20 years ago. At that time, it was basically an agro-based economy with significant industrial inputs. The service sector was largely state controlled and poorly developed and what was described as "services" was basically income generated from the services of various public corporations. The presence of a large and professional service sector was largely unknown.

Today, services are driving the economic growth. However, this has lead to congestion in the urban areas, with significant rural migration to the large cities. India has significantly improved on its problem solving capability regarding urban infrastructure development. There are proper frameworks in place; the large municipal corporations have acquired the capacity to raise their own funds; and structuring and policy framing skills are indigenously available, on a steadily increasing basis.

While all these developments are there in the urban areas, the lack of the same in the rural and semi-urban areas has been a cause for serious concern among policy makers. Taking cognizance of this fact, the authorities have looked for effective measures to develop rural infrastructure, without which the rapid growth of the rural economy would not be possible. We would like to point out that "rural" does not strictly point to "agrarian" for the purpose of this article. There is a considerable scope for other services to come up, provided the support infrastructure comes up as well. The problem is that the rural people in many cases are not used to pay for such infrastructure. There are also a number of vested interests in the rural areas which cannot be monitored in the same way as an urban municipality can. Therefore it is clear that the state has to take up a large part of this burden, if the development of the rural areas is to take off. The Rural Infrastructure Development Fund (RIDF) plays a crucial role, in that it is being operated and monitored by National Bank for Agriculture and Rural Development (NABARD) which has been the apex body for such development, over the past few decades.

The present government has also launched schemes such as National Employment Guarantee Bill (NEGB) 2005, which aims to fulfill the mission and vision of Bharat Nirman. While NEGB promises to build up rural infrastructure projects, one of its demerits is that the idle wage payment is allowed even if the projects are not run or cannot run because of some un predictable reasons such as climatic, terrorism and red tape problems. Though NEGB promises to build the better rural infrastructure, its main aim is to provide 100-day employment to each member of a family in the selected district. Hence, it is really a tough task to balance the development works and the employment generation.

Recently, the Confederation of Indian Industry (CII) in the year 2005 arranged Suminfra conference where it was opined by almost all speakers that India lacks not only sufficient capital for rural infrastructure projects but also financing models and attractive policies. On account of this, India is unable to visualize development in the rural areas. Though the Government of India has launched several schemes and policies since the 1960s, the actual implementation record has been very poor. But ultimately, it is the RIDF which has emerged as the key driver for the development of rural infrastructure.

The Evolution of RIDF

The Rural Infrastructure Development Fund is like a Special Purpose Vehicle (SPV) for creating and strengthening rural infrastructure. One of the major aims of developing rural infrastructure is to generate additional employment opportunities and to improve the quality of life of the rural people. In sum, the objectives of the RIDF is multidimensional and it focuses on how to accelerate the overall growth rate of the Indian economy by taking care of building rural infrastructure and providing a better amenities.

Montek Singh Ahluwalia, Deputy Chairman of the Planning Commission, said that, "India has had a lending facility for rural infrastructure since 1995-96, perhaps the only one of its kind anywhere in the world. The RIDF is a demand-driven non-concessional scheme targeted at sub-national state governments. The success of schemes like RIDF depends on redressing inter-state inequities and imbalances.[1]

---

1 "Economic Performance of States in Post Reforms Period", *Economic and Political Weekly*, 35, 1637-48.

The RIDF, has a much better success path than the earlier programs because it:

i. is clear and specific as to its objectives;

ii. uses State balances monitored by the Reserve Bank of India; and

iii. is managed by NABARD, the apex bank for such activities.

It was ten years back when RIDF was set up by the Government of India, having a single focus of building rural infrastructure projects. Till now when ten tranches have been completed, and it is very important to evaluate its pros and cons as well as the developmental work done till now. This article is an attempt to address this issue.

RIDF Tranches and Corpus

The RIDF was started in 1995-96 with a corpus amount of Rs.2000 cr. The main aim of RIDF is to finance rural infrastructure projects such as rural roads, water harvesting systems, forest development, plantation and horticulture, developing market yards, drainage system, rural education institutes, village knowledge centers, soil conservation, protection from flood, etc. (Refer to Annexure). As the number of projects went on increasing, the corpus amount also increased over a period and today approximately 10,000 projects are undergoing/are completed because of RIDF.

However, the interim government in the year 2004-05 announced to dismantle RIDF and planned to set up an Agriculture Infrastructure and Credit Fund. This was a real setback to RIDF but the regular budget of 2004 announced its revival and announced a corpus of Rs.8000 cr. This shows that the government also felt the need of having RIDF and developing rural infrastructure projects by such effort (Table 1).

A close look at Table 1 reveals the fact that RIDF corpus has increased over the period and by RIDF XI, a total amount of Rs.50,000 cr was sanctioned. The 300% increase in corpus from RIDF I to RIDF XI implies that RIDF is going to cover more rural infrastructure projects and it is just not limited to developing road, bridges, water system, education institutes but it now also covers areas

Table 1: RIDF Tranches and Corpus Amount

RIDF Tranches	Year	Corpus (Rs. cr)	No. of Projects
RIDF I	1995-96	2000	4168
RIDF II	1996-97	2500	8167
RIDF III	1997-98	2500	14346
RIDF IV	1998-99	3000	6173
RIDF V	1999-2000	3500	13272
RIDF VI	2000-01	4500	43407
RIDF VII	2001-02	5000	25056
RIDF VIII	2002-03	5500	21870
RIDF IX	2003-04	5500	19625
RIDF X	2004-05	8000	60015
RIDF XI	2005-06	8000	–
RIDF XII	2006-07	10,000	–
Total		**60,000**	

Source: www.nabard.org

such as plantation, horticulture and developing mandi system. This also implies that the idea of having Agriculture Infrastructure and Credit Fund in place of RIDF was not just a nightmare when RIDF can take care of agricultural infrastructure.

Figure 1: Sanction and Disbursements Under RIDF

(Rs. cr)

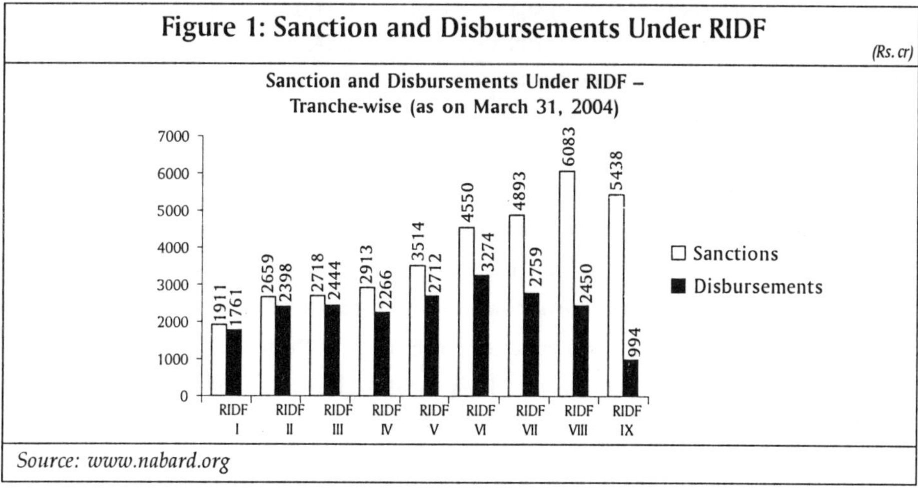

Source: www.nabard.org

However, as far as utility of RIDF is concerned, the government is very cautious to have its proper use so that the target audience should be benefited. With this aim, in the budget 2006-07, the budgetary allocation for RIDF has been increased to Rs.10,000 cr. As there are numerous projects in the pipeline, it is important to complete the uncompleted projects than starting new projects, as it involves the sink investment. NABARD is very selective in appraising, monitoring and implementing the project wisely. The reasons for the gap between sanctioned and disbursement include:

- Delay in project appraisal and bureaucratic levels in sanctioning the amount, and
- Delay in finding the right NGOs/Self-Help Groups (SHGs).

Table 2 shows the linkage between SHGs and banks.

Table 2: SHG-Bank Linkage Program: Cumulative Progress (As on March 31, 2005)

(Rs. cr)

Year	SHGs Financed (No.)	Bank Loans Disbursed*	SHGs Refinanced (No.)	Refinanced Disbursed
2001	2,63,825	480.87	2,13,213	394.98
2002	4,61,478	1,026.34	3,40,131	790.24
2003	7,17,360	2,048.67	4,93,634	1,412.71
2004	10,79,091	3,904.20	6,11,043	2,118.15
2005	16,18,476	6,898.46	8,24,888	3,085.91

* Includes repeat loans issued to existing SHGs.

Source: www.nabard.org

Another argument is that releasing the fund to SHGs by RIDF is somewhat difficult, as the process is complex and SHGs do not have mastery in preparing the project proposal and they can be put in the backseat if they are not able to communicate their business proposals. Therefore, NABARD must pay a close observation to such affairs, as it sanctions the fund to those parties whose proposal is found suitable by the committee. It is meaningless to mention that SHGs are a social guardian of the downtrodden and the poor section of society and they should not be neglected. However, NABARD has achieved significantly when it comes to the matter of how fund is sanctioned to SHGs.

Methodology of Project Sanctioning

Figure 2 is self-explanatory. Sanctioning of project involves the scrutinizing of applications by Community Based Organizations (CBOs), followed by NABARD staff members and the project is also appraised by field visits. Once the project report is found suitable, it is sent to the state steering committee. After that the project approval comes into picture and NABARD, involving in capacity building exercise, prepares once the project appraisal is done. The loan is sanctioned by a committee constituted by the NABARD Board based on project. Thus, the RIDF basically takes care of capacity building of the state government and other development agencies. Once the project is completed, project completion report

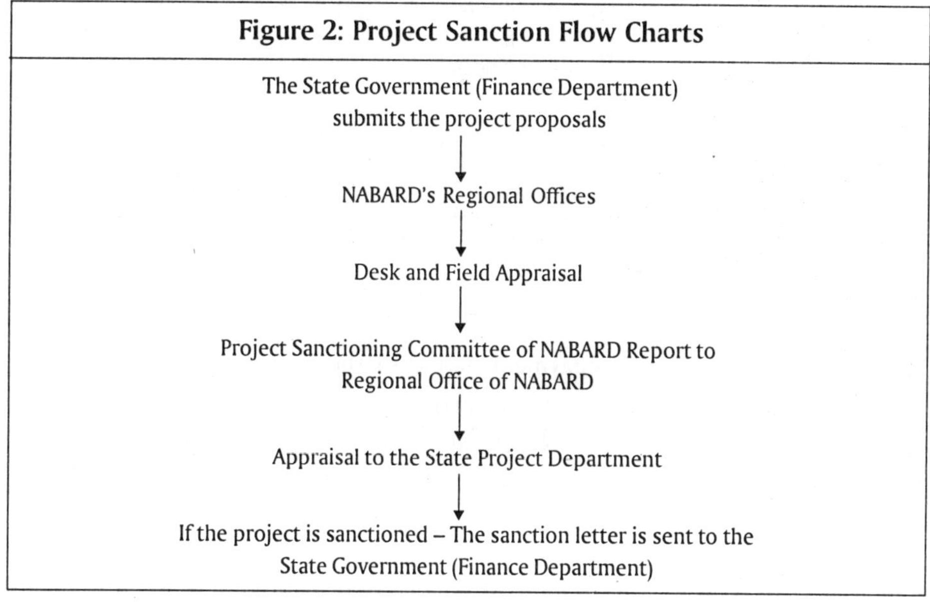

Figure 2: Project Sanction Flow Charts

is prepared by NABARD staff members and the same is sent to the Staff Steering Committee for the review. Thus NABARD is involved in appraising, monitoring, implementing and reviewing the project.

Project Sanctioning Committee (PSC) is the sole decider as to who and which projects will be sanctioned based on the appraisal report. PSC includes the members such as Chairman of NABARD; Managing Director of NABARD; Secretary (Banking), Ministry of Finance, Government of India (GoI), on the Board of

NABARD; Secretary, Ministry of Rural Development, GoI, on the Board of NABARD; Secretary, Ministry of Agriculture, GoI, on the Board of NABARD; Deputy Governor, RBI, on the Board of NABARD; and two State Government Representatives from the Board of NABARD.

Table 3: Rate of Interest

Tranche	Rate of Interest (Per Annum)	
RIDF-I	13.00	
RIDF-II	12.00	
RIDF-III	12.00	
RIDF-IV	8.50@	7.00*
RIDF-V	8.50@	7.00*
RIDF-VI	8.50@	7.00*
RIDF-VII	8.00@	7.00*
RIDF-VIII	6.50	
RIDF-IX	6.50	
RIDF-X	6.50	
RIDF-XI	6.50	

@ w.e.f. April 16, 2005 for loans disbursed on or before October 31, 2003

* On loans disbursed w.e.f. November 01, 2003.

Source: www.nabard.org

In the earlier years, the repayment period of the loan amount in RIDF was five years including 2-3 years gestation period, but it has now extended to seven years. RIDF provides the loan to NGOs, SHGs, Panchayati Raj Institutions (PRIs), and the state governments. In earlier days, the Rate of Interest (ROI) was as high as 13% but it has now been lowered to 6.5%.

Table 3 shows the rate of interest on the sanctioned amount. It is praiseworthy that the ROI has decreased with a higher rate of 13.0% per annum to 6.5%. This step is aimed to cover more projects and also for the upliftment of the rural sector. The higher interest is surely a burden to the beneficiaries but the current ROI is reasonably good, as most of the other financial institutions provide the loan at a much higher rate. The lower ROI has encouraged the target audience to arrange the loan through RIDF.

Achievements of Projects

Table 4 and Figure 3 show the amount sanctioned in different projects. A close observation shows that major sectors covered by the RIDF were irrigation, rural roads and bridges, social and power. Among these sectors, the percentage of amount sanctioned to the irrigation sector was the highest.

Table 4: Sector-wise Projects and Amount Sanctioned

(As on March 31, 2005)

(Rs. cr)

Sector	RIDF X	Share (%)	RIDF (I to X) (Total)	Share (%)
Irrigation				
No.	3,060	5.1	79,317	36.7
Amount	2,486.82	30.0	14,788.14	34.4
Rural Bridges				
No.	455	0.8	9,332	4.3
Amount	592.59	7.2	4,785.41	11.2
Rural Roads				
No.	5,046	8.4	44,144	20.4
Amount	2,472.08	29.8	14,498.28	33.8
Social Sector*				
No.	45,838	76.4	68,675	31.8
Amount	1,556.41	18.8	3,877.25	9.0
Power Sector**				
No.	–	–	723	0.3
Amount	–	–	1,348.33	3.1
Others@				
No.	5,616	9.3	13,908	6.5
Amount	1,174.85	14.2	3,651.10	8.5
Total No.	**60,015**	**100.0**	**2,16,099**	**100.0**
Amount	**8,282.75**	**100.0**	**42,948.51**	**100.0**

* Social Sector includes Rural Drinking Water, Primary/Secondary Schools and Primary Health Centers.

** Power Sector includes System Improvements and Mini Hydel Projects.

@ Others include: Watershed Development, Flood Protection, CADA, Drainage, Inland Waterways, Soil Conservation, Forest Development, Rubber Plantations, Fisheries, Animal Husbandry, Seed/Agriculture/Horticulture Farms, Market Yards/Godowns, Cold Storages, Citizen Information Centers, Food Parks, etc.

Source: www.nabard.org

During RIDF I-X, a sum of Rs.14,788.14 cr (out of Rs.42,948.51 cr) was sanctioned in irrigation projects and 3060 projects were covered in different states like Punjab, Tamil Nadu, Orissa, etc. This shows the unequal distribution of RIDF amount as approximately one-third of the sanctioned amount went to the irrigation sector. Although the irrigation sector has improved a lot because of such effort but other areas should be equally emphasized, only then can total development be expected.

Figure 3: Sanctions and Disbursements under Various Tranches of RIDF Projects (As on March 31, 2005)

(Rs. cr)

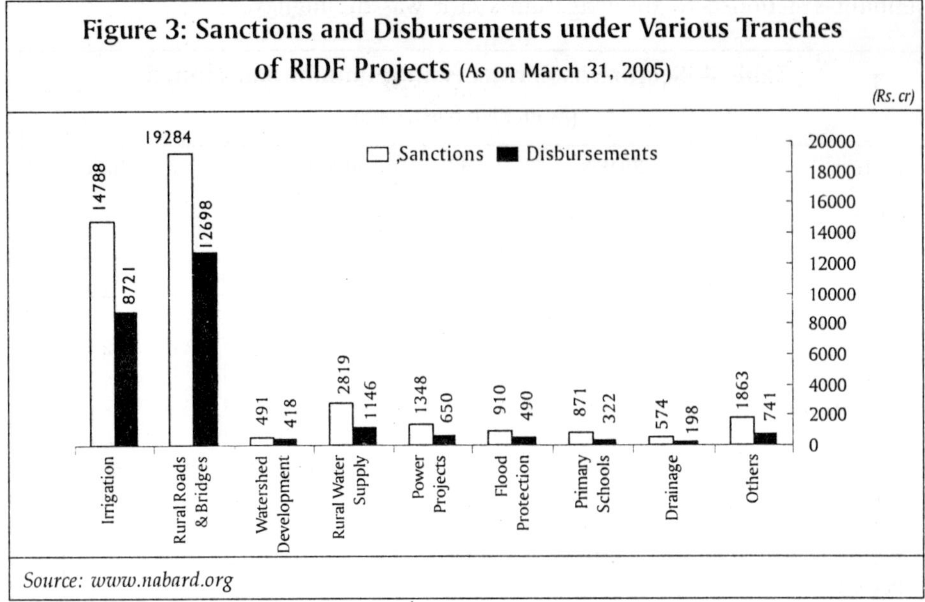

Source: www.nabard.org

Next to irrigation, rural roads and bridges projects got more focus by RIFD. A total non-recurring employment of 1,89,738 person days were generated through rural road projects (Table 5). The major states that benefited were Punjab, Haryana, Tamil Nadu, Gujarat and Orissa.

Since RIDF has a limited amount and the projects are numerous, the state government prioritizes the projects. The important criteria while prioritizing are: substantial return, employment opportunities in tribal and drought prone areas, short gestation period, technically feasible and financially viable.

Benefits

The benefits of RIDF are very significant. A total of 67.7 lakh ha area has been covered by irrigation projects and an addition of 1.31 lakh km., long rural road network and 231 km bridge length were built up. Due to the completion of these projects, a total amount of Rs.7813 cr has been contributed to the GDP

Table 5: Benefits Derived from Infrastructure Development Projects under RIDF

Sr. No.	Type of Investment	State/ Reference Year	No.	Total Length (km.)	Capital Cost (Rs.'000)	Net Incremental Income (Rs.'000)	Additional Employment Generation (Person days)	ERR (%)
1.	**Rural Road Projects**							
	i. Construction of new link roads	Punjab/2002	3	12.59	13,412	5,082	60,038$	33
	ii. Reconstruction of roads		2	16.38	44,105	8.638	1,89,738$	17
	iii. Strengthening and black topping of roads	Tamil Nadu/ 2002	2	19.60	51,332	5,620	28#	20
	iv. Construction of roads	Rajasthan/ 2001-02	4	11.50	12,520	2,396	15#	28
	v. Construction of Roads	Gujarat/ 2001-02	10	61.00	43,940	12,704	–	37
2.	**Rural Bridge Projects**							
	i. On river Mahanadi	Orissa/ 2003-04	1	1,858.66A	4,12,510	3,10,917	11,96,000$	>50
	ii. On river Kharasrota		1	471A	2,32,065	69,617	2,41,800$	38

$: Non-Recurring Employment A: Length in Metres #: Person days per worker

Source: www.nabard.org

and has generated a recurring employment of 37.70 lakh jobs and non-recurring employment of 9,860 lakh person days, due to increased irrigation while 11,178 lakh person days of non-recurring employment is expected from non-irrigation projects.

By the end of December 2004, public sector banks have issued 167.9 lakh Kisan Credit Cards (KCCs) with limits amounting to about Rs.46,000 cr. Cumulative sanctions and disbursements under various tranches of RIDF (RIDF I to X) amounted to about Rs.42,000 cr and Rs.24,000 cr, respectively, by February 2005. With a view to further increasing the flow of credit to agriculture, the following measures have been initiated.[2]

- RBI has set up an Expert Group to formulate strategy for increasing investment in agriculture and the report is expected by end of May 2005.

[2] www.banknetindia.com/banking/6policyapril05.htm

- In order to make an assessment of customer satisfaction on credit delivery in rural areas by banks, it is proposed to conduct a survey with the help of an outside agency.
- Keeping in view the importance of post-harvest operations, it is proposed to increase the limit on loans to farmers through the produce marketing scheme from Rs.5 lakh to Rs.10 lakh under priority sector lending.
- There is a realisation amongst bankers that there are increasing business opportunities in financing agriculture, banks are, therefore, urged to continue their efforts to step up credit to agriculture.

In addition to this, Mission 2007 has been launched by an alliance comprising nearly 80 organizations including civil society organizations. Their goal is to set up a Knowledge Center in every village by the 60th Independence Day. The government has decided to join the alliance and route its support through NABARD. The Finance Minister has also proposed to allow NABARD to provide Rs.100 cr out of RIDF.[3]

Conclusion

Rural finance needs to be monitored properly if the project has to succeed. This is true in most developing countries. Rural Communities, by their very nature, are somewhat traditional when it comes to understanding and appreciating the modern ways of life. The educational level is generally very poor and the quality of the administration, insipid. All this points to a need for a major central body (in this case NABARD) to take a hands on interest in the same. It is much easier for the various ministries to interact with NABARD and get a real-time idea of what is happening. NABARD can also represent to the Central Government in case of any need for changes in policy or working rules. This is most essential for the proper development of a scheme. Otherwise, the energies would be scattered among many regions and states. There could also be a case of NABARD empaneling the best NGO, to secure even better implementation. The track record shows that they do a far better job on average than the panchayats, block development offices, etc. It terms of implementing the various programs. The

[3] www.mssrf.org/iec/601/index.htm

commitment and know-how are generally there. The NGO's are usually in close touch with the pulse of the local community. This is an often ignored aspect of implementing rural development schemes. Without community participation and consent, all schemes will fail, particularly in a democracy. However, mala fide it has to be checked, hence the empanelment is important.

Given all these factors, and the proposed manifold expansion of the RIDF (boosted by healthy revenues from taxes on services), we could expect the RIDF to really kickstart the growth of rural economy in the next decade or so.

The political ramifications are also to be examined of going either fully, or partially with the NGO scenario. This method of subcontracting or enfranchising NGO's to do most of the work (including the financing) of NGO schemes would necessarily mean that the traditional network would have little say in the matter. While all studies have shown that a partial devolution is eminently desirable, there is likely to be strong resistance from the Block Development Officers, Village sarpanch, etc. These could cause a potential political time bomb and has to be managed. One solution could be to involve them in the process, but give the final say to the NGO. Another option would be to start in a phased manner and see how it goes. In any case the decentralization of all these schemes to meet the unique needs of various parts of the country, would have to be done and the body carrying out all these activities would have to be substantially superior in both technical and managerial know-how, as well as accounting standards, to the departments carrying on the activity presently. Otherwise, rural development will forever remain an elusive pipe dream.

(Deepak Kumar, Former Associate Consultant, The Icfai University Press, Hyderabad. He can be reached at bornwaldeepak_11@rediffmail.com).

Annexure: Eligible Activities by RIDF

1.	Rural Roads
2.	Rural Bridges
3.	Minor Irrigation Projects/micro irrigation
4.	Soil Conservation
5.	Flood Protection
6.	Watershed development/reclamation of waterlogged areas
7.	Drainage
8.	Forest Development
9.	Market yard/godown, apna mandi, rural haats and other marketing infrastructure
10.	Cold Storage, public or joint sector cold storage at various exit points
11.	Seed/agriculture/horticulture farms
12.	Plantation and horticulture
13.	Grading and certifying mechanisms such as testing and certifying laboratories etc.
14.	Community irrigation wells of irrigation purposes for the village as a whole
15.	Fishing Harbor/jetties
16.	Riverine Fisheries
17.	Animal Husbandry
18.	Modern Abattoir

Source: http://www.nabard.org

Structure of RIDF, Experiences and Quantum of Funding

The RIDF was set up by the Government in the year 1995-96 in order to fund the ongoing rural Infrastructure projects. The Fund is maintained by the National Bank for Agriculture and Rural Development (NABARD). Domestic commercial banks contribute to the Fund to the extent of their shortfall in stipulated priority sector lending to agriculture. The main objective of the Fund is to provide loans to State Governments and State-owned corporations to enable them to complete ongoing rural infrastructure projects. Till the end of 2003-04, nine tranches (I to IX) of RIDF have been completed. In the Interim Budget for the year 2004-05, an announcement was made regarding setting up of Agriculture Infrastructure and Credit Fund and discontinuation of RIDF mechanism. This decision was reconsidered; and the regular Budget presented on July 8, 2004 proposed revival of RIDF with a corpus of Rs.8,000 crore during 2004-05. Accordingly, RIDF (X) is currently under implementation. The total corpus of RIDF (RIDF I to RIDF X) amount to Rs.42,000 crore. Cumulative sanctions and disbursements under various tranches of RIDF stood at Rs.37,718 crore and Rs.22,940 crore, respectively, on December 31, 2004. Out of 1,36,486 projects sanctioned under RIDF I to VIII, 84,584 projects have been completed. During the current year till December 31, 2004, sanctions and disbursements under RIDF X amounted to Rs.3,048 crore and Rs.52 crore, respectively.

The shortfall in disbursements of RIDF funds as compared to sanctions continues to remain a matter of concern in the implementation of RIDF. The Government has taken a number of steps to address this problem. The scope of RIDF has been widened to include activities such as rural drinking water schemes, soil conservation, rural market yards, rural health centers and primary schools, mini hydel plants, shishu shiksha kendras, anganwadis, and system improvement in the power sector. From RIDF V onwards, the ambit was extended to projects undertaken by Panchayat Raj institutions and projects in the social sector covering primary education, health and drinking water. The activities to be financed under RIDF X include minor irrigation projects/micro irrigation, flood protection, watershed development/reclamation of waterlogged areas, drainage, forest development, market yard/godown, apna mandi, rural haats and other marketing infrastructure, cold storage, seed/agriculture/ horticulture farms, plantation and horticulture, grading and certifying mechanisms such as testing and certifying laboratories, etc., community irrigation wells for irrigation purposes for the village as a whole, fishing harbor/jetties, riverine fisheries, animal husbandry and modern abattoir.

Compiled from the http://www.indiabudget.nic.in

7

The Community Led Infrastructure Finance Facility (CLIFF)

Ian Morris and Malcolm Jack

Effective urban development strategies can help in reducing the global incidence of poverty in order to achieve the Millennium Development Goals and "funding to finance community-based slum upgrading" has been identified as a 'Quick-win' solution to the situation. This article discusses in detail about CLIFF (The Community Led Infrastructure Finance Facility), how it operates, its financial products, its sources of funding, its achievements and the significance of community capacity. The Community Led Infrastructure Finance Facility (CLIFF) is distinctly different from municipal Development Fund mechanisms as it provides venture capital and other financial products directly to organisations of the urban poor, rather than to government, to support community-led slum upgrading schemes conceived in partnership with city authorities. Community involvement is vital if slum development is to be locally appropriate, effective and sustainable, in addition to the human rights argument and could well assume a much greater importance in community infrastructure financing in the days to come.

The Challenge

Poverty is becoming increasingly 'urbanised' – between 2000 and 2030, the urban areas of the less developed regions will absorb 95 percent of the world's population growth[1]. At least 900 million people live in slums[2], and the UN estimates that as many as 55% of the world's poor people currently live in urban areas[3]. Effective urban development strategies can contribute to reducing the global incidence of poverty and to achieving the Millennium Development Goals—indeed Jeffrey Sachs' recent report *Investing in development – a practical plan to achieve the Millennium Development Goals*[4] specifically identifies "funding to finance community based slum upgrading" as a 'Quick-win' solution. Yet current strategies tend to rely on traditional arrangements in which municipalities are expected to finance slum development projects designed and delivered by conventional private contractors. Poor communities have limited say or involvement in slum 'solutions', and mobilisation of local financial resources is often limited. But community involvement is vital, if slum development is to be locally appropriate, effective and sustainable, in addition to the human rights argument for doing so.

Background

The Indian Alliance of SPARC (an Indian NGO), Nirman (a not-for-profit company which acts as the financial and construction arm of SPARC) and two community-based networks (Mahila Milan and the National Slum Dwellers Federation) is a leading example of how communities have organised themselves and developed capacity in tackling the complex issues of housing and infrastructure in slums. There are other community-based organisations across the world that have formed along similar lines, such as those that make up the Slum/Shack Dwellers International (SDI) network, in which the Indian Alliance is also actively involved. The Indian Alliance has been working together for around 20 years, although NSDF was established almost 30 years ago. The membership of NSDF

1 UN-Habitat (2003), *Slums of the World: the face of urban poverty in the new millennium?*, Nairobi: UN-Habitat.

2 UN Millennium Project (2005), *Investing in Development: A practical plan to achieve the millennium development goals*, [The Sachs Report], New York: UNDP

3 Tibaijuka, Anna (2002), *Opening statement at workshop on urban policy implications of enhancing food security in African cities*, Nairobi, Kenya, May 2002.

4 UN Millennium Project (op.cit), p66.

and Mahila Milan has grown to well over 750,000 households nationwide, spanning several states in India, and continues to grow.

Over the 20 years that the Alliance has been working together, their capacity, activity, impact and credibility has also grown. Towards the end of the 1990s, the Alliance had developed a portfolio of housing and infrastructure projects that would either set, test or challenge existing slum development policies and practice. The Alliance has had to overcome numerous obstacles to reach this stage, but access to finance to complete these large-scale projects emerged as a major blockage. SPARC and Nirman had built up their own 'bridge finance' fund for lending to projects, but this had become insufficient given both the growing number and size of projects. Banks were often positive about the prospect of lending for such projects in the initial stages of engagement, but proved unreliable when it came to delivery. Without sufficient finance the Alliance had to drip-feed the projects in their portfolio with finance from their own bridge funds, which prolonged implementation and hampered the further development of the Alliance in terms of capacity, activity, impact and credibility.

Homeless International acted upon this and, with the support of DFID, carried out a 4-year research project entitled 'Bridging the finance gap in housing and infrastructure' that essentially examined how easy or difficult it was for communities to carry out their own habitat developments in a number of countries in Africa, Asia and Latin America. Homeless International and international partners used the research to examine regulatory frameworks which affected slum upgrading, and analysed examples where communities had achieved this. This research is what led to the development of CLIFF.

What CLIFF Does

The Community Led Infrastructure Finance Facility (CLIFF) is distinctly different from municipal Development Fund mechanisms. It provides venture-capital and other financial products directly to organisations of the urban poor, rather than to government, to support community-led slum upgrading schemes conceived in partnership with city authorities—CLIFF can only therefore work where poor communities have built the capacity to manage slum-upgrading initiatives. CLIFF uses finance as a tool to bring poor communities (and the organisations which support them) right into the heart of urban development planning and action by:

- Allowing communities to demonstrate strategies, processes and initiatives in practice that will either set, test or challenge existing slum development policies.
- Acting as a forum for engagement between the poor and other stakeholders.
- Helping communities consider city-wide development issues through prioritising flagship projects.
- Supporting organisations of the urban poor in taking, managing and mitigating risks to achieve slum improvements at scale.

Slum areas like Dharavi (reputedly India's largest slum) are characterised by high density, poor housing and inadequate infrastructure

Homeless International manages the global facility, which is currently operational with the Alliance in India and with a similar Alliance in Kenya.

CLIFF and Homeless International Financial Products

Meeting the challenge of slums, particularly in large cities, generally requires collective housing and infrastructure solutions, as opposed to separate individual/household solutions. Consequently, CLIFF has been designed as a venture capital facility rather than a microcredit institution—in other words it supports flagship community-led slum development projects rather than providing credit to individual households. CLIFF therefore offers the following forms of financial support:

- Technical assistance grants – so that professional help can be brought in to help communities to "package" projects in a way that banks and state authorities can deal with.
- Loan financing to projects – to kick start community-led flagship initiatives while further negotiations with formal finance institutions and public officials to unlock local financial resources take place. Providing schemes at least break-even, CLIFF finance gets fully repaid to Nirman from income streams, which can then be recycled to pre-finance further projects.
- Knowledge grants – for exchanges, visits and workshops so that as many people as possible are able to learn from the projects as they are developed and implemented.
- Grants for core operational and administration costs – for the agencies managing CLIFF.
- Guarantees – Homeless International's Guarantee Fund can also be used to complement CLIFF, by providing financial guarantees to underwrite some of the risk taken by banks when lending to projects.

Loan financing will be recycled as projects are completed and revenues received, thereby establishing Nirman as a sustainable, long-term financing facility in India.

Sources of Funding

The facility is financed through Cities Alliance with funds from DFID (approximately £6.8 million) and Sida (approximately £3 million). Homeless International has also generated £0.6 million to date in its Guarantee Fund. CLIFF began implementation in 2002, and was designed as a pilot with an initial timeframe of 6 years.

CLIFF loan finance was provided to this housing project in Dharavi, Mumbai, whilst negotiations with banks and government authorities took place. Later, the National Housing Bank provided loan finance which took over the majority of the CLIFF loan finance that had been approved for the project, freeing up CLIFF loan finance for helping to kick-start other new schemes.

How CLIFF Operates

Mahila Milan and the National Slum Dwellers Federation (NSDF) generate numerous project opportunities through their ongoing negotiations with city authorities across India. Mahila Milan and NSDF work with Nirman and SPARC to analyse projects' viability and cashflow options. Larger-scale projects are then considered for CLIFF support, based on certain criteria. To obtain CLIFF financing, projects must:

- Have the potential to be implemented as a flagship that will provide a precedent for future scaling up, replicability and pro-poor policy change.
- Build on established local organisation by communities of the urban poor and their existing relationships with local authority and municipal officials, and have the potential to strengthen such city-community relationships.

- Actively include and benefit the poorest and most marginalised members of the community in the area where the project is to be implemented.
- Be properly costed; be financially viable; and offer options for negotiating loan finance from commercial banking institutions and municipal/state subsidies where necessary.
- Include an analysis of the major project risks, identifying what form these risks will take, who will bear the burden of these risks, and how CLIFF will assist in the management and mitigation of these risks.
- Incorporate a management strategy that identifies how project responsibilities will be allocated and undertaken.
- Include long-term planning for sustainability and maintenance of the assets developed as a result of the investment.
- Incorporate a learning and knowledge-sharing agenda to ensure that other communities and actors in urban development can benefit from the experience.

The Milan Nagar scheme in Mumbai received CLIFF support because it was the first community-led development to test how Mumbai's slum upgrading policies could provide affordable housing solutions for pavement dwellers in practice. There are estimated to be over 20,000 families living on the pavements in Mumbai.

Homeless International manages the global CLIFF facility. In practice this includes activities such as supporting local partners with the implementation of CLIFF where relevant (e.g. provision of financial guarantees to banks, assistance with the development of certain aspects of organisational development and management, such as policies, systems and procedures), monitoring, documentation and dissemination of experiences, liaising with other governing bodies within CLIFF, and research into demand and supply (i.e. country contexts and sources of funding support). However, as local CLIFF facilities become established and local organisations take on a greater number of activities, Homeless International's roles and functions will continue to evolve. Cities Alliance administers CLIFF on behalf of the donors, and the CLIFF Advisory Group, which is made up of the implementing agencies of CLIFF and other stakeholders, meets twice a year to discuss and decide strategic issues relating to CLIFF.

Achievements so far in India

CLIFF had, by November 2006, supported 14 community-led housing projects benefiting more than 5,300 families and a further two sanitation programmes benefiting over 259,000 families. Several other projects are under appraisal for CLIFF support, whilst Mahila Milan and the National Slum Dwellers Federation continue to conceive and develop numerous new projects which may demand CLIFF financing in future.

CLIFF has been successful in helping leverage and blend financial and other resources from a whole range of actors including municipalities and the private sector (e.g. banks and land owners) to catalyze scaling-up and replication of community-led slum upgrading schemes.

By November 2006, more than £5.8 million had been obtained from contracted government payments, government subsidies, residential/commercial unit sales, sales of Transferable Development Rights[5], grants and community contributions. Around a further £25 million is projected by the time the current

---

5 For an explanation of the Slum Rehabilitation Act, associated policies and the systems relating to the sale of Transferable Development Rights (TDR) see report by Sundar Burra (2003) downloadable from http://www.sparcindia.org/documents/Changing%20the%20Rules%20Regulatory%20Guidelines%20and%20the%20Urban%20Poor.htm

Figure 1: Anticipated Income Leveraged by CLIFF-Supported Projects

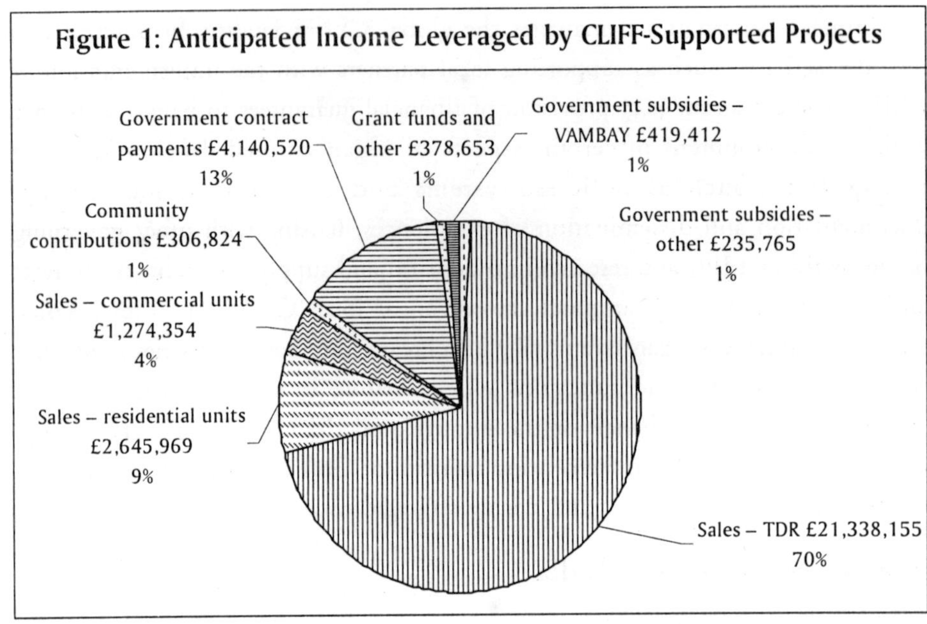

portfolio of CLIFF projects is completed. The projects supported by CLIFF loan financing are therefore projected to leverage over £30 million in revenue streams (see Figures 1 and 2).

Land is one of the most valuable, and therefore hotly contested, assets in cities—particularly in commercially vibrant cities like Mumbai and Bangalore. The success of the Alliance, supported by CLIFF, in securing land and tenure for the urban poor is impressive in this light. By November 2006, the Alliance had secured more than 135,000m^2 of land for housing developments and sites for 280 toilet blocks through projects supported by CLIFF in five cities across India.

Many project revenues cannot be released until projects are completed, or are only receivable after certain construction phases have been completed and approved. For scaling-up and replication to occur, sources of finance other than locally owned funds and CLIFF are required. Banks in India, although generally positive about the business opportunities of lending for slum upgrading schemes, have few precedents with which to compare assumptions about timings and volumes of

The Sunnuduguddu scheme enabled the Indian Alliance to take up an offer of land made for the first time by city authorities in Bangalore. The Alliance began the scheme with loan finance from SPARC, but construction was slow due to a shortage of loan finance. CLIFF loan financing enabled the pace of construction to increase to a more natural level.

revenue streams in politically and physically complex slum upgrading schemes. CLIFF has played several important roles in helping to draw in bank financing, by:

- Providing up-front loan financing to test cashflow/viability assumptions in practice.
- Provide up-front loan financing to share the financial risks for a particular scheme.
- Exposing bankers and associated professionals to communities' experiences and capacities in successfully developing and implementing projects—experience has shown that bankers require an illusive 'comfort factor' that is not always related purely to the financial picture for projects.

- Deepening capacity within the Indian Alliance to 'package' or articulate complex community-managed projects in a manner that formal institutions can deal with.
- Providing guarantees which underwrite loan financing to community-led projects.

So far, the Indian Alliance have convinced three banks (Citibank, National Housing Bank and ICICI Bank) to provide loan financing for housing schemes totalling over £3 million (projected requirement over £2 million), with support from Homeless International's Guarantee Fund and USAID's DCA facility (see Figure 2). The Alliance has also persuaded a fourth bank (UTI Bank) to provide £0.75 million as loan finance and performance bond, using a local guarantee provided by Nirman, which enabled the Alliance to secure a municipal contract for a large-scale sanitation programme in Mumbai. The Alliance is currently in negotiations with several banks with respect to both the provision of finance for new projects, and the mainstreaming of lending for slum development projects within banks and the banking sector in India.

Finally, the Alliance has started to negotiate pre-finance from commercial construction contractors involved in CLIFF-supported schemes, which have constituted around 30% of total project costs. This reduces both the amount of financing that is required and duration that finance is required for, thereby reducing the costs of finance and improving the viability of the schemes developed by the Alliance.

A second CLIFF has been in operation since 2005 in Kenya, to support *Muungano Wa Wanavijiji* (a network of community-based savings groups), the Pamoja Trust (a Kenyan NGO) and the Akiba Mashinani Trust (AMT – the financial arm of the Pamoja Trust). CLIFF in Kenya is just moving out of its development and testing phase, supporting five smaller-scale projects (two housing, two land-banking and one sanitation). CLIFF loan financing of almost £80,000 are projected to leverage almost £160,000 in revenues from these projects, all from community contributions. The reasons why all revenues are in the form of community contributions as compared to in India with the Alliance, are because of the differences in political and economic context, and the relatively early stage

Figure 2: Anticipated Financing Leveraged by CLIFF-Supported Projects

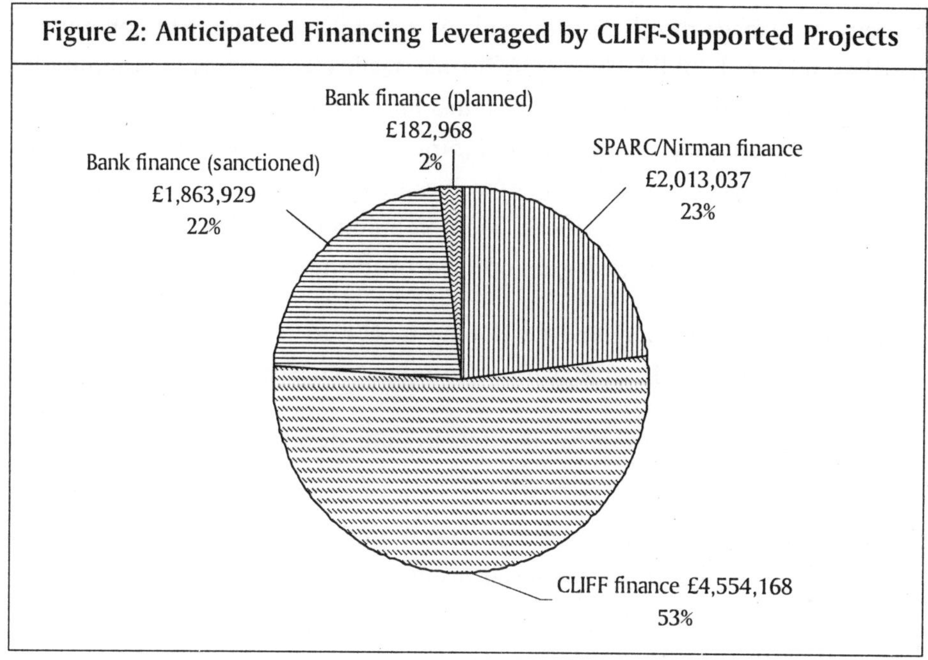

the Kenyan Alliance is at in terms of its development—e.g. negotiating for subsidies or special permission to construct for-sale units to cross-subsidise construction costs of units for families from the government. *Muungano*, Pamoja Trust and AMT are developing further projects, and exploring options for diversified revenue streams and the involvement of banks.

Homeless International also carried out feasibility studies for the application of Community-Led Infrastructure Finance Facility (CLIFF) operations in Ghana, Ethiopia, Zambia and Uganda for UN-Habitat's Urban Management Programme (UMP). These studies outlined opportunities and possible next steps in supporting community-led slum upgrading in those countries.

Community Capacity is Vital

CLIFF is particularly innovative in that it responds to local demand and local capacity. It does not seek to plan, manage and implement slum development projects conceived by professionals, rather to catalyze support for large-scale solutions developed by poor communities and the organisations with whom they work. On the financial side, poor communities and their networks must have the capacity to manage money, usually built up through experiences of community-based savings and credit schemes. A finance facility to support community-led development cannot therefore be parachuted into a context where no such capacity exists within networks of poor communities. In contexts where communities' technical and financial management capacities are weaker, a CLIFF-like programme would need to include a significant grant component and longer timeframe to build up such capacities, and scale up loan financing gradually.

Experiences in planning and developing CLIFF so far offer some lessons for developing finance facility mechanisms in other contexts:

- Community involvement is vital, if slum development is to be locally appropriate, effective and sustainable.
- Poor communities cannot easily access venture capital for large-scale flagship projects, so finance facility mechanisms which provide loan finance directly

Prince Charles meets members of Mahila Milan and the National Slum Dwellers Federation to learn how they plan, implement and manage complex slum upgrading projects

to them, like CLIFF, are required if communities' solutions are to be demonstrated, scaled-up and replicated.

- Community capacity building must take place alongside the development of such loan finance mechanisms, which also promotes replication and learning.

For More Information Visit

- www.homeless-international.org – *for more information about CLIFF and Homeless International, including the most recent* CLIFF Annual Report *and* CLIFF Monitoring Report, *copies of papers produced following Homeless International's* Bridging the finance gap research *and* Feasibility studies for the application of Community-Led Infrastructure Finance Facility (CLIFF) operations in Ghana, Ethiopia, Zambia and Uganda
- www.sparcindia.org *and* www.nirman.org – *for more information about the Alliance of Nirman, SPARC, NSDF and Mahila Milan in India*
- www.sdinet.org – *for more information about SDI*

(Ian Morris, Financial Services Co-ordinator, and Malcolm Jack, International Grants Co-ordinator, Homeless International.)

Views of Hernando de Soto

Hernando de Soto first came to attention in his native country. In 1979, after a successful career in business in Europe, a 38-year-old Hernando de Soto returned to a Peru plagued by poverty and years of military rule. As an author and an activist, and later as adviser to President Alberto Fujimori in the early years of his administration, De Soto moved to bring his impoverished fellow countrymen out of the shadow economy and unlock their potential to build wealth, a process that continues today.

From his Peruvian roots, De Soto now can be seen traveling throughout the world, meeting with current and future heads of state. President Vicente Fox of Mexico sought out De Soto for help when he was the governor of the state of Guanajuato, and today De Soto is working with the Fox administration on property rights reform. Egyptian president Hosni Mubarak's son, Gamal, approached De Soto to seek his views for implementing a program on property rights in Egypt. Both Philippine presidents Joseph Estrada and Gloria Arroyo have invited De Soto to help. De Soto tells these heads of state that their poor citizens are lacking formal legal title to their property and are unable to use their assets as collateral. They cannot get bank loans to expand their businesses or improve their properties. Hernando De Soto has truly revolutionized the understanding of the causes of wealth and poverty. While many scholars have pointed to and explained the importance of property rights to rising living standards, de Soto has asked the hard question of what it takes to get the state to recognize the property rights that function within the communities of the poor. Can they transform the mere physical "extralegal" control of assets into capital, a key to sustained economic development?

De Soto affirmed that they can attain legal status and developed a guide to the "capitalization process" for poor countries. In his activism and in his books *The Other Path* and *The Mystery of Capital*, Hernando de Soto has done much more than applying the lessons of economics to old problems; he has asked new questions and provided both new understanding and new hope for transforming poverty into wealth. He has won support from many political leaders including former president Bill Clinton, former British Prime Minister Margaret Thatcher, World Bank president James Wolfensohn and Russian President, Vladimir Putin.

In 1980, De Soto founded the Institute for Liberty and Democracy, which has conducted breakthrough research on the lack of property rights and has prodded many governments to consider change. For his work on behalf of the poor, the Peruvian Marxist terrorist organization Shining Path launched two assassination attempts on his life. The Shining Path is history, but De Soto continues to help governments and inspire the poor to look ahead to economic freedom and prosperity.

Compiled from the source http://www.cato.org

Section II

A Sectoral Overview

8

Financing of Renewable Energies

Usha N Raghunandan

The role of Renewable Energy (RE) is vital to counter adverse global climate change, addressing issues relating to regional and local environment, poverty reduction and in increasing energy security. This article describes how renewable energies are different in comparison to the conventional energy projects and its impact on their financing needs and ability to attract finance. It also discusses various types of financing instruments used for financing renewable energy in India, while highlighting the barriers and financing gaps that make its funding difficult. It also provides useful insights on the role of Ministry of Environment and Forest, India and its guidelines with respect of renewable energy in India; financing support provided by IREDA towards promoting renewable energy in India besides discussing aspects like Clean Development Mechanism and Kyoto protocol and Carbon Credits in brief. The current momentum of renewable energy development, together with the geographic advantage of availability of resources, can prove to be a major strategic advantage in developing renewable energy provided India gears up for the challenge by creating more instruments for financing the renewable energy.

Introduction

The role of Renewable Energy (RE) is of utmost importance towards alleviating adverse global climate change, addressing the regional and local environmental concerns, reducing poverty and increasing energy security. In fact renewable energy is the most dynamic sector of the global energy market besides being a multi-billion dollar industry. The renewable energy sector constitutes a very insignificant segment of the world's energy industry owing to certain finance-related risks that cause hindrances in their growth. The process of harnessing renewable energy is site-specific and unfortunately most sites suitable for the process are yet to become cost-competitive. Moreover, renewable energy projects are known to have huge capital costs in comparison to competing technologies and relatively low rates of return. As a result investors show aversion to investments in such projects they are seen as "High risk – low return options". This applies particularly to the developing countries, where low-cost finance is not easily available and hence relies mostly on targeted subsidies.

Renewable Energy Projects vs Conventional Energy Projects

When compared to the existing energy-supply options, renewable energies are believed to be taking a huge leap towards innovation. The renewable energy technologies are substantially different from the conventional energy systems in terms of capacity, scale, characteristics of energy resources and a host of other factors. Such differences generally do not get mislaid as they carried on to the financiers since financing a renewable energy plant is completely different from financing the conventional energy plants that necessitate innovative thinking both in terms of new modes of financing as well as risk management techniques.

As most of the financiers are generally averse to new things, the differences between renewable and conventional energy systems and the associated risk perceptions may act as the most major barriers to investment, even if certain RE technologies are known to be cost effective in comparison to the conventional energy-supply options. The following paragraphs will explain how renewable energy projects are different from the conventional energy projects and the impact it would have on their financial requirements and consequent ability to attract capital.

Financing of Renewable Energies is New: Planning to invest in the renewable energy sector for the first time is considered to be an investment by itself. And if financiers are looking at becoming effective in investing in renewable energy markets, they need to move up the learning or experience curve. Market failures may sometimes act as barriers to enter the market and hinder such learning process. In order to function efficiently, markets depend on timely, appropriate, and reliable information. Energy markets are mostly far from perfect, more so a renewable energy market, which is in the stage of a technological and structural transition. Generally, there is a lack of accurate information that enables proper assessment of a project's viability for, there is, limited economic justification for any single market participant to obtain such information. Lack of sufficient information thus may result in a project's risk being overrated thereby increasing transaction costs.

Financial Structure and Scale: Renewable energy projects are generally known to have higher capital costs and lower operational costs as compared to the conventional fossil-fuel technologies. As a result, external financing requirement is quite high and necessitates its repayment to be spread across the life of the project. This results in making the risk-exposure of the project—a long-term challenge that would also bring along with it, political-risk implications like changes in government policy.

Renewable energy projects like solar PV and mini-hydropower being typically small, involve substantially huge transaction costs that are mostly disproportionate, in comparison to the conventional infrastructure projects. As is well known huge investments require initial feasibility and due-diligence work but unfortunately, the costs involved in this work do not vary significantly with project size. The impact on the transaction costs of RE projects, therefore tend to be higher owing to a proportionately higher pre-investment costs, including legal and engineering fees, consultants, and permitting costs. Moreover, the size of the RE projects which is generally smaller in nature results in lower gross returns, in spite of the rate of return being well within market standards of what is considered to be an attractive investment.

Developers Face Financing Problems and have Limited Track Records: Financiers often consider renewable energy projects as highly risky ventures and are therefore disinclined to provide non-recourse project finance. It is but natural for the financiers to see experienced construction contractors, operators and suppliers with proven equipment being involved in such projects thereby adding to the development costs of the under-financed developers in the phase of due diligence which may sometimes put a project at great risk.

RE Technologies are Commercially Unproven – Perception of Financiers: Financiers consider the cost and long-term performance risks of renewable technologies to be higher than the conventional technologies with some exceptions like onshore wind energy. There operates a vicious circle in case of most of the new technologies, financiers and manufacturers are generally reluctant to invest the required funds in order to reduce costs when demand is low and uncertain. However, without investment being made, demand continues to remain low for potential economies of scale cannot be achieved at lower levels of production.

Fuel Supply Risk – Concern for RE: Though the fuel requirement of renewable energy plants is usually available either at low cost or for free, financiers consider its availability as serious concern both in terms of evaluating the resource (like hydro, wind, solar, geothermal, etc.,) and contracting its supply (bio-energy). For instance, if we consider a wind project, a minimum of one year of on-site wind speed measurements is required for a financier to consider seriously about investment in that project.

Sources of Finance

Some of the most popular forms of financing used in funding renewable energy plants are explained below:

Private Finance: It refers to the finance that is generally provided out of personal savings or bank loans secured by private assets. This form of finance is generally considered in case of small projects that do not require a huge initial outlay.

Equity Finance: This form of funding includes equity investment by venture capitalists, strategic investors besides the developers' own equity and private finance to provide for new projects.

Mezzanine Finance: Also known as quasi-equity finance, this form of finance involves grouping of a variety of configuration in the financing package that range between high risk/high upside equity position and lower risk/fixed returns debt position.

Corporate Finance: It refers to the debt provided by banks to developers having a proven track record, by using 'on-balance sheet' assets as collateral and hence often referred to as 'on-balance sheet corporate finance'.

Project Finance: This type of finance includes debt extended by banks to those single-purpose companies, whose energy sales are guaranteed by power purchase agreements (PPA). This form of financing is also known as 'off-balance sheet or non-recourse finance' for the reason that financiers depend mostly on the certainty of project cash flows to repay the loan and not the credit standing of the project sponsors.

Participation Finance: It may be described as an extension of project finance, wherein the 'lender' is not a single person/entity but a group of investors. A co-operative wind fund, which enjoys the benefits of fiscal incentives and tax exemption, is an example of 'Participation Finance'.

Third-Party Finance: As the name implies, it refers to a mode of financing in which an independent party finances many individual energy systems. It may be carried out in the form of hire purchase, fee-for-service and leasing schemes.

Consumer Finance: It refers to a form of financing often used by the clients in rural areas so as to make modern energy services affordable. For instance, many micro-credit schemes are now being offered in the solar home system market, that involve risk-sharing at the local and institutional levels. Once clients' credit standing is established, such a portfolio may be considered as an asset and used as a collateral for further financing.

Lines of Credit: These are often used by development finance institutions (DFIs) in order to promote the creation of credit windows in national or local banks for lending to specific areas like renewable energy projects. This form of refinance is considered to be the quickest way to engage the participation of donors/DFIs by providing them utmost autonomy towards setting the financing terms.

Credit Enhancements: These include a variety of subsidies generally offered by DFIs/donor programs with the aim of softening the loan finance, either to the lender or to the borrower. The concession may be provided in the form of risk sharing or reduction in the interest-rates. Partial Risk Guarantee is one such form of credit enhancement instrument that ensures debt-servicing payments to selective lenders/investors of a project, for specific period of time or up to a certain level of exposure to risk. Partial Credit Guarantee is another form of credit enhancement instrument that provides for extension of loan repayment periods, thereby improving the project's cash flows. Interest Rate Subsidy is another type of credit enhancement that aims to lower the cost of financing for the borrower and therefore is considered to be an effective means of helping banks to build their loan portfolios in specific renewable energy sectors. The bank's interests are hence fully in sync with that of the donor by taking up the entire credit risk, both in terms of minimising defaults as well as continued lending even after the donor support has been phased out.

End-User Financing: There have been many instances of the renewable energy projects being financed through the end user, in developing countries with mixed results. Two of the most popular ones are:

- The Supplier Credit Model is the most basic form of financing of a renewable energy enterprise by the end users and is usually short-term finance that ranges between 3 and 12 months. The model requires that the enterprise either provides funds for its purchases, or secures manufacturer credit, which may sometime extend to six months, but not longer.
- The Fee-For-Service Model is a form of financing wherein the customers pay for an energy service thereby making the renewable energy products and services more affordable. This model is also believed to minimize the long-term risks that are inherent to the credit models like technology risk, rural electrification risk, etc.

Renewable Energy Sector in India

India has been bestowed with a vast pool of renewable energy resources like wind energy, solar energy, biomass and small hydro which are widely scattered across the country, and may be made use of, to generate power with the help of commercially viable technologies. An increased use of such sources is expected to play a vital role towards achieving environmental objectives. The following table provides an idea of the potential of various renewable energy technologies in India.

Renewable Energy Potential in India

Energy Source	Estimated Potential
Solar Energy	20 MW/ sq.km
Wind Energy	20,000 MW
Small Hydro	10,000 MW
Ocean Thermal Power	50,000 MW
Sea Wave Power	20,000 MW
Tidal Power	10,000 MW
Bio Energy	17,000 MW
Draught Animal Power	30,000 MW
Energy From MSW	1,000 MW
Biogas Plants	12 Million Plants
Improved Wood Burning Stoves	120 Million Stoves

Source: MNES Annual Report; Financing Renewable Energy Projects – Raising Local Capital, Dr. V. Bakthavatsalam

The renewable energy programme undertaken by India is the largest and the most extensive in comparison to those by other developing countries of the world. The Government of India (GoI) has been promoting an increased use of renewable energy technologies by offering a variety of policy and support measures. This renewable energy programme is monitored by the Ministry of Non-Conventional Energy Sources (MNES)—nodal ministry of the GoI, which is entrusted with the charge of renewable energy sector of the country in terms of planning, policy making, promotion and co-ordination of various aspects of renewable energy.

Ministry of Environment and Forests, India – Guidelines

The Ministry of Environment & Forests is mainly responsible for the planning, coordination promotion, and supervision of the implementation of environmental and forestry programmes in India. The most important responsibilities of the Ministry of Environment and Forests include conservation and survey of forests and wildlife, flora and fauna, prevention and control of pollution, afforestation and regeneration of degraded areas in the environment, within the framework of legislations.

Protection of Environment and Sustainable Development are considered to be the cornerstones of the policies and procedures that govern various developmental activities in India. In this regard, The Ministry of Environment & Forests has initiated several policies and has also enacted legislations relating to the environmental and pollution control with a view to prevent unwarranted exploitation of natural resources towards promoting integration of environmental concerns in developmental projects. Notification on Environmental Impact Assessment (EIA) of developmental projects is one such initiative that deserves a special mention. Issued on 27.1.1994 under the provisions of Environment (Protection) Act, 1986 the notification made EIA mandatory for 29 categories of various developmental projects. In the year 2000, one more item was added to the list. Currently the 39 categories of projects require EIA as per notification by the Environmental Impact Assessment Division, Ministry of Environment & Forests, Government of India as on 14th September 2006.

Indian Renewable Energy Development Agency (IREDA)

Indian Renewable Energy Development Agency (IREDA) was set up as a Public limited company in the year 1987 under the Ministry of New and Renewable Energy (MNRE) with the aim of promoting, developing and extending financial assistance to renewable energy efficiency/conservation projects with the motto "Energy for Ever".

The primary objectives of IREDA include:

- Operating a revolving fund for promoting, developing and commercializing New and Renewable Sources of Energy (NRSE);
- Extending financial assistance to Energy Efficiency & Conservation projects and schemes; and
- Providing support in upgradation of technologies.

IREDA's Financing Activities: IREDA's lending activities cover a wide spectrum including those related to energy efficiency and conservation. Currently IREDA extends finance mainly in the following sectors –

- In Wind Energy sector – for setting up grid connected wind farm projects.

- In Solar Energy Technologies – for manufacturing & Utilization of Solar Thermal and Solar Photo Voltaic systems.
- In Bio-Energy Technologies – to support biomass based cogeneration and power generation projects, biomass gasification, energy from waste and briquetting projects.
- In Small Hydro power sector – for setting up Small, Mini and Micro Hydel Projects.
- Energy Efficiency and Conservation.
- Hybrid Systems.

The extent of finance that can be provided by IREDA is generally determined by its exposure limit, which is a set based on the client's credit standing and the collaterals offered for the term loan. Some of the popular instruments offered by IREDA include:

- Lease financing.
- Equipment financing.
- Debt financing in the form of soft term loans to different sectors of renewable energy.
- On Lending through financial intermediaries.

Highlights of the Financing Norms of IREDA: Debt instruments offered by IREDA include project-financing schemes, equipment financing schemes and manufacturing loans. The quantum of assistance provided by IREDA involves upto 80 percent of the project cost and up to 90 percent of the equipment cost. Rate of interest ranges between 0 percent and 15 percent per annum with a moratorium up to 3 years and a repayment period of 10 years.

A cautious approach followed by IREDA with respect to its financial policies has enabled it to tap resources from the internal market through various instruments as well as International institutions such as Asian Development Bank, World Bank, Danish International Development Agency, etc., for funding various renewable energy plants. Further it has also various received bilateral and multilateral grants and many more external lines of credit are in the pipeline.

Kyoto Protocol

The Kyoto Protocol refers to an agreement made under the United Nations Framework Convention on Climate Change (UNFCCC). According to this agreement, countries that have accepted this protocol make a commitment to reduce emissions of carbon-di-oxide and five other greenhouse gases[1], or engage in 'Emissions-Trading'[2] if they maintain or increase emissions of such gases. At present, the Kyoto Protocol covers more than 160 countries across the globe and over 55% of global greenhouse gas (GHG) emissions. Some of the core principles of the protocol include:

a) Kyoto is underwritten by governments and is governed by global legislation enacted under the guidance of the United Nations.

b) Under this agreement, governments underwriting the Kyoto are divided into two general categories:

- Developed countries referred to as Annex 1 countries, which have accepted the obligations relating to Greenhouse Gas emissions and are required to submit an annual greenhouse gas inventory.
- Developing countries referred to as Non-Annex I countries, which do not have the obligations towards Greenhouse gas emissions but may participate in Clean Development Mechanisms (CDMs).
- Any country under Annex 1 failing to meet its Kyoto target will be penalized in the form of having to submit 1.3 emission allowances in a second commitment period for every ton of GHG emissions exceeding their cap in the first commitment period (i.e, 2008-2012).
- By 2008-2012, Annex 1 countries are required to reduce their GHG emissions by an average of 5% below their 1990 levels (in case of many countries, like the European Union member states, this corresponds to some 15% below their expected GHG emissions in 2008). While the emissions reduction is 5% on an average, national targets range from

---

1 Greenhouse gases refer to those components of atmosphere that contribute to the Greenhouse Effect. The natural greenhouse gases include water vapor, carbon dioxide, methane and ozone while the non-natural greenhouse gases include nitrous oxide, sulphur hexaflouride, hydrofluoro carbons, perfluoro carbons, chlorofluoro carbons etc.

2 Emissions trading (or cap and trade) is an administrative approach used for pollution control by providing economic incentives for achieving reductions in the emissions of pollutants.

8% reductions for the European Union to a 10% emissions increase for Iceland. These reduction targets-expire in 2013.

Thus, stabilization of greenhouse gas concentrations in the atmosphere at a level so as to prevent dangerous anthropogenic interference with the climate system is the main objective of the Kyoto protocol.

Clean Development Mechanism

The Clean Development Mechanism (CDM) refers to an arrangement made under the Kyoto Protocol that allows the industrialized countries committed to Greenhouse Gas Emission reduction to make investments in emission reducing projects undertaken in developing countries as an alternative to what is generally considered to be more expensive emission reductions in their own countries. Theoretically, CDM is believed to result in cost reductions for the industrialized countries substantially, though the quantum of emission reduction achieved is the same without the CDM. On the flipside, the critics have, for long, opposed the CDM and have been of the opinion that the benefits accruing from CDM may be imaginary for it—was severely criticized in the early 2007 in respect of a payment of 4.6 billion euros for the destruction of Hydrofluorocarbon (HFC) gases while a study put the actual cost at 100 million euros if it were funded by development agencies.

India is an active participant of the United Nations Framework Convention on Climate Change (UNFCCC) whose primary objective, as mentioned earlier, is to achieve stabilization of greenhouse gas concentrations in the atmosphere at a level which would prevent dangerous anthropogenic interference with the climate system. India assented to the Kyoto Protocol in August 2002 and one of the objectives of its consent was towards fulfilling the prerequisites for implementation of Clean Development Mechanism (CDM) projects, in accordance with priority accorded for achieving sustainable development.

The National Clean Development Mechanism (CDM) Authority is the nodal agency constituted by the Government of India to oversee evaluation and approval of CDM projects based on the guidelines and general criteria laid down in the relevant rules and modalities pertaining to CDM over and above the guidelines issued by the Clean Development Mechanism Executive Board and Conference of Parties that serves as a 'Meeting of Parties' to the UNFCCC.

Carbon Credits: These refer to the certificates issued to those countries that have been successful in reducing the emissions leading to global warming. For trading purposes, one credit is considered to be equivalent to one tonne of reduced carbon dioxide emission. Such credits may be traded in the international market at the prevailing market rate and such a trading generally takes place in open market. Generally, developed countries that exceed the permissible levels of carbon emissions either cut down their emissions, or borrow or buy carbon credits from developing countries. Increasing awareness about the need to control pollution brought the concept of 'Carbon Credit' into existence which took a formal structure as a result of the afore described international agreement between 141 countries popularly known as 'Kyoto Protocol'.

Conclusion

Funding renewable energy projects continues to be a Herculean task across the globe more so in developing countries. Inspite of the challenges facing the sector, particularly, the financial difficulties, it appears to be vibrant and optimistic in an otherwise crisis-plagued investment environment highlighted by uncertainty, turmoil and risk aversion currently. Increased environmental, social and energy-security concerns along with advanced renewable energy technologies, have accelerated the support for renewable energy projects to a great extent in the recent times. The onus lies on the governments now towards introducing right policy frameworks as well as financial tools to help the renewable energy sector to achieve its true market potential. This becomes all the more important in case of developing countries, where investments are generally not forthcoming owing to geo-political, economic, and regulatory risks besides the absence of well developed financial markets and products thereby placing the entire risks on the investors. It is here that the financiers can play a vital role by taking up the social responsibility towards developing and delivering appropriate market solutions that pave the way for a free energy market with less carbon, less fuel and fuel-price risk, besides providing more and better access to the poor.

India has initiated one of the world's largest programmes on renewable energy, far more diverse in terms of applications and technologies, in comparison to similar efforts by other developing countries. Optimum utilization of India's vast potential for generating energy from renewable sources to overcome the severe power crunch faced by the country facilitates the integration of renewable energy into the national energy planning to enable a balanced energy-mix. This, in turn, would require taking renewable energy technologies a step beyond the research, development and demonstration phase to commercialization by creating appropriate financing mechanisms.

(Usha N Raghunandan, Research Associate, Icfai Books.)

References

Mobilizing Finance For Renewable Energies (International Conference for Renewable Energy, Bonn, January 2004).

Financing Renewable Energy Projects - Raising Local Capital, Dr. V. Bakthavatsalam, Managing Director, Indian Renewable Energy Development Agency Ltd.

Financing Structures for CDM Projects in India and Capacity Building Options for EU-Indo Collaboration, Vinay Deodhar, Axel Michaelowa, Matthias Krey (HWWA Discussion Paper, 2003)

ttc-environment.ic.gc.ca

www.renewingindia.org

www.renewableenergyaccess.com

http://www.mnes.nic.in/

www.ireda.in

http://envfor.nic.in/

http://cdmindia.nic.in

en.wikipedia.org/

9

Financing of Power Projects

Dr. M V S Birinchi

Power is a critical infrastructure for the overall growth of country's economy. A commercially and financially viable power sector can alone accelerate the economic growth.

Around 1,00,000 MW of capacity additions in next 10 years is needed to erase deficit scenario and the finances required during 11th plan are estimated at Rs.5,000 billions. However comfort for lending agencies depend upon the credibility of the off takers, the Transmission and Distribution entities.

The Ministry of Power, Government of India has ushered in power sector reforms under which SEBs are restructured, and has also taken a number of strategic initiatives like APDRP (Accelerated Power Development & Reform Program), a six level intervention strategy (National, State, Utility, Distribution Circle, feeder and consumer levels) with focus on reduction in AT&C (Aggregate Technical & Commercial losses), improve quality in power supply and service, to achieve commercial viability.

The FIs are now favourably disposed to invest in power sector and an insight into the issues & challenges in financing of power projects is attempted in this paper.

Introduction

The installed capacity of Power Generation was mere 1362 MW at the time of independence (1947) and it has been increased to 1,24,287 MW by the end of 2005-06. Despite this significant progress in capacity additions and also phenomenal improvement in operational efficiency country is suffering from a deficit of 12.3% in peak power capacity and 8.3% in energy due to ever increasing demand far in excess of capacity additions. The main conventional resources for power generation are coal and hydro power. While coal mines are available in states like AP, Bihar, Jharkhand, Orissa and West Bengal large quantum of hydro resources are available in the Himalayan Region.

The year-wise on fuel-wise capacity in the last decade are shown in the graphs and the changes in fuel-wise mix of capacities from 1996 to 2006 are indicated in the pie diagrams given below:

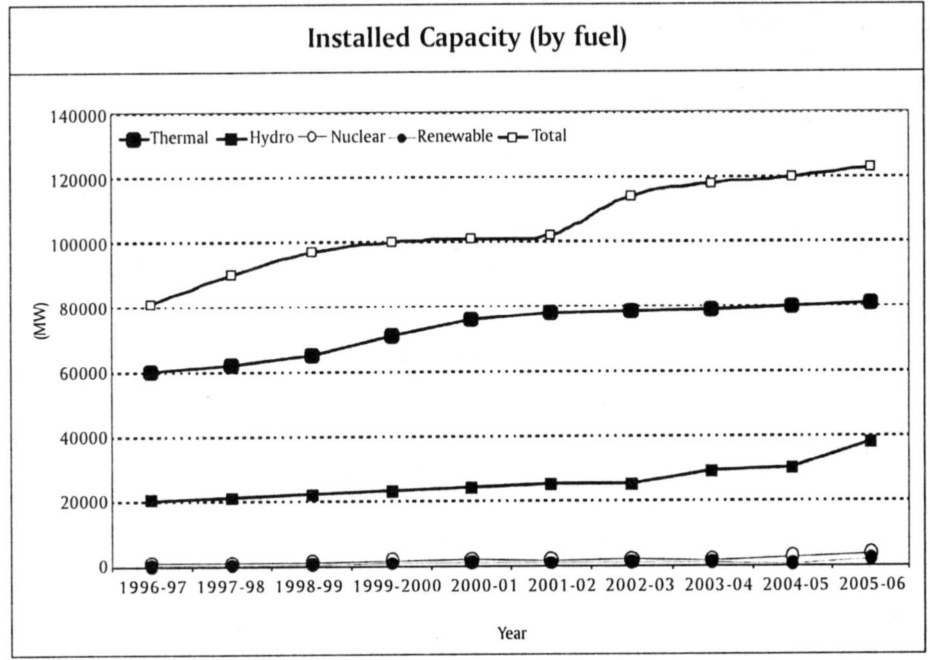

Paradigm Shift in Power Sector

Electricity Act 2003 which came into force from 10th June, 2003 and the National Electricity Policy enunciated in 2004 emphasizes the following goals and initiatives.

1996-97 (MW)

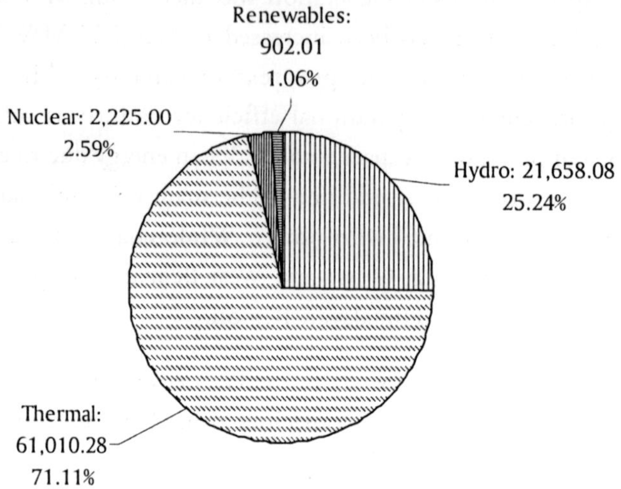

Renewables: 902.01 1.06%

Nuclear: 2,225.00 2.59%

Hydro: 21,658.08 25.24%

Thermal: 61,010.28 71.11%

Total: 85,795.37 MW

Source: CEA General Review

2005-06 (MW)

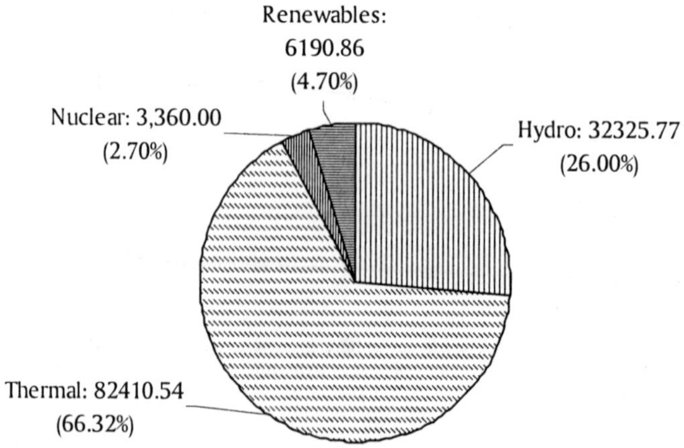

Renewables: 6190.86 (4.70%)

Nuclear: 3,360.00 (2.70%)

Hydro: 32325.77 (26.00%)

Thermal: 82410.54 (66.32%)

Total: 124,287.17 MW

Source: CEA General Review

Installed Capacity (by Sector) (Central, State & Private)

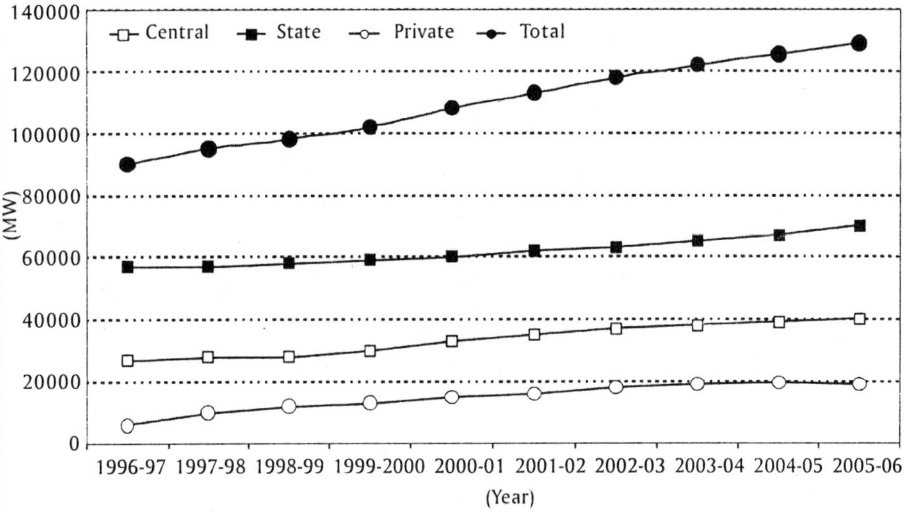

140000
120000
100000
80000
60000
40000
20000
0
(MW)

Central State Private Total

1996-97 1997-98 1998-99 1999-2000 2000-01 2001-02 2002-03 2003-04 2004-05 2005-06
(Year)

Source: CEA General Review.

1996-97 (MW)

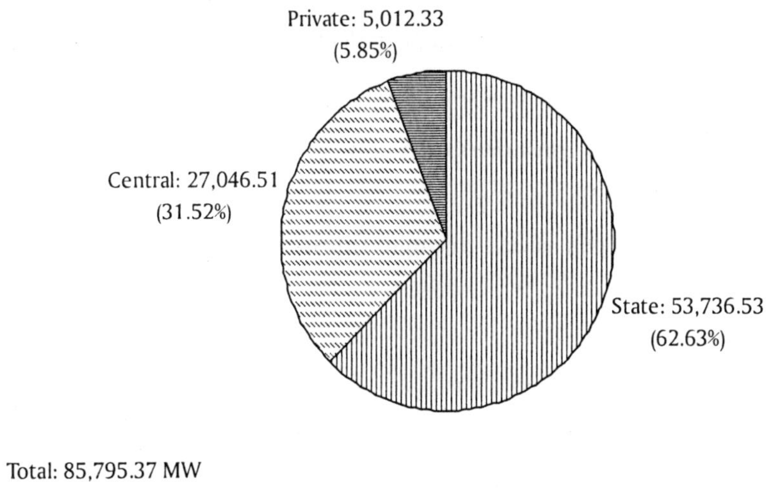

Private: 5,012.33
(5.85%)

Central: 27,046.51
(31.52%)

State: 53,736.53
(62.63%)

Total: 85,795.37 MW

Source: CEA General.

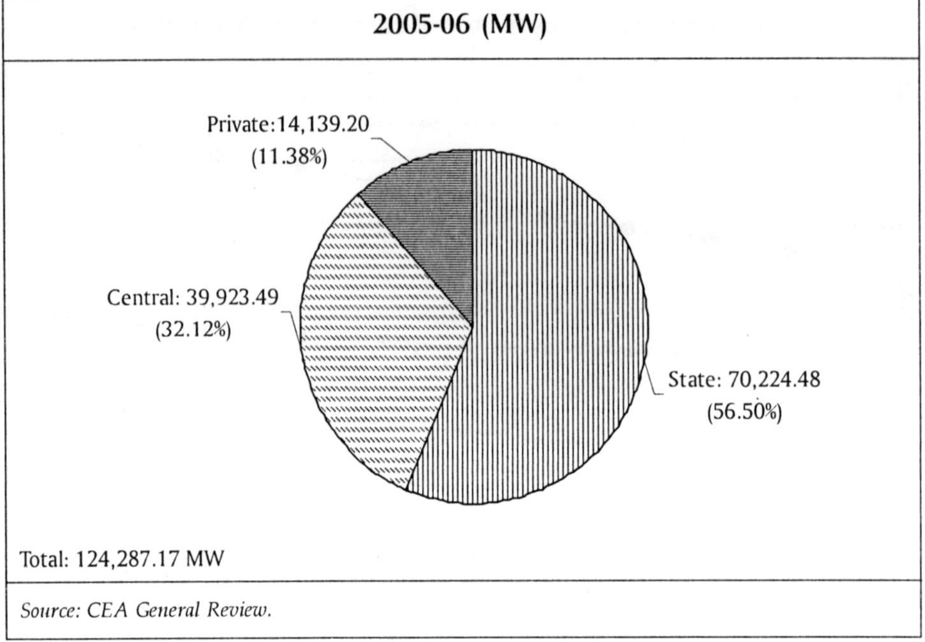

Source: CEA General Review.

- Delicensing of generation except reservoir based hydro.
- No controls over captive plants.
- Groups of consumers can do bulk purchases of power.
- Purchase of power directly or though traders.
- Setting up of power markets [Power Exchange Px] Discoms or traders.
- IPPs can sell power to consumers or trading companies and not necessarily to state power utilities.
- Non discriminate open access through Transmission & Distribution net works.
- Multiyear tariffs.
- Debt equity ratio can be 70:30 [now moving to 80:20]
- Assured return on equity at 14% post-tax
- All power projects should be developed through competitive bidding. [and not through MOU route].

Results of Strategic Initiatives by MOP (GOI)

Due to several strategic initiatives taken by Ministry of Power, Government of India, finances of State Sector Power Companies have registered good improvement. Financial Institutes are now favourable towards lending for power projects. Discoms have improved performance by reducing AT&C losses, technological advancements, improved metering, promptness in billing and efficient collections.

The strict regulatory regime has enhanced the levels of efficiency at which incentives would be given to generators and retail tariffs are now close to cost to serve.

Power projects management require early financial closure, flow of funds on time at each stage, avoid cost over runs, and time over runs, as otherwise the project will become unviable.

Debt Market

As per statistics of planning commission and CEA; the investment requirement during 11th plan stands at Rs.5,000 billions. Where as the aggregate disbursements during 2004-05 by AIFIs were Rs.259.42 billion. The AIFIs are PFC, REC etc.

The debt equity ratio is 80:20 and the financial system in India does not have active liquid and debt market large enough to provide required amount of debt funding.

Equity Participation

Regarding equity participation, power sector was not able to attract investors in view of large funding required and Pre-reforms scenario of high rate of T&D losses, ineffective MBC (Metering, Billing & Collections) and regulated tariffs.

The situation has now changed with power utilities achieving financial turn around by improving operational and fiscal efficiency and the Discoms have started earning marginal profits.

Generation Planning

As per National Electricity Policy capacity additions in generation to the tune of 1,00,000 MW is envisaged during 10th and 11th plan periods to achieve per capita availability of 1,000 units by 2,012.

Procurement of power by Distribution Companies will be through competitive bidding. Setting up of large sized mega power stations of 4,000 MW each is envisaged to obtain cheaper as well as reliable power supply.

The issues and challenges are:

- Debt funding is difficult with present exposure norms.
- Indian financial system does not have an active, liquid and large "debt market" and is presently dominated by banks, mutual funds and large investors.
- Demand for investments in areas other than power is also increasing.
- IPOs can offer opportunities for power companies to avail funds from capital markets and power companies can be permitted to form IPOs at the fag end of constructions so that investors in equity investments in short term projects can be attracted.
- PSUs like NTPC, NHPC, PTC can participate as Central Government IPOs.
- Investments in Power Bonds are to be encouraged and the Bonds can be in smaller denominations.
- Concession for investments in power bonds.
- New customers can subscribe at the rate of a couple of thousands of rupees per kilowatt as per connected load to be repaid say in five years.

Conclusions

While returns for the equity investor in power sector are encouraging, long gestation periods are retarding the process. It is being suggested by experts in power financing that notional dividend during the construction period can be allowed to be capitalized in the form of equity which will give new impetus to equity investment in the sector and for this all enabling provisions are to be made in Electricity Act, Companies Act and Income Tax Act etc.

(Dr. M V S Birinchi, a Former Director (Tech) A.P. Transco is presently Advisor & Head (Power & Energy) for "Engineering Staff College of India" An ISO 9001: 2000 Certified Institute, A Forum of the IEI and recognized by AICTE. He can be reached at mbirinchi@yahoo.co.in).

10

Infrastructure Investment in Indian Telecom Sector

Kalyani Rampilla

Communication has become a major part of governance, as it requires wider accessibility of the public to the government. This has brought the telecom sector into focus. The objective of the Telecom policy – more accessibility and affordability—requires upgrading technology for better and quicker access networks at affordable prices. Keeping pace with rapid technological developments and growing demand requires massive investments, which may not be met by the government alone. Being a lucrative and growing sector, attracting investments has not been too difficult for the telecom sector. Besides attracting foreign investment, the government must generate revenues from domestic players by reforming its policies. Indigenous development of telecom equipment manufacture appears to be the most viable option to increase access and also cut costs.

The telecom sector has come into focus in recent years, which is the result of rapid developments in the information technology sector. The distinction between information technology and communications is becoming gradually blurred. India has a relative advantage globally in the field of information technology. This is critically dependent upon high quality infrastructure. Hence, infrastructure development in the telecom and information technology sector has been given high priority. Linkage between telecom and information technology has a marked influence on the telecom policy. In India, presently, the number of mobile telephones far outstrips the number of landlines. The demand for telephones is growing with the rapidly increasing consumer class. The government has to reform its policies to develop infrastructure to meet the growing demand. Infrastructure development on such a large scale would require huge investments. The government cannot raise such large amounts by itself and hence has to open up the sector to domestic private and foreign players to enable inflow of necessary funds. "Telecom companies today are facing the twin challenge of having to maintain affordability of services on the one hand and generate enough surplus cash to fund the requirements for network expansion and growth on the other," says COAI (Cellular Operator Association of India).

The Indian Telecom sector was initially a wholly government-owned sector monopolised by the Bharat Sanchar Nigam Limited (BSNL), the operating arm of the Department of Telecommunication (DoT). BSNL provides fixed line and wireless services throughout India except in Delhi and Mumbai, where the state-owned Mahanagar Telecom Nigam Ltd. (MTNL) is dominant. The state also has a minority stake in Videsh Sanchar Nigam Ltd (VSNL), India's international long-distance carrier and sole Internet Service Provider until 2000. In 2002, the government sold a controlling stake of 45% to the Tata group. The Tata group was among the first to set up privately owned cellular and fixed networks following liberalisation of these sectors. The national long-distance service was opened up to competition in November 2001 and the international long-distance service in April 2002. The investment was mainly from domestic government sources. It was only in the 1990s that the process of opening up of the telecom sector to private sector was started. The National Telecom Policy (NTP) was formulated in 1999 to enable market-based reforms in the telecom sector. It was envisioned to open up the entire sector to the market, streamline regulatory process and rationalize licenses.

Teledensity in India has risen from 5.14% in 2003 to 16% in 2006. This has been mainly due to the rise in mobile telephone use. The number of telephones has been increasing, especially cellular phones. The share of PSUs in market has been higher in fixed line services as compared to cellular services. But, gradually there seems to be an overall movement towards mobile phones from both PSUs and private services.

Table 1: Number of Telephones – Fixed Lines and Mobiles (millions)

Year	Fixed Line		Mobiles incl. WLL	
	No. in million	Share of PSUs	No. in million	Share of PSUs
2001-02	38.42	98.65	6.54	3.98
2002-03	41.63	97.36	12.99	20.32
2003-04	42.85	94.49	33.69	17.78
2004-05	46.20	88.98	52.17	21.03
2005-06	47.71	85.31	78.08	21.11

Source: Economic Survey 2005-06.

The rising demand for telephones has to be met by the government by investing in infrastructure in the sector. Policies have to be restructured to attract investment into the sector.

The N K Singh Committee Report suggested a required investment of Rs.165,216 cr to achieve teledensity of 12. It suggested 30% contribution from private sector, which comes to around Rs.50,000 cr. To help generate funds, two measures were proposed – increasing FDI limit and reduction in revenue sharing. The revenue share comprises USO and administrative costs. But, the major issue was, if there was a reduction of USO, how would the required investment be met? Universal Service Obligation is a source of funds by levying 5% of adjusted gross revenues of telecom companies.

Compiled from "NK Singh Report: Fund Raising Features", Pravin Prashant, http://www.indiaonestop.com/ict/it_overview.htm, Monday, October 14, 2002.

The share of telecom sector in the central plan outlay has witnessed a rise. This augurs well for the sector as this will open up opportunities for investments in this sector. The share of this sector in the VIII and the IX Plans was around 6%. It rose to 7.8% in the X Plan outlay.

The major Indian business houses are Birlas, BPL, Escorts, Essar, Reliance, RPG and Tatas. Currently, the dominant players are Bharti Televentures, Reliance Infocomm and Tatas.

Table 2: Central Plan Outlay for the Telecom Sector – 1999-00 to 2006-07 (Rs. cr)			
Year	Telecom	Total	Share of Telecom
1999-00	14038.6	160608.2	8.74
2000-01	31880.9	185736.8	17.16
2001-02	18083.0	186315.2	9.71
2002-03	19540	144038	13.57
2003-04	14903	147893	10.08
2004-05	11730	163720	7.16
2005-06	12140	211253	5.75
2006-07	19884	254041	7.83

Source: indiabudget.nic.in

The requirement of additional phones is 81.71 million – 14.72 (rural) and 66.99 (urban); fixed lines 50.16 and cells 31.55m. The investment required in the manufacturing sector would be Rs.6250 cr.

Table 3: Investment Requirement During X Plan

Years	Amount in Rs. Cr.			Share in Total	
	Public	Private	Total	Public	Private
2002-03	20700	2581	23281	88.91	11.09
2003-04	21735	4544	26279	82.71	17.29
2004-05	22822	8768	31510	72.24	27.26
2005-06	23963	12261	36224	66.15	33.85
2006-07	25161	18137	43298	58.11	41.89
Total	114381	46291	160672	71.19	28.81

Source: Economic Research Unit, DoT.

The commonly viable source of funds can be (a) Revenue from subscribers; (b) USOF (Universal Service Obligation Fund); (c) Surplus revenues from telecom companies; and (d) Foreign investments.

Revenue from Subscribers

The increase in cellular subscribers should result in generating revenues. With the growing importance of data services, companies have recognised it as a potential for improving operating margins.

The "Song Catcher" option is an innovative way to generate revenues for the mobile companies. This is more relevant in a nation obsessed with films and music. To download a song one likes, dial 393 and hold for 15 seconds. The song is downloaded in a matter of 15 seconds, but at a cost of Rs.20.

Innovation is absolutely necessary in a country, which uses its mobile more to answer and receive calls; such technological innovations are necessary to generate surplus income. With presence of cable TV in majority of households and increasing interest in serials, game shows, cricket matches etc., companies have found an easy and entertaining way to generate revenues. Almost every show on TV is replete with quizzes, questions, opinion polls etc., urging viewers to SMS their responses or call to a advertised number. These calls are charged relatively higher, but the lure of winning luxury goods/services as prizes makes the viewers overlook the call charge.

The growth in net subscribers for Tata Teleservices is nearly 20 percent in some states. It launched a new scheme, Tata Indicom Rhythm, a package that includes a Huawei make FM handset with double talk time benefits at Rs.1,799. This is a relatively competitive price and is sure to attract more subscribers, thereby generating more revenues.

Reliance Offers Virtual Rakhi Experience!

Move over postal rakhis. This Raksha Bandhan Reliance Infocomm plans to bring brothers and sisters living thousands of miles apart face-to-face, albeit through video conferencing.

Siblings could avail of this service 'ab raksha, no bandhan of distance' by signing up with 240 Reliance WebWorld centres across the country. "The charges for 10-minute facility within the country would be Rs.250 and Rs.1,200 to Rs.3,000 abroad depending upon the countries they reside in," a company statement quoting Mr Sundeep Saksena, head, Reliance WebWorld (UP circle), said today. The scheme would remain open on Raksha Bandhan (August 19) and also on August 20 and 21.

Source: The Tribune, Lucknow, August 18, 2005.

USOF

The Universal Service Obligation Fund (USOF) is funded by imposing a levy of 5% of adjusted gross revenues of telecom companies. This is used to provide provision of services at low cost in rural areas. Fiscal support to pay phones and individual household lines is delivered through USOF. The amount collected from various sources towards USOF during the period 2002-03 to 2005-06 was Rs.8796.4 cr. In 2006-07, the USOF would be Rs.1500 crores.

Table 4: USOF

2002-03	2003-04	2004-05	2005-06	2006-07
1653.6	2143.0	3457.7	1542.07	1500.00

Compiled from Thirtieth Report Standing Committee on Information Technology (2005-2006) (Fourteenth Lok Sabha) Ministry of Communications And Information Technology (Department of Telecommunications) Demands for Grants (2006-2007). P.7.

Surplus Revenues from Telecom Companies

Since there is a boom in the telecom sector with many telecom players making profits, it has been suggested that the surplus revenues can be redirected for investment into the sector. This will benefit both the government as well as the telecom companies. The telecom companies need to provide better accessibility and services to the consumers at relatively lower cost to be competitive. This requires upgradation of technology, which is again capital-intensive. These surpluses, used as investments, will definitely reap better profits and expand the market.

The Indian Telecom sector has a valuation of over $100 bn or Rs.4.5 lakh crore. Listed companies like Bharti Airtel and Reliance report valuations ranging between $26-27 bn and $19-20 bn respectively. Even yet-to-be-listed companies like BSNL and Idea report valuations of over $30 bn and $8-9 bn respectively. (Telecom Sector valuation tops $100 bn, *Economic Times*, January 17, 2007).

Bharti Airtel registered an increase in net profit of 123% in the quarter Oct-Dec, 2006 as a direct result of a widening subscriber base. It has a capex of $2 bn in the financial year 2006-07 and is planning to invest $2.5 bn in the financial year 2007-08.

Tata Teleservices Limited plans to invest around Rs.4000 crore for expanding its network to states where it does not already have a presence. The States include Jammu and Kashmir, Assam and the North East regions. Tata Teleservices Ltd would invest Rs.200 crore for expanding the Optical Fibre Network (OFC) in West Bengal, Orissa, Bihar, Jharkhand and Kolkata telecom circles.

Reliance Communications may start its second GDR to raise $1.2 bn. This will raise its foreign direct holding to 22.09%. The company will have to take the approval of FIPB in case foreign investors raise their equity in the company. It had earlier raised $500 bn in March 2006. These will be included in the capex of $2.5 bn in 2007-08. The company has $1 bn worth of FCCBs in the international markets; these are expected to be listed in the Singapore Exchange soon.

BSNL plans to invest Rs.2000 cr to augment its broadband infrastructure in urban and rural areas. BSNL announced a huge investment of Rs.17000 cr. to GSM, CDMA, broadband services, besides the billing segment. "A major investment of Rs.6,000 crore has been earmarked for GSM expansion. About Rs.3,000 crore will be spent for expanding broadband services and a similar investment will be made in CDMA-based services in various parts of the country. The entire investments would be funded through internal accruals and there is no plan to borrow from the market at this juncture." BSNL Chairman and Managing Director AK Sinha said. They have started procuring land and other infrastructure in order to facilitate the rollout for the over 63 million GSM lines that could begin as and when the equipment is received. (The Tribune, September 18, 2006.)

Foreign Investment

The increasing consumer base and limited resources has forced the government to reform its policies regarding foreign investments. The growing domestic market, cost-friendly service providers are making India more and more attractive for investors. The ceiling on foreign investment has been raised from 49% to 74% as a measure to attract more foreign investment. The FDI, to the extent of 74% can be made directly to the company or through a holding company. The investment beyond 49% is subject to government approval. There have been suggestions to increase the FDI share to 100% in some exceptional cases. Though the foreign investors will hold a major share in the company, the major Directors on the Board will be mainly Indian. Moreover, DoT retains its authority to restrict licenses in sensitive areas due to growing security concerns.

On 22nd March 2007, the Union Government revised the guidelines for foreign investment in the Indian Telecom sector. In lieu with the controversial issue of remote access and security and intelligence agencies, additional security norms were included. The Cabinet has laid down five protectionist measures in this regard.

"*One, remote access to networks in India will be allowed only from approved locations. Two, remote access will only be offered to equipment suppliers, manufacturers and affiliates. Three, remote access cannot be used for monitoring content. Four, a mirror image of remote access information must be made available online in India to the security agencies. Five, a complete audit trail of remote access activities must be maintained for six months.*" (Centre clears decks for 74% telecom FDI, Nivedita Mookerji, Thursday, March 22, 2007, DNA Daily News and Analysis.)

The deadline for telecom companies to meet these guidelines is April 2, 2007. Regarding the stipulations of having only resident Indians as CEOs/CTOs/CFOs, Tata Teleservices, which has a foreign CEO, has put forth a case to exempt companies with up to 49% FDI from this norm.

The total amount of FDI inflows received into the telecom sector between August 1991 and June 2006 was Rs.15780 cr or US$3692 cr., which accounted for 11% of total FDI inflows. The surge in foreign investments in the telecom sector emphasises the vast potential for investors.

The growth potential of the Indian telecom sector has not gone unnoticed by the European Banks, which have already committed over Rs.2000 crore for infrastructure development in the country. The German banking major KFW Bankengruppe, European Bank JB and Swedfund were among the others to have committed to invest in the country. These investments are in the form of foreign currency convertible bonds (FCCBs), provided at low-cost and for a long duration of 8-10 years.

Independent Mobile Infrastructure Mauritius Ltd (IMIML) has offered an investment of Rs.3000 cr. It is spread over a five-year period and IMIML or its affiliates can make investments. The government has approved the investment conditionally. Companies listed in other parts of the world are bound to divest 26% equity in favor of the Indian public*.

---

* "Rs.3000 crore FDI by Telecom Infrastructure firm" *http://www.domain-bcom/industry/telecom/20070118_infrastructure.html*, January 18, 2007.

Table 5: Money Power

Bank/Fund	Company	Investment
KFW Group	IL&FS Fund	Rs.114 cr
	IDFC Fund	Rs.22.8 cr
	SREI Infrastructure	Rs.114 cr
	GTL Infrastructure	Rs.114 cr
Bank JB	GTL Infrastructure	Rs.88.35 cr
FMO	India Infrastructure Equipment	17.24% stake
Swedfund	India Infrastructure Equipment	17.24% stake
Standard Chartered-led Consortium	GTL Infrastructure	Rs.1500 cr.

Source: "European Banks Line up to Invest in Telecom", Rajesh S Kurup, Business Standard, January 18, 2007.

Sequoia Capital has made a 1.5% stake in Idea Cellular for $42 mn. The other stakeholders in Idea Cellular are US-based Providence Equity Partners – 15% or $400 mn; UK-based GLG Partners – 8% or $213 mn.

vJive, India's first broadband media and digital signage network has received Rs.20 cr as part of an overall Rs.100 cr investment plan by Matrix Partners India (MPI). MPI is India's first consumer services risk capital fund. It strives to provide risk capital to build market by leading consumer companies.

Maxis Communications, Malaysia's leading telecom service provider will invest Rs.22 bn into Aircel Cellular to support existing and additional subscribers targeted by the company.

"Baring Private Equity Partners (BPEP) is currently investing its second India-specific fund of $175 million. It is investing in Indian companies focused on new telecom applications, wireless solutions and telecom infrastructure."*

Need for Improving Indigenous Manufacture

The country's premier telecom manufacturing institute, ITI was established with a view to meet the telecom equipment requirements of the telecom companies. It is a paradox that in the current booming telecom market scenario, this institute has

* "Baring sees big bucks in Indian Telecom", *The Economic Times of India,* December 12, 2006.

been neglected and allowed to turn sick. In the present context—growing market for telecom sector—meeting the demand through upgradation of technology by investing in infrastructure seems to be the most reasonable solution. Investing in infrastructure and indigenising manufacture of equipment will reduce the costs as also cut down on outflows of foreign exchange in the form of equipment imports.

Now, Alcatel has decided to collaborate with C-DoT to develop the breakthrough technology—WiMax. WiMax can provide broadband wireless access at high data rates with a range of 15 kms in rural areas and 700 metres in urban areas. WiMax can be a major radio access solution integrated in both fixed and mobile network architectures. Alcatel's tying up with Intel will further benefit C-DoT to define, standardise and market WiMax products. It will also offer better quality of service, enhanced security and higher data rates. BSNL's tie-up with Alcatel will increase its broadband penetration, especially in rural areas, where its telecom infrastructure is limited.

The government has proposed to set up a 1-lakh electric service centres in rural areas, catering to 6 lakh villages and make the government more accessible to the public. The total cost of the project is estimated at Rs.5742 cr with private sector contribution of Rs.4093 cr. These kiosks/centres would act as front-end for e-governance initiative. They would have broadband connectivity and be operated by local entrepreneurs.

In the face of increasing consumer class and increasing incomes and purchasing power, the consumer is also well aware of technological developments globally. The demand for better and quicker quality service is growing. But, competition among the telecom companies is driving them to slash prices of services and products, resulting in a drag on profits. Importing manufactured parts will increase costs, which will be passed on to the consumer. Indigenous manufacture of telecom parts and improving the infrastructure will cut down the dependence on imports, thereby resulting in reduction of costs and, in turn, prices. The government has initiated a proposal for setting up Telecom Equipment and Services Export Promotion Council and Telecom Testing and Security Certification Centre (TETC). Companies like Alcatel, Cisco have come forward to set up their own research and development (R&D) centres in India. This could lead India to be a manufacturing hub for telecom equipment, besides being a hub for IT.

The major steps to be taken up by the government to capitalise on the current boom in the telecom sector are:

- Generate funds from surplus revenues of telecom companies for reinvestment;
- Reform policies to create a competitive and business-friendly environment for private investors;
- Channelise investment for development of infrastructure for Research and Development (R&D); and
- Upgrade technology to meet the objective of expanding the network of course, at affordable prices.

(Kalyani Rampilla, Sub-Editor, Icfai Books a division of the Icfai University Press.)

References

1. "Top Sector for Foreign Direct Investment in India", *//indiaonestop.com/fdi-telecom.htm*
2. IndiaCore.com – "The online resource for information on the Indian core sector".
3. "Telecom reforms and opportunities for small and medium entrepreneurs" Shyamal Ghosh, *www.connect-world.com*
4. "Increased FDI ceiling in telecom sector notified", *The Hindu,* November 8, 2005.
5. "Investments surge in the telecom space", *The Economic Times,* December 8, 2006.
6. "European banks line up to invest in telecom", Rajesh S Kurup, *Business Standard,* January 18, 2007.
7. *Economic Survey* 2005-06.
8. Telecom Sector valuation tops $100 bn, *Economic Times,* January 17, 2007.
9. "Baring sees big bucks in Indian Telecom", *The Economic Times of India,* December 12, 2006.

FDI Investments in Telecom Sector (Main Projects) 2005-06

Name	Location	Nature of Project	Amount Proposed to be invested	Present Status
Ericsson	Jaipur	Telecom manufacturing	$ 50 mn (already invested)	Inaugurated on 11.03.05. Unit in operation
Ericsson	Chennai	R&D facility, Global service delivery centre and facility for manufacturing base stations and mobile switching equipments	$100 mn in first phase	Inaugurated on 25.02.06. unit in operation.
Ericsson	Other than Tamil Nadu	-do-	$100 mn in first phase (within 2-3 yrs)	Announced on 11.03.05. Under implementation
Elcoteq	Bangalore	Telecom manufacturing	$100 mn, $18 mn already invested	Inaugurated on 11.04.05. Unit in operation.
LG	Pune	Telecom manufacturing	$12 mn	Unit in operation
Nokia	Chennai	Mobile handset manufacturing	$200 mn	Inaugurated on 11.03.06. Unit in operation
Nokia	Chennai	To set up global network operation centre for customers in Asia Pacific region, Europe, Middle East and Africa		Inaugurated on 11.03.05. Unit in operation.
Alcatel	Chennai	Wimax Centre	$60 mn	Inaugurated on 03.09.05. Unit in operation
Samsung	Manesar, Gurgaon, Haryana	Handset manufacturing	$15 mn. Expansion plan of $200 mn in next 3 years.	Inaugurated on 07.03.06. Unit in operation.

Contd...

Contd...

Siemens	Chennai, Hyderabad, Kolkata	Telecom equipment manufacturing	$100 mn	Announced on 09.08.05
Flextronics	Chennai	Telecom hardware manufacturing	$100 mn	Announced on 14.09.05. Under implementation.
CISCO	Chennai	NGN Lab at Chennai; e-governance networking in IT & Telecom across the nation	$1.1 bn	Announced on 19.10.05. Under implementation.
HonHai (FoxConn) Precision Industry Co. Ltd.	Chennai	Manufacturing of mobile handsets and components and electrical hardware and related services	$110 mn	MoU to be signed.
Motorola	Chennai	Manufacturing of Motorola's first "Made in India" low-cost GSM phone	$70 mn	Released in Delhi on 22.12.05. Unit in operation.

Source: http://www.indiaonestop.com/ict/it_overview.htm

11

The Financing of Water Projects: An Overview

Deepak Kumar

Financing water projects had been a Herculean task until the private sector came into picture. This paper lists a few such projects, drawn from India and overseas, which could have never been successful without involving private sectors. Moreover, the role of different international agencies like USAID, the World Bank, UNDP and the World Economic Forum can't be ignored in this development. However, the word of caution here is that each project, being unique in itself, should not be replicated elsewhere without understanding the macro- and micro-environment. The paper concludes by saying that the record of stakeholders in the water sector has not been particularly satisfactory as on date due to the tendency to put the developed country methodologies into practice in developing countries and thus, need an integrated coordination among themselves.

Introduction

Like other projects, water projects were traditionally financed and dependent on budget allocation, in most countries. However, a few initiatives and policy

Source: The Icfai Journal of Infrastructure, Vol. IV, No. 3, 2006. This article was originally published as "The Financing of Water Projects: A Study".

regulations have changed the financing scenario of the infrastructure projects; the water sector was no exception. Meanwhile, the governments also tried to encourage the people to invest in bonds, but with a few exceptions, nothing worked in a great way. The governments also encouraged municipals to arrange the funds to develop their own infrastructure. This was the time when the private participation was found to be the need of the hour. The private sectors, no doubt, focussed to mitigate the risks *vis-à-vis* the best return of the money invested. On the other hand, there were also challenges to safeguard the interest of the masses. One argument was commonly seen in earlier days that too much private participation in water projects might deplete the water levels and other resources. Therefore, encouraging the investment was a crisis management task and safeguarding the interest of masses through regulations and polices was a big challenge in most of the countries.

Here is the need as how to balance the situation and the public-private participation comes into the picture. The need to have private participation is to leverage the limited government funding and access the private sector management efficiencies. Among other reasons are fiscal constraints and poor cost recovery which, in simple words, decreases the social and economic development, thereby resuling in poor quality operation and limited expansion of networks.

Involving private sector in water projects is not an easy task, as it involves risks to them, such as regulation, stability of economy, growth prospects and developmental risks. The other types of risks are operational and construction risk. It is often seen that the time and cost are overrun in different infrastructure projects and water projects are not an exception in this regard. As far as operational risk is concerned, the main risk is how to get the tariffs, as the private sector is very much concerned of this. The tariff must be transparent and should protect commercial interests of private investors. On the other hand, it is important to safeguard the consumers' interest by internal cross subsidy and limited government subsidy, besides setting up a regulatory body.

Types of Financing

Based on the involvement of private parties, types of ownership, source of financing and mode of operation, the following types of model are commonly seen in water sector (Table 1).

Table 1: Types of PSP (Private Sector Participation) Models			
PSP Model	**Ownership of Facilities**	**Financing**	**Operation**
Service Contract	Public	Public	Public and Some Private
Management Contract	Public	Public	Private
Lease Contract	Public	Public	Private
Concession Contract	Private for Contract Duration	Private	Private
BOOT	Private and Public	Private	Private
Reverse BOOT	Public and Private	Public	Private
Joint Ownership	Private and Public	Private and Public	Public and Private
Outright Sale	Private	Private	Private
Source: www.wdm2004.org/new_web/technical_session/files/rashid_al_hmoud.pdf			

Table 1 depicts the common methods of financing in different countries but Elie Elhadj, the School of Oriental and African Studies (SOAS), University of London, in his paper, "Financing Major Water Projects in the Poorest Economies", summarized the findings as in Table 2. Elhadj is of the opinion that in the poorest countries, the financing of water projects is done by government, US financing sources, domestic private sectors and foreign private sectors (Table 2).

Indian Examples

In the Indian context, three projects have been dealt with here which are only indicative in nature. These are:

- Tirupur Water Supply and Sewerage Project, Tamil Nadu.
- Sri Sathya Sai Drinking Water Project, Ananthapur, Andhra Pradesh.
- Visakhapatnam Industrial Water Supply Project, Andhra Pradesh.

Table 2: Financing Major Water Projects in the Poorest Economies

	Equity	Long-term Debt	Short-term Debt
A. Government-owned Projects			
A.1. Local currency financing from:			
A.1.a. Government sources			
– Taxation	Yes	Yes	Yes
– Printing of currency	Yes	Yes	Yes
A.1.b. Domestic private sector sources			
– Domestic commercial banks	–	No	Yes
– Government bonds	–	Yes	No
A.2. US$ financing sources			
A.2.a. Domestic private sector holdings in US$	–	Yes	Yes
A.2.b. Foreign governments and multilateral financial aid institutions	–	Yes	Yes
A.2.c. Foreign private sector			
– Foreign commercial banks	–	No	Rarely
– Foreign bond markets	–	No	No
– Foreign private sector equity	Rarely	Rarely	Rarely
B. Domestic Private Sector-owned Projects			
B.1. Local currency financing from:			
B.1.a. Domestic commecrical banks	No	No	Yes
B.1.b. Domestic bond markets	No	Yes	No
B.1.c. Domestic equity markets	Yes	No	No
B.2. US$ Financing source from:			
B.2.a. Domestic private sector holdings in US$	Yes	Yes	Yes
B.2.b. Foreign governments and multilateral financial aid institutions	IFC, MIGA only	No	No
B.2.c. Foreign private sector			
– Foreign commercial banks	No	No	No
– Foreign bond markets	No	No	No
– Foreign private sector equity	Rarely	Rarely	Rarely

Source: www.soas.ac.uk/waterissues/occasionalpapers/OCC35.pdf

Tirupur Water Supply and Sewerage Project

This project was based on the Concession Model, i.e., Build-Own-Operate-Transfer (BOOT) and the total concession period was 30 years. The Concessionaire of this project was "New Tirupur Area Development Co Area Development". The total cost of the project was Rs.1023 cr ($220 mn).

The project aimed at supplying 185 Million Liter per Day (MLD) of water and is allocated to industries, domestic uses and wayside villages at 115 MLD, 33.7 MLD, and 36.3 MLD, respectively.

Figure 1: Tirupur Water Project

(Figures in $ million)

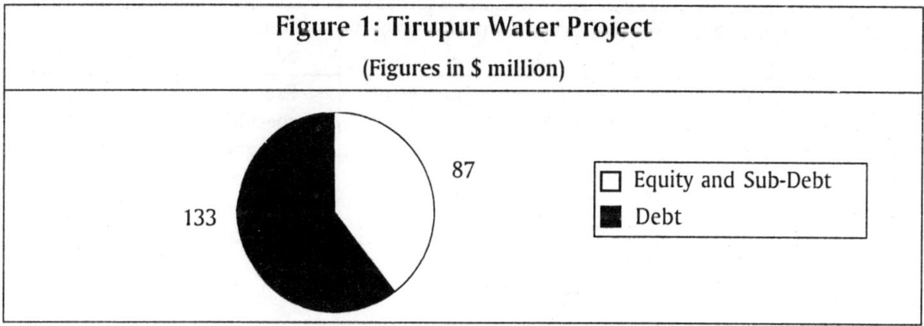

However, there is problem in this project as the cost of water is as high as Rs.30 per KL. This is because of high capital cost, high operating cost and investment in building sewerage network. However, as far as tariff structure is concerned, the industries are charged as high as Rs.45/KL while households in rural areas are charged at Rs.3.50/KL. Thus, recovering the investment cost is problematic in this case. To address this issue, tariff revisions are done on annual basis for water supplied for households in Tirupur town. As per one estimation, the subsidies of Rs.25/KL and Rs.26.5/KL are given to industries and rural households. This incurs the burden of Rs.65 cr of subsidy to the government. Thus, it cannot be ignored that the investment can be incurred in a very short-term and the government has also to be accountable to provide the better drinking water facility. In the coming years, it is expected that the project will benefit a larger section of society and industry, taking care of social development.

Sri Sathya Sai Drinking Water Project, Ananthapur, Andhra Pradesh

This is a classic model of public-private and people partnership, which could never have been possible without the support of the people of Ananthapur. The following stakeholders participated actively in the whole project (Table 3).

Table 3: Stakeholders of the Project

1.	Sri Sathya Sai Central Trust (henceforth-Trust)	Funding and coordinating agency of the project	Funded the project through voluntary contributions received from individuals of the civil society
2.	The Andhra Pradesh Government	The facilitator of the project	Technical and administrative support
3.	L&T	The actual implementer of the project	• Executed design and specifications. • Designed all overhead service reservoirs. • Powered the team to avoid any delay of project.
4.	People of Ananthapur	Contributed their physical man-days	—

Ananthapur is one of those districts which faced drought during 1970-90 and drinking water was a major problem before this project actually came into operation. The people had to go 2-3 km to get two vessels of water and one can imagine how the man-days would have been lost because of that situation. The available drinking water was not sufficient to the villagers and it had excessive fluoride. All this affected the quality of life of the villagers and they had to face the problems of food security and income generation.

This project now provides access to more than 1 million poor in 731 villages and three towns who had hitherto no safe drinking water supply. Ananthapur is a semi-arid district in the State of Andhra Pradesh, which is the third poorest state in India. The whole district, with a population of nearly 1.5 million, was facing extreme shortage of drinking water in its 1,000 villages and towns. This was what led to the implementation of the Sri Sathya Sai Drinking Water Supply Project in 1998.[1]

1 http://www.cin.gov.cn/Habitat/en/media/media02-22.htm

Thus, there was no way out than an organization which could make the whole system to work. The Sri Sathya Sai Trust came in front and determined to provide the drinking water facility to villagers of Ananthapur, having the population of 1.5 million (Table 4).

Table 4: Salient Features of the Project		
1.	Project Cost	Rs.3000 mn
2.	Project completed in a record	18 months (February 1995–July 1996)
3.	Establishment of public stand posts	1,700
4.	Establishment of concrete cisterns with four taps each	1,000
5.	Source of water supply	60% from nearby three rivers and 40% groundwater

Financing of the Project

The project is an excellent example of public, private and people participation. The whole project was funded through voluntary contributions received from individuals of the civil society. Once the project was completed in July 1996, the next task was how the whole system would be operated and maintained. Once the project was completed, the whole system was handed over to the state government but the government had another set of mind like how to sustain the system, as it is also found that the people have a strong sense of belonging to the project and the Sathya trust which cannot be ignored. To create a win-win situation, Sri Sathya Sai Water Supply Project Board was established. This board is now solely responsible for operating and maintaining the system.

To maintain the whole system, it was decided to collect the user fee from institutions for the usage and the government will allocate the amount from budget for usage by villagers.

As of now, 70% of the O&M amount is allocated by the state government and other 30% is being collected from the institutions and volunteers (Figure 2). The water bill is generated each month and the payment form institutions are requested without any delay. The panchayat bodies are also facilitators in the whole system, as it does not want to disturb the existing system. Besides these, the AP government bears the O&M cost of project like machinery, plant and staff.

Visakhapatnam Industrial Water Supply Project

Another example of water project is again from Andhra Pradesh, India. It is the first Build-Operate-Transfer (BOT) Industrial Water Supply Project in India, which was completed in record time of 12 months at the cost of Rs.450 cr. After completion of this project, Godavari water has been brought to Visakhapatnam connecting through pipeline.

Figure 2: O&M Cost Incurred in Sri Sathya Sai Drinking Water Project, Ananthapur

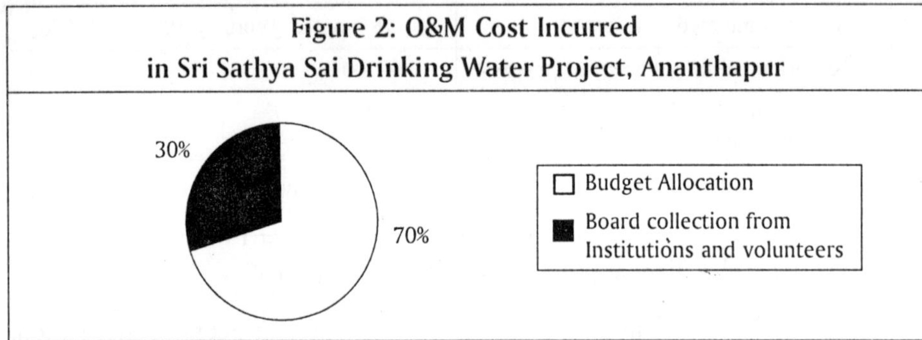

This project is unique as it is jointly developed by Public Institutions (APIIC, RINL, VMC and NTPC) with L&T as private contributor. Some unique features of this project are: securitization of Project financials by an Independent Auditor, monitoring of Project deliverables by an Independent Engineer, and Water Price Review was done by an Independent Committee.

Figure 3: Visakhapatnam Industrial Water Supply Company (VIWSCo) – Special Purpose Vehicle (SPV)

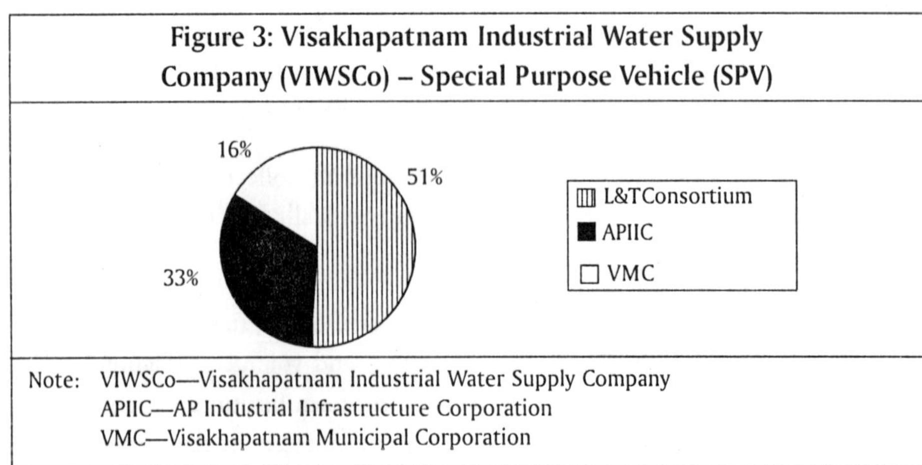

Note: VIWSCo—Visakhapatnam Industrial Water Supply Company
APIIC—AP Industrial Infrastructure Corporation
VMC—Visakhapatnam Municipal Corporation

As far as implementation of this project is concerned, VIWSCo (Visakhapatnam Industrial Water Supply Company) acted as Special Purpose Vehicle (SPV). The debt fund was raised from beneficiaries like different industries and the direct subsidy was provided by the State Government so that the initial fixed charge burden could be decreased. The subsidy was an alternative of commercial loan (Figure 3).

International Examples

The international examples from China and Peru have been quoted in Annexures 1 and 2.

Private Sector Participation in Water Sector in China[2]

A large proportion of funds to develop China's water infrastructure is expected to be raised by means of overseas investment, loans and market financing. The political trend is clearly in favor of attracting foreign capital and joint funding to achieve the required water supply and sewage treatment targets. However, private participation in water sector in China is very poor in comparison to other infrastructure sectors. As sponsors get the finance through bank lending in a few cases, they also take out the money from their corporate balance sheet.

The interest in such sector is very low because individual investment in such sector is less than $30 mn, a threshold at which the approval by the State Development Planning Commission is done. The models that have come up in financing the water sector are management contract, BOT contracts, official or tender BOT schemes, and concession contract.

BOT contracts can be further divided into three broad categories:

- **Negotiated cooperative joint venture BOT schemes** – Follow cooperative joint ventures, which are controlled either by provincial or municipal authorities but the central government supports in a limited way.
- **Negotiated wholly privately-owned BOT schemes** – Where the local government agencies only act as the granting authority and regulator and do not take any equity stake. This is in order to avoid any conflict (e.g., Shanghai Dachang).

2 P Nair and Deepak Kumar, "Private Participation in Infrastructure in China", *The Icfai Journal of Infrastructure*, September 2004.

- **Official or tender BOT schemes** – Which involve competitive bidding, central government and off-taker credit support provided by provincial or municipal governments (e.g., Chengdu Water Supply and Beijing Water # 10).

Figure 4: USAID Drinking Water Supply and Sanitation Obligations by Region (Totaling Over $161 mn in 2005)

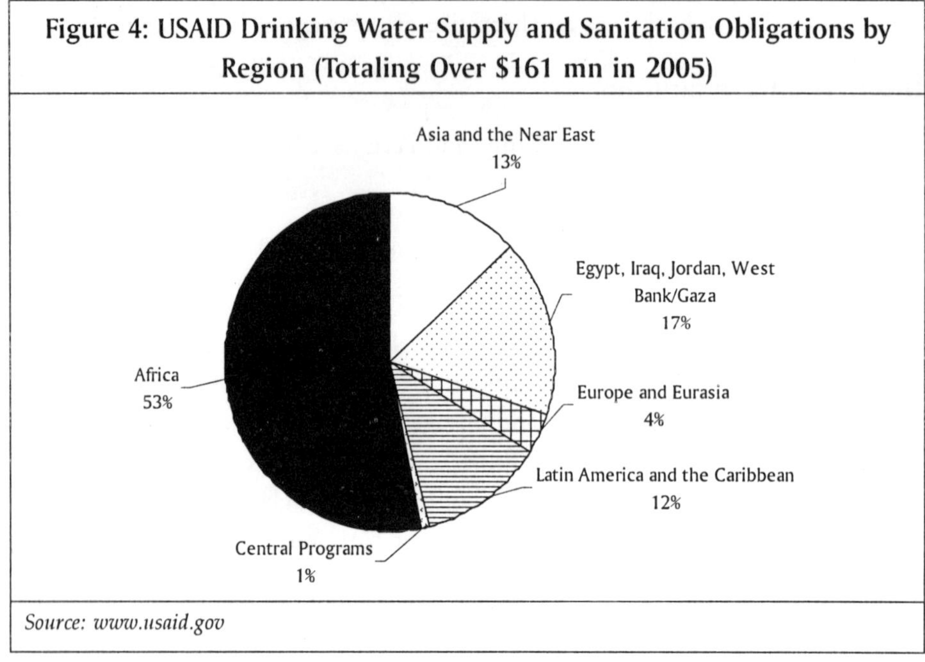

Source: www.usaid.gov

Role of Different Agencies

Different agencies such as the USAID, the World Bank, UNDP and the World Economic Forum are contributing for water projects in a big manner. They are having alliance with local, state and central governments to facilitate the whole system. Here are some examples:

- USAID has worked in Ethiopia, Pakistan, and Haiti, etc. In these countries, it has established water treatment plants in alliance with corporates. It has also encouraged the local people to participate. In Ethiopia, Pakistan, and Haiti, USAID involved Procter & Gamble to provide the water purification products, and the diseases like diarrhea have decreased by almost 30-40%. Moreover, it has been observed that the major financing by USAID in the year 2005 went to African countries (Figure 4). There is need here for

Table 5: Funding for Selected Water and Sanitation Projects

Project Site, Type and Date	Project Cost	Debt/Equity	Country Rating	Source and Maturity of Debt
Malaysia, Concession (1993)	US$2.4 bn (about US$500 mn in first two years)	75/25	A+	Government soft loans due to severe tariff collection problems
Buenos Aires, Argentina; Concession (1993)	US$4 bn (US$300 mn in first two years)	60/40	BB–	10-year IFC A-loan, 12-year IFC B-loan (recourse to Argentina government in event of early termination)
Izinit, Turkey; BOT (1995)	US$800 mn	85/15	B	13-year export credit agency loans, 7-year MITI[a] loan, 7-year commercial bank loan (recourse to Turkish government)
Chihuahua, Mexico; BOT (1994)	US$17 mn	53/15/32[b]	BB	8.5-year commercial bank loan with limited recourse to Banobras
Johor, Malaysia; BOT (1992)	US$284 mn	50/50	A+	10-year project finance loan from Public Bank Bhd (nonrecourse)
Sydney, Australia; BOO (1993)	A$230 mn	80/20	AAA	15-year commercial loans (State government stands behind Sydney Water Corp. payment.)
England and Wales, Full Privatization (1989)	US$5.24 bn	25/75	AAA	Capital markets, corporate finance, European Investment Bank, and other sources.

Note: [a] Ministry of International Trade and Industry of Japan.
[b] Debt/equity/grant.

Source: www.worldbank.org

USAID to refocus its attention on the Asian countries as these countries contain a major chunk of world's population.

- The World Economic Forum has also launched Indian Business Alliance on Water to facilitate the water supply in Rajasthan. Several programs have been conducted in Jaipur in this regard.
- The World Bank is also involved actively in financing and facilitating the water projects across the world. Table 5 provides a brief summary.

Recommendation of World Bank for Water and Sanitation Sector

The promotion of a broad range of private participation models in water is what is being encouraged. In addition to concession schemes, the Chinese Government has been urged to look at other models of encouraging private participation in the water sector. Two of them could be the Management Contract model and the Leasing Contract model. The Management Contract model looks at getting the private party, essentially to handle the management operations, without incurring much of the financial risk. The Leasing Contract model allows all the facilities to be leased by the private parties at a regular rent. Here, commercial risks as well as operating risks are borne by the private party. However, the ownership responsibility, and hence financing of the capital investment, would not be borne by the private party.

Conclusion

The record of coordination among stakeholders of the water sector has not been particularly happy as on date due to the tendency to put the developed country methodologies into practice in developing countries. These countries have different requirements at various levels and need an altogether a different approach. Customized approaches should be the norm, rather than standardizing everything at some macro level.

(Deepak Kumar, Former Associate Consultant, The Icfai University Press, Hyderabad. He can be reached at bornwaldeepak_11@rediffmail.com).

Disclaimer: The views expressed here are the author's own and they are not of the organization he represents.

References

1. *http://www.cin.gov.cn/Habitat/en/media/media02-22.htm*
2. Nair P and Kumar Deepak, "Private Participation in Infrastructure in China", *The Icfai Journal of Infrastructure*, September 2004.
3. *Siteresources.worldbank.org/ INTWDR2004/Resources/22487_plummerWDR.pdf*
4. *www.wdm2004.org/new_web/technical_ session/files/rashid_al_hmoud.pdf*
5. *www.aquamedia.at*
6. *www.soas.ac.uk/waterissues/occasionalpapers/OCC35.pdf*
7. *www.usaid.gov*
8. *www.worldbank.org*

Annexure 1: Water Tanker Service Delivery in Peri-Urban Areas of Lima, Peru

In the late 1980s, informal settlements in peri-urban Lima were riddled with water and faecalborne diseases because of the poor water quality and arid conditions. The creation of a partnership in 1990 involving the municipality, communities and the small-scale independent water-tanker drivers (together with a successful community mobilization program) has contributed to significant upgradation in the quality, quantity and reliability of water supply to poor residents and a sustainable alternative in settlements not connected to the network.

The inclusion of small-scale providers at the core of the partnership acknowledged that the *ad hoc* tankers represented an asset and not a liability to be discarded. The strategic design of the program (with EU support) included these small-scale water suppliers as a vital link in the utility delivery process. Efforts were made to regulate the quality and price of the water supply to ensure that delivery became fair, viable and sustainable.

Perhaps the most significant step in this process was the formalization of the water tanker provision, through registration as small businesses and the development of tanker driver associations. The new system requires that the tanker drivers obtain treated water from one of the four official pumps provided for this purpose by the Lima Water Utility. Although sometimes insufficient in quantity, this water is of the same quality as that supplied to the city network. The tanker drivers pay the utility per tanker filled. The tankers are annually contracted by the community management organizations to provide water to local storage reservoirs, to which a small independent network has been constructed. The tanker drivers are paid a fixed amount agreed by the community and regulated by the municipality. These small enterprises vary. Some are single owner-drivers; others are local businessmen with five to ten tankers, employing 10-20 workers. In order to ensure ongoing work, the businesses maintain their tankers regularly (although there is some concern about some of the hygiene standards). At the city level, the Directorate of Environmental Health carries out monitoring of the quality of water supplied at the pump and the conditions of the tankers. The municipality regulates and monitors the service at the local level.

Initially operated for some years in the informal sector, a key characteristic of these enterprises is their lack of managerial and administrative capacity. They have had few opportunities for developing skills in formal accounting and management or technical proficiency. Consequently, they lacked knowledge of their responsibilities as water distributors and in relation to taxation and fees.

Source: siteresources.worldbank.org/INTWDR2004/Resources/22487_plummerWDR.pdf

Annexure 2: Examples of Foreign Investments in Water and Sanitation Sector in China

- In late 2001, US Filter won a $3.1 mn contract to supply the city of Karamay, China's new Waste Water Treatment Plant (WWTP) with biological and clarification technology.
- In August 2002, Thames Water announced its plan to acquire 48.8% stake in the Hong Kong-based China Water Co for $72 mn, thus, expanding its operational and technical expertise in China.
- Ondeo has a contract for the equipment and site supervision of a drinking water purification plant (150,000 m3/d.) in Changzou.
- In may 2002, Ondeo signed two new contracts in China for a total value of almost €460 mn. In Qingdao, Ondeo was chosen to manage a 25-year contract to supply drinking water to 2.3 million residents. In Shanghai, Ondeo is reconstructing two drinking water treatment plants located in Nanshi and Yangshupu.
- Vivendi recently signed a 23-year contract worth $307 mn with the Chinese municipality of Baoji (population 500,000) for the refurbishment and extension of two drinking water treatment plants and their operation.

Source: www.aquamedia.at

12

Airport Privatization and Financing: Experiences from Countries and Lessons for India

Padmalatha Suresh

With the privatization of the British Airport Authority (BAA) in 1987, the participation of the private sector in airport infrastructure has increased substantially. A better air transport sector also contributes significantly to the development of an economy. With this sector making a positive contribution to the expanded economy, the respective governments of different countries could focus on safety and security regulation, along with competitive policies, and economic and environmental regulations, as well. The commercial viability of operating the airport infrastructure for the private sector arises from (i) being able to price its services effectively, and (ii) the customers being able and willing to pay for these services. Airport infrastructure privatization is promising to be a global mega trend, with more and more governments and private players being pushed in that direction. Most mature airports remain profitable through the vagaries of the airline industry largely

Source: The Icfai Journal of Infrastructure, Vol. IV, No. 2, 2006.

due to the fact that they earn a high proportion of their income from non-aeronautical revenues. Bangalore International Airport Ltd., is the first Public-Private Partnership (PPP) Greenfield project in India. It has been recently project-financed with a substantial amount of bank funding. However, international experience suggests that markets also have a greater role to play in airport financing. With airport privatization already gaining momentum, the government machinery, financing and contractual structures have to gear up to keep pace.

Why Privatize?

Since the privatization of the British Airport Authority (BAA) in 1987, private sector participation in airport infrastructure has expanded and evolved by leaps and bounds.

A well functioning air transport sector offers significant economic development benefits, contributing to poverty alleviation (World Bank). The sector has the potential to be financially self-sustaining because of:

- Rapid technological change,
- Industry consolidation,
- The Low Cost Carrier (LCC) business model,
- The existence of adequate pricing models and mechanisms, and
- Consumer willingness to pay for safe, cost effective services.

When this sector starts making a positive contribution to the expanded economy, the respective governments, which currently have substantial involvement in the existing air transport infrastructure, could focus on safety and security regulation, along with competition policy and economic and environmental regulation.

The air transport industry can be viewed in four components—aircraft manufacturing, airline operations, airport infrastructure and air navigation services.

The private sector has had a dominating presence in aircraft manufacturing and airline operations. Hence, it is only logical that the sector plays a larger role in airport infrastructure as well. However, provision of Air Navigation Services (ANS) still remains a core public sector responsibility, due to the strategic nature of airport assets, and the increase of security concerns and threats. The only exception to this at present is the UK's 'for profit' ANS: Even here, the primary partners are the major UK airlines and the Government.

In almost all countries, the bulk of airport infrastructure had traditionally been created by the public sector. In the United States, many airports are still overwhelmingly owned by local governments.

The transfer of major UK airports to the BAA marked a major shift of air transport infrastructure to the private sector. Private sector participation has increased substantially over the last two decades in the airport sector through a variety of schemes and models[1], such as:

- Sale of a concession to a private sector entity (consortium of operator, financier and developer) to operate and develop a single airport for a stipulated concession period ranging from 20 to 50 years (Public-Private Partnership).
- Sale of a concession to a private sector entity to operate and manage a system of several airports on behalf of one or more strategic investors, or on behalf of the public at large as shareholders, for a stipulated concession period (Operations and Management Contracts).
- Sale of shares in a national airports authority to the private sector (entirely or in partnership with government), such that the authority becomes an entity in the private sector (divestiture).
- Sale of a concession to a private sector entity to develop and operate a facility of a government-owned airport (passenger terminal, cargo center etc.) for a stipulated period of time, after which ownership in the facility may revert to the state. This is the typical Build-Operate-Transfer (BOT) project.

Table 1 shows how the above models have been used internationally in some airport privatizations.

[1] www.icao.int/icao/en/ro/nacc/aps/09_pp_craig_e.pdf

Table 1: Models of Airport Privatizations – Examples	
Model	**Where Implemented**
Full Privatization	United Kingdom: Privatization of the British Airport Authority responsible for operation of seven airports.
	Australia: 17 airports sold on long-term leases of 50 years, with an option to extend for additional 49 years.
BOT/Concession agreement	Columbia: BOT contract to build second runway and operate both runways at El Dorado International Airport, Bogota.
	Canada: Private entity to build and operate a third terminal at Pearson International Airport, Toronto, on a long-term lease basis.
Partial Divestiture/ Strategic partner	Thailand: A strategic partner invited to develop and operate a second International Airport at Bangkok.
Management Contracts	Hong Kong: Private company awarded management contract of Kai Tak new airport.

The commercial viability of operating airport infrastructure for the private sector arises from being able to price its services effectively, and the customers being able and willing to pay for these services. Sound pricing helps in generating cash flows that can be used to pay for the operations, maintenance, and development of the facility. The cash flows also allow for debt service and adequate returns to equity holders.

Under the traditional nonprofit, public service model, the tasks of airport's management were to get planes in and out, move passengers on and off, and cover their costs (not necessarily all costs as measured by real world accounting). By contrast, under the new commercial model, management is expected to run the entire enterprise at profit, seeking adequate returns for its shareholders. The management style has to be entrepreneurial, endeavoring to maximize all possible revenue sources (subject to any regulatory constraints), meet the needs of all customers, cover all costs (as measured by GAAP) as efficiently as possible, pay taxes, and make a real return on the overall capital investment. It is noteworthy that this commercial model is being used not only by privatized airports like Heathrow or Gatwick, but also by several other government-owned but separately incorporated airports like Auckland, Frankfurt or Schiphol, which operate like any other business, making profits and paying taxes.

Experts opine that Australia and New Zealand have taken the commercial model more further than any other country has done so far. In both countries, any fee-charging enterprise is in government hands must be set up as a corporation, keep its books using GAAP, earn a return on its capital, pay all normal business taxes, and borrow at taxable rates. New Zealand applies this commercial model even to its highway system. It is seen that the commercial model dramatically changes the corporate culture—the entity is transformed into a different kind—which is entrepreneurial and customer-driven because it is profit-seeking.

The prime concern with all privatization of public goods and services is that the profit will emerge from squeezing the users. Are these legitimate fears of the public justified in the context of privatized airports?

Take the case of London Heathrow and Gatwick, which have been privately-owned now for over 15 years. Their airside charges today are lower in real terms than they were in 1987 when they were privatized. Yet, BAA is highly profitable, worth over three times as much as it was at the time of privatization. The value has been added through greater passenger and cargo volume, larger commercial revenue, and significantly lowered operating costs.

Take the instance of Brisbane, Melbourne, and Perth airports as well. Three international consortia paid a total of $2.6 bn to the Australian government to acquire 50-year franchises for these airports. The investors would not have parted with such stakes unless they were convinced of the returns on their investment.

Global Trends in Airport Privatization and Financing

With the worldwide slowdown in air travel in the wake of the 9/11 terrorist attacks, a number of pending airport privatizations were put on hold. However, the momentum resumed by the mid-2002. Let us look at some of the recent major airport privatizations and how they were financed:

- The winning bidder for the 99-year lease to Sydney's Kingsford Smith Airport was Southern Cross Airports Corporation. This consortium, led by Mcquarie Bank and Hochtief Airport, paid US$3 bn for the acquisition, financed by a combination of debt and equity. Debt providers include Commonwealth Bank, Barclays Capital, Royal Bank of Scotland, Societe

Generale and Fliers. The equity investors are Macquarie, Hochtief, Ferrovial Aeropuertos, Abbey National Treasury Services, Ontario Teachers' Pension Plan Board, and the Motor Traders Association of Australia Superannuation Fund. The high price paid for the airport stirred a hornet's nest, with one news report stating that "Macquarie Bank has left open the possibility of a public float of Sydney airport".

- The second largest airport in Australia, Melbourne International Airport, is indeed in for a 'public float', with an estimated A$1.2 bn share offering. The 99-year lease to Melbourne Tullamarine Airport was acquired in 1997 by Australia Pacific Airports Corporation, a consortium led by BAA. Though the purchase price was A$1.3 bn, the airport's present estimated market value stands at around A$2.4 bn. The public float is intended to pay down the A$1.1 bn debt funding.
- In New Zealand, the Auckland City Council offloaded its 26% stake, and the government, its 52% stake in Auckland International Airport, through a public share offering.
- The Chinese government permitted foreign investors to hold a majority stake, over and above the stipulated 49%, in civil airport joint ventures. The decision prompted the move to list Halkou Meilan airport on the Hong Kong Stock Exchange, to raise $111 mn from the share offering. The Chinese government also instructed all domestic airports to increase their user fees, to enable them become self-supporting.
- Japan privatized the New Tokyo International Airport Authority in 2004, with shares to be sold in tranches over the subsequent five years.
- A consortium led by Vienna International Airport, SNC-Lavalin, and local firm Vianchi and Company, acquired a 65-year lease of 40% of Malta International Airport.
- Two main airports of Cyprus were privatized with 25-year concessions.
- Oman became the first country in the Middle East to privatize its airports when it awarded a BOT concession to a consortium headed by BAA.
- The $2 bn Berlin Schonefeld airport privatization, operated through a 99-year lease, was financed by the Hochtief led consortium.

- Milan's airports joined Rome and Naples as privatized entities with SEA, the government corporation owning the city's airports, divesting 25% stake to strategic investors.
- Ecuador has signed a 35 year BOT agreement to build a $300 mn Greenfield Airport.
- YVR, the outsourcing division of Vancouver Airport, paid $22 mn for a majority stake in Tradeport International, which operates as the John C Munro International Airport in Ontario.
- Jamaica awarded a 30 year BOT contract to a consortium headed by Grupo Dragados and YVR to expand and operate Sangster International Airport in Montego Bay, the country's principal tourist getaway.
- Even the United States, which had been closed to the PPP option of airport privatization, is now changing its stance. Most airports in the US are at present financed by a combination of federal grants, local operating surpluses, special purpose user taxes, bank loans, revenue bonds and general obligation bonds.

Thus, airport infrastructure privatization is promising to be a global mega trend, with more and more governments and private players being pushed in that direction. The reasons for the shift are quite obvious:

1. World passenger growth forecasts speak of a 3.4% Compound Annual Growth Rate (CAGR) to reach about 6 billion in 2020 (Airports Council International). The capital investment in airport infrastructure to support this growth is estimated at over US$60 bn. Hence, the government has to look for alternative financing sources to fund such massive expansion.
2. The overseas track record of privatized infrastructure is becoming so impressive that policymakers in all countries want to improve and upgrade airports, highways, and environmental infrastructure to obtain better technology, more robust economic performance, better management, and customer-friendliness.
3. Economic cycles will push many cities to cash-out their investments in non-core businesses (such as airports and municipal electric and water utilities), as cities in Europe, South America, and Asia/Pacific are doing.

4. Some of the better-run airports in countries like the US will demand privatization, both for the freedom to operate as a business and for the ability to compete for opportunities to run other airports.

The new commercialized approach to airport management will, therefore, result in both airlines and passengers getting significantly better airports.

This is begining to look like an important trend. In fact, the December 23, 1997 issue of Airports Newsletter quoted IATA stating that it "generally supports privatization as a way of making airports and air traffic control facilities more efficient, accountable, and customer-oriented."

Financial Structure of Privatized Airports

Table 2 provides a view of the financial structure of major privatized airports around the world:

Overall, the listed airports were seen to be financed by a combination of debt, equity (private investors) and government stake in the proportion of 33:50:17. Of the debt, bonds constituted 49%, bank loans 36%, and hybrid financial instruments 15%. (Bloomberg, 2002). The proportion of debt is borne out by the average for listed airports in Table 2.

However, going by the limited data available in Table 2, it appears that at least two of the listed airports could support a higher than average financial leverage of around 50-60% (Copenhagen and Zurich). In the case of other listed airports, the financial leverage appears lower, probably due to the fact that repayment of debt is well under way, or increased public shareholding. The heartening fact about the data is that all airports in the table show healthy interest coverage ratios.

The unlisted airports appear to take on more financial risk than their listed counterparts, as is evidenced by their leverage ratios, substantially higher than the average for listed airports. Understandably, the interest coverage could be lower, but only slightly.

The data in Table 3, though limited, could lead to one important conclusion—airport operations are quite profitable, and the cash flows from operations can sustain even higher doses of debt. This inference is borne out by the data in Table 3, which compares the four year average EBIT (Earnings Before Interest and Taxes) margins of the privatized airports with the EBIT margins of the biggest airline patronizing the airport.

Table 2: Financing Structure of Major International Privatized Airports

Airport	Standard and Poor Rating	Market Cap in 2003 (USD million)	Financial Leverage (Book value of debt/ book value of debt + equity) (percent)	Interest Coverage Ratio (times) (EBITDA*/ Interest)
Listed Airports				
Auckland	A+ (stable)	1128	32.3	8.1
British Airways Authority (BAA)	A+ (stable)	8012	40.1	5
Beijing Capital International Airport (BCIA)	n/a	1134	17.7	11.3
Copenhagen	A (stable)	763	56.2	5.9
Fraport	n/a	2328	33.4	10.4
Hainan	n/a	309	18.9	11
Malaysia	n/a	492	4.1	n/a
Zurich	BBB (negative)	133	68.6	4.2
Vienna	n/a	786	0.5	n/a
Average			**30.2**	**8.0**
Unlisted Airports				
Changi	n/a	n/a	0	n/a
Hong Kong	A+ (stable)	n/a	17.4	12.1
Sydney	BBB (negative)	n/a	68.3	n/a
Melbourne	A (stable)	n/a	81.4	2.1
Average			**55.7**	**7.1**

* EBITDA = Earnings before interest, taxes, depreciation and amortization, signifying cash flows available to meet interest payments.

Source: Bloomberg, Company Financials, Deustche Bank estimates.

Table 3: EBIT Margin of Few Privatized Airports			
Privatized Airport	**Four Year Average EBIT Margin (1999-2002) of the Airport (approximate %)**	**Biggest Airline Operating Out of the Airport**	**Four Year Average EBIT Margin (1999-2002) of the Airline (approximate %)**
Auckland	55	Air New Zealand	5
Aeroporto di Firenze, Italy	20	Alitalia	– 5
British Airways Authority (BAA)	30	British Airways	2.5
Beijing Capital International Airport (BCIA)	40	China Southern	10
Copenhagen	35	SAS-Scandinavian Airlines	1
Fraport	17.5	Lufthansa	5
Malaysia Airports Berhad (MAB)	22	Malaysian Airlines	– 5
Vienna International (VIE)	25	Austrian Airlines	1
Source: Bloomberg, Company Annual Reports.			

Table 3 clearly shows that airport operations are profitable, notwithstanding the individual airlines' profitability. How is this possible? Most mature airports remain profitable through the vagaries of the airline industry, due to the fact that they earn a high proportion of their income from non-aeronautical revenues.

What are the constituents of aeronautical and non-aeronautical revenues?

Aeronautical revenues arise primarily from the following activities at the airport:

- Route Navigation Facilitation Charges (RNFC).
- Landing, housing and parking charges.
- Terminal Navigation Landing Charges (TNLC).
- X-Ray baggage charges.

The sources of non-aeronautical revenues are as follows:

- Duty-free shopping.
- Catering and restaurants.

- News, shops, banks, communication facilities, etc.
- Airline terminal rents and real estate.
- Others, such as hotel and travel services.

Table 4 depicts the proportion of aeronautical and non-aeronautical revenues earned by major international privatized airports:

Table 4: Airports Revenue Structure

Airport	% of Aeronautical Revenues in Total Revenue	% of Non-Aeronautical Revenues in Total Revenue
British Airports Authority (BAA)	28	72
Toronto	38	62
Sydney	29	71
Houston	19	81
Heathrow	47	53
Kuala Lumpur	46	54
Los Angeles	57	43
Changi, Singapore	42	58
Paris	51	49
Zurich	49	51

Source: CRISIL.

It, therefore, follows that if privatized airports are to be profitable on a sustained basis, the airport infrastructure should include non-aeronautical facilities developed to mitigate the airline industry risk.

Privatization and Financing of Indian Airports

Airports are an important gateway to India's globalization and fast-track economic development agenda. At present, there are 449 airports/airstrips in the country. Of these, the Airports Authority of India (AAI) manages 126 airports (89 domestic, 11 international, and 26 civil enclaves at defense airstrips). With the opening up of the civil aviation sector, the process is on for upgrading metro airports through the PPP route. Indian airports at present, derive bulk of their revenue through aeronautical sources, with the metro airports contributing the bulk of non-aeronautical income. Even in such cases, non-aeronautical income hovers around 20% of total income. It is evident at the present level of aeronautical revenue generation, no airport would be viable. Therefore, it is pertinent to note that the development of airports should be based on international standards, which may also bring up the investments.

The Bangalore International Airport Ltd, the first PPP Greenfield project, has been recently financed with substantial amount of bank funding. However, international experience suggests that, along with bank lending, the financial markets would have to play a greater role in airport financing. Some of the recently concluded international transactions are a pointer—BAA's convertible bond issue of GBP 425 mn, Schipol's Euro 300 mn of Medium Term Notes, Perth International Airport's convertible bond offering of A$45 mn, and Airport Authority of Hong Kong's dollar denominated bond issue.

Airport privatization projects, though profitable, carry risks for all parties involved. The private investor's consortium, entering into the concession agreement with the host government faces construction and completion risks. Thereafter, operational and market risks could impact the expected cash flows. The host government runs the risk of project sponsors being unable to generate sufficient returns to carry the project through the concession period, or having to make substantial capital investment for upgradation after the concession period. The project company's highly leveraged capital structure implies that any development impairing expected cash flows or project assets would directly hit the debt service capacity of the project and the lenders' bottomline. Government policy changes and environmental impact could also turn out to be decisive risk factors in many projects.

If India is to make the airport privatization model successful, the following issues have to be looked into:

- The government should take the lead in specifying the terms of reference for various bids from the private sector. Leaving the determination of the project's form and scale to bidders (to suit their profit objective) would be a sure prescription for failure in this sensitive sector.
- Contracts work best when risks are identifiable, outcomes verifiable and contracts are enforceable. Since risks would be allocated to various parties through contracts, it is imperative that the government institutes a sound

legal framework and arbitration mechanisms to ensure proper risk management.

- Due diligence is typically carried out by bankers and the government at the time of financing. At this juncture, some drawbacks may be rectified at huge cost or may be beyond rectification. The government will, therefore, have to carry out financial and technical reviews periodically, right from the project planning stage.
- Insurance is a powerful risk mitigating mechanism in large projects. The government should take steps to deepen the insurance market to guard stakeholders against all insurable risks, including major political risks.
- The financial markets should be able to generate public interest in subscribing to airport bonds and other public issues. Structures resembling General Airport Revenue Bonds (GARBs) in the US could be introduced. This will call for substantial widening of the bond markets.
- The rating agencies should be encouraged to develop the appetite for rating various types of risks, and equipped to handle increased demand from the private sector and public looking for investment grade securities.
- The banking sector should prepare to assess risks unique to airport projects and finance the projects through innovative instruments. Growth in high risk-high return financing has to be supported by a strong and well structured securitization framework.
- Where required, the assistance of Multilateral Agencies such as the World Bank can be sought for. The World Bank and its arms have gained enormous expertise in funding and facilitating airport privatization projects over the world.
- Users of privatized retail facilities, such as airports or toll roads, should be educated on the need for and advantages of paying user charges.

Conclusion

International experience suggests that airport privatization is beneficial to all stakeholders—the government, the private investors, the financial system and the public at large. With the opening up of the civil aviation sector in India, there is no reason to doubt that India can make a success story of airport privatization. However, with airport privatization already gaining momentum, the government machinery, financing and contractual structures have to ramp up to keep pace.

(Padmalatha Suresh, Director, DMS Financial Services Ltd., Chennai, India. She can be reachd at padmalathasuresh@yahoo.com).

References

1. Fitch Ratings (2003), "Airport Project Finance and Special Facilities Debt—Very Different Credits", Project Finance Special Report (November).
2. Infrastructure Economics and Finance Network, "Air Transport Infrastructure—The Role of Public and Private Sectors", The World Bank.
3. Padmalatha Suresh, "Greenfield Airport Projects—Time for Public Private Partnerships to Take Off", *Business Line,* July 29, 2005.
4. Robert Scott (2003), "Airport financing—An Investor Perspective", Deutsche Bank PECC International Roundtable (September).
5. Sanjay K Sinha (2005), "Mobilizing Private Investment in Airport Development in India", Presentation in India Infrastructure Summit, CRISIL (March).
6. Victor Craig, "Risk and Due Diligence in Airport Privatization", Air Transport, Halcrow Airplan, Malaysia.
7. Various International Airport Websites.

Funding of Airports at Bangalore, Hyderabad, Delhi and Mumbai

With the increase in traffic for both passenger & cargo aviation services in India, the government has put in place a program for directing investments in the airport infrastructure—through both internal resource mobilization, as well as through private sector participation in modernizing specific Airports. A Model Concession Agreement is also being developed for standardizing and simplifying the PPP transactions for airports.

Greenfield Airports: 100% FDI is allowed through the automatic route for Greenfield Airports in the country. In Bangalore and Hyderabad, the government has initiated the construction of Greenfield airports through Build Own Operate and Transfer (BOOT) basis with private sector participation. The project at Bangalore will cost Rs 14 billion, while the project at Hyderabad will cost Rs.17.6 billion. In both these projects, AAI holds 26% equity and private stakeholders hold the rest 74%. AAI has also proposed to establish a Greenfield airport in Navi Mumbai to meet the long-term requirement of air traffic of the Mumbai region.

Bangalore International Airport Ltd. (BIAL)

The BIAL Master Plan has been developed to fulfill the need for an operationally efficient and passenger friendly airport. This new airport will be able to handle up to 11 million passengers and will be ready for operation by April 2008. A consortium led by Siemens, Germany with Unique Zurich, Swizerland and Larsen & Toubro India Ltd. as other members have been chosen as the strategic Joint Venture Partners. GoK is extending Rs.3.5 billon as State support and is providing approximately 4000 acres of land on concessional rent. AAI's investment in the equity is capped at Rs.500 million, while the approximate cost of the project is Rs.14 billion.

Hyderabad International Airport Ltd. (HIAL)

HIAL is a public-private joint venture between GMR Group, Malaysia Airports Holdings Berhad and both the State Government of Andhra Pradesh and Airports Authority of India (AAI). GMR Group holds 63% of the equity, MAHB 11%, while the Government of Andhra Pradesh and Airports Authority of India each hold 13%. This new airport will be operational by August 2008. A Special Purpose Vehicle has been set up for the construction of this airport AAI's equity is being capped at Rs.500 million, while the approximate cost of the project is Rs.17.6 billion.

Modernization of Existing Airports in Delhi & Mumbai

The existing International airports in Delhi and Mumbai are being restructured and modernized through Private sector participation. In the Joint Ventures, AAI and other Government PSUs hold 26% equity, with the balance 74% being held by the strategic partner. As per the current policy of the government, the FDI in existing airports has a sectoral cap of 49%. The development plans for Delhi and Mumbai airports envisage an investment of Rs.5,270 crore and Rs.6,130 crore respectively (totaling Rs.11,400 crore) during the period of 2006-07 to 2013-14 for development of these two airports.

Compiled from the source http://www.ibef.org

13

Private Sector Participation in Transport Infrastructure Development

Pradeepta Kumar Samanta

Transport system is considered as the artery and the nerve, which connects the entire economy of the country. An efficient transport system is the prerequisite for attaining higher level of economic growth. The growing manufacturing sector in India is highly dependent on the transport sector for attracting FDI as well as global market players. In India, the freight cost is 11% of the landed cost of goods as against the global average of 6%. In terms of infrastructure spending, China spends 20% of its GDP, amounting to $260 bn, while in India it is only $1 bn i.e., 6% of the GDP. In the last few years keeping in tandem with the on-going economic reform process, the Government has taken a number of steps to attract private players and reduce the demand and supply gap in various infrastructure sectors. In this context, the port sector needs special attention as it accounts for 90% in volume and 75% in value of our foreign trade. Private sector participation is highly essential to

Source: The Icfai Journal of Infrastructure, December 2005. This article was originally published as "Private Sector Participation in Transport Infrastructure Development: A Study of the Port Sector".

supplement the efforts of the public sector to augment the capacity expansion and for a sustainable economic growth. This paper highlights the increasing role of private players in the transport sector in the global arena and the scope for its participation in the port sector in India.

Introduction

Infrastructure is fundamental to create improved marketability, efficient resource utilization and increased opportunities for the public to participate in the economic development process of a country. During the last two decades, increased globalization and intensified competition in world trade have resulted not only from the liberalization of trade policies, but also significant advances in the infrastructure sector, especially transport, communication, energy, banking, insurance, science and technology, education and health. An appropriate and well-managed infrastructure is one of the most important factors that allow a higher level of exploitation of the comparative advantages of regions and countries. The transport infrastructure acts as a catalyst for both domestic and international transactions. However, the technical inefficiencies in roads, railways, power, and water alone caused losses estimated at $55 bn a year in early 1990s—equivalent to 1% of the GDP of all developing countries, a quarter of their annual investment in infrastructure, and twice the annual development finance for infrastructure in the developing world.[1]

In the context of an increasingly competitive international environment for manufactured goods, the cost incurred in transportation has a significant bearing on the competitiveness of Indian products[2]. With the liberalized industrial and trade policies, India is striving to carve a niche market for itself in the global economy. As the cheapest mode of transport the sea-mode of transport has acquired prominence and popularity throughout the world. With a vast coastline of more than 6,000 kms, India has 12 major ports and 160 minor ports in the country, which handle about 90% in volume and 75% in value of the foreign trade. India has set itself an ambitious

---

1 ppi.worldbank.org/book/Chapter1.pdf

2 indiabudget.nic.in/es2001-02/chapt2002/chap913.p

growth target of 8% in the 10th Plan, which requires a 10 to 12% annual growth in transport system capacity in the coming years. To compete with the international ports, the Indian port sector needs large scale private sector participation. Against this backdrop, an attempt has been made in this paper to analyze the present state of transport infrastructure in general and scope for increased level of private sector participation in the port sector in particular.

Infrastructure Investment: Public vs Private Sector Finance

The global infrastructure markets have undergone a sea change and institutional restructuring during the last three decades. Technological advances in all sphere and conscious changes in public policy have brought deregulation and competition in mature markets and liberalization in the developing world. Efficient transport, reliable energy, safe drinking water, and modern telecommunication systems are critical to attracting foreign direct investment, expanding international trade, and achieving long-term investment and growth.[3] Worldwide, most future demand for infrastructure is likely to come from the developing world (home to 85% of the world's population), where access to infrastructure services falls well behind the levels in the developed world. During the period from 1992 to 2003, total international investment in developing countries' infrastructure is estimated to have been $622 bn—an average of $52 bn a year, and 3.85% of the total gross domestic investment in the developing world. The world's infrastructure stock today can be valued at about US$15 tn. Of this total, about 60% is in high income countries, 28% in middle income countries and 13% in low income countries as against the population shares of 16%, 45%, and 39% respectively (Fay and Yepes 2003).

The multilateral agencies such as ADB, EBRD, IBRD/IDA, IDB and EIB etc., played a significant role in financing the infrastructure sector during the 1990s.

There are two main benefits of development of new infrastructure assets through private rather than public financing for a country. First, the new asset is financed from the government's balance sheet, thus preserving the government's borrowing capacity. Second, in many cases, private financing and operation is expected to

---

[3] rru.worldbank.org/PapersLinks/Open.aspx?id=3738

result in lower costs and higher operating efficiency, flowing from the stronger commercial disciplines operating on private firms.

Table 1: Multilateral Development Bank Commitments to Infrastructure Sectors, 1995-2002

$ billions

	1995	1996	1997	1998	1999	2000	2001	2002
Total	17.770	18.266	16.612	17.687	13.842	14.957	14.684	16.591
As percentage of total commitment	33.984	24.708	36.130	40.998	31.205	34.147	34.171	38.973
ADB	3.424	2.849	1.903	2.337	1.752	2.655	2.261	2.879
AfDB	0.176	0.087	0.210	0.372	0.277	0.135	0.375	0.463
EBRD	1.404	1.631	1.077	0.874	0.916	0.792	1.164	1.458
EIB	2.465	2.425	3.067	3.483	2.993	3.735	3.552	4.401
IBRD/IDA	7.384	7.954	6.616	6.674	5.278	4.248	4.980	4.599
IDB	2.221	2.666	2.805	3.117	1.782	1.702	0.988	0.998
IFC	0.335	0.358	0.496	0.394	0.289	0.472	0.321	0.486
IsDB	0.219	0.148	0.295	0.260	0.351	0.468	0.475	0.445
MIGA	0.142	0.148	0.143	0.176	0.204	0.749	0.568	0.862

Infrastructure sectors considered are energy, water supply and sanitation, transport, urban development, and communication (information and communications technologies).

ADB: Asian Development Bank.

AfDB: African Development Bank.

EBRD: European Bank for Reconstruction and Development.

EIB: European Investment Bank.

IBRD/IDA: International Bank for Reconstruction and Development/International Development Agency.

IDB: Inter-American Development Bank.

IFC: International Finance Corporation.

IsDB: Islamic Development Bank.

MIGA: Multilateral Investment Guarantee Agency.

Source: Global Development Finance 2004, World Bank.

Studies have shown that private projects can be built with fewer time overruns as compared to their public-financed equivalents. A case study making a comparative analysis of privately financed and publicly financed infrastructure projects in developing countries has revealed that private projects had average time overruns that were 54-68% of public projects. In case of public financing, the performance and other risks are left with the taxpayers. Private financing presents opportunities to shift this risk to private investors and users. This sharpens incentives for prudent risk management and efficiency while strengthening the government's own financial position. Efficient risk allocation involves assigning risks to the party best able to manage or mitigate the risk. On this principle, commercial risks are best borne by investors and users, while noncommercial risks such as those associated with a change of government policy or nationalization are best borne by government and hence the taxpayers.[4]

The firms going for participation into the infrastructure sector have three comparative advantages in the developing countries. First, the utilization of modern technology; second, access to capital at a lower cost than that available to the host countries' governments. And, third, a capacity to operate at a global level, implying, among other things, an ability to draw on synergies involved in structuring business relationships in the form of joint ventures and special purpose vehicles (Global Development Finance – 2004).

Transport Infrastructure Investment

Transport infrastructure has both forward and backward linkages. An efficient transport system can boost trade and greater volume of trade can, in turn, create demand for investment in the transport network. It is now widely acknowledged that efficiency in the transport sector has major spillover effects on the competitiveness of both goods and services. Competition and increased efficiency in maritime transport services, resulting in lower freight rates, contribute directly to a country's international competitiveness. Increased commercialization and growth of international trade have led to considerable pressure on the operating environment of the existing transport infrastructure, forcing it to adapt new, improved and more reliable technology. Commercialization has also enhanced competition among trading nations to increase their share in the world's trade.[5]

---

4 rru.worldbank.org/PapersLinks/Open.aspx?id=539

5 www.unescap.org/ttdw/Publications/TPTS_pubs/bulletin73/bulletin73_ch2.pdf

Financing infrastructure has turned into a global challenge. Further, it is increasingly difficult to finance the investment required to sustain the growth of transport infrastructure. The large multinational corporations and their alliances, which emerged in the Globalization era, have the willingness, financial strength and technical know-how to operate and manage the advanced transport network. This has changed the scenario whereby countries, which had once closed door for foreign investment, are now opening up their corridors for privatization and foreign investment.

During the period 1985-2003, commitments worth US$684 bn were made around the world for 1137 new transport projects, making an average project size of US$600 mn per project. Of these, the toll roads account for 50% while rail, airports and ports account for 22%, 16% and 12% respectively, of the total projects. About 60% of these projects are committed to developing countries, and 55% amounts committed are for developed countries. Two-thirds of the private projects credited to developed countries accrue to five countries: US (122 projects), Spain (66), UK (64), Australia (46) and Canada (37). (Antonio and Tomas, 2004).

Table 2: Different Forms of Private Sector Participation in Infrastructure

	Service or Management Contracts	**Concessions**	**Greenfield Projects (BOT or BOO)**	**Divestitures**
Ownership of Assets	Public	Public	Public/Private	Private
Capital Investments	Public	Private	Private	Private
Operational Efficiency	Limited	Yes	Yes	Yes
New Services	No	Yes	Yes	Yes
Typical Duration	1-5 years	25-30 years	20-30 years	Indefinite unless limited by license

Source: World Bank.

Forms of Private Sector Participation in Transport

Generally, there are four different forms of private sector participation in transport sector such as (a) Divestitures, (b) Greenfield Projects, (c) Service or Management Contracts, and (d) Concessions.

Again, it varies from one country to another and sub-sectors also. In *Divestiture* contracts, the ownership of the business is transferred to the private sector in the form of public offerings of shares or private trade sales of assets. *Greenfield* contracts are applicable to specific projects such as new toll road or airport terminal. Under this contract, new investment projects will be commissioned by the private sector in the form of Build-Operate-Own (BOO), and Build-Operate-Transfer (BOT). The commercial risks associated with the project will be the responsibility of the private constructor, while the exchange or political risks can be shared to varying degrees with the public sector through various types of legal instruments. Greenfield projects, which are confined to building roads and seaport facilities, were the second most common type of private participation in the developing countries during the period of 1990-2002.

In *Service or Management contracts,* the private operator is allowed to manage the service without any investment. The duration of these contracts is one to five years, and the government continues to take all risks involved in the project except for the management risk. *Concessions* are the most common form of private sector participation in the transport sector. This is a long-term contract, in which the responsibility for operation and management is passed on to a private operator. In developed countries, divestitures and asset sales have been the main instruments of private participation in transport infrastructure. In developing and transition economies, concessions are the most common form of private sector participation in transport infrastructure. World Bank data reveals that concession contracts accounted for 58% of all transport projects between 1990 and 2002 (Table 3).

Latin America had the most private activity in transport, followed by East Asia. The growth of the sector in these two regions coincided with the opening of other infrastructure sectors to private activity, and with progress towards establishing legal and regulatory institutions that promote private participation (Table 4). In the other developing regions, private participation in transport took place mostly in the second half of the 1990s, and mainly in one or two sectors[6]. Further, the private participation in developing countries by sub-sector reveals that, the road sector occupies the top position in terms of number of projects as

[6] www.dgroups.org/groups/worldbank/ GDF04/docs/Transport_Infrastructure.pdf?ois=no

well as amount of investment followed by Railways in investment and seaports in number of projects (Table 5).

Table 3: Transport Projects with Private Participation by Type in Developing Countries, 1990-2002

Type of Private Participation	Number of Projects	Total Investment (US$ mns)
Concessions	390	69.5
Divestures	58	7.0
Greenfield projects	211	43.3
Management and lease contracts	45	0.3
Total	704	120.1

Source: World Bank, PPI Project Database.

Table 4: Private Participation in Transport Projects by Region, 1990-2002

Region	No. of Countries	Projects	Investment (2001 US$ bns)
East Asia and Pacific	9	238	43.9
Europe and Central Asia	10	43	4.6
Latin America and the Caribbean	20	320	64.0
Middle East and the North Africa	7	18	2.2
South Asia	4	46	2.8
Sub-Saharan Africa	18	39	2.6
Total	68	704	120.1

Source: World Bank, PPI Project Database.

Table 5: Private Participation in Transport by Sub-sector in Developing Countries, 1990-2002

Sub-sector	Projects	Investment (2001 US$ bns)
Airports	85	12.2
Railways	78	26.8
Seaports	199	19.3
Roads	343	62.6
Total	705	120.9

Source: World Bank, PPI Project Database.

Why Private Sector Participation?

In most of the developing countries, the public sector infrastructure providers have a poor track record in operating efficiency. There are weak incentives to reduce costs and to deal with technical and non-technical losses. Staffing levels are also often inflated to meet political goals, and labor productivity is often further reduced by labor systems that offer few incentives for performance. Under public ownership, infrastructure prices are often controlled to meet short-term political objectives. This resulted in significant efficiency losses, and limited funds for maintenance and expansion, usually to the detriment of the poorest members of society who paid much higher prices for inferior substitutes.[7]

The participation of private sector in infrastructure can help to improve the existing situation in various ways. In certain cases where competition can be introduced, firms face strong incentives to perform efficiently or lose customers to their competitors and ultimately go out of business or be taken over. In another case, the firms operating in a monopolistic market can be motivated to minimize costs by subjecting themselves to regulatory frameworks. It may be added here that the private firms and their managers are usually free of civil service regulations that can inhibit operating flexibility and innovation.

Private Sector Participation in Transport Infrastructure: The Scenario in Developing Countries

An efficient transport system is a prerequisite for sustained economic development. But the developing countries' transport sector exhibits a poor performance in attracting only about 18% of the total investment flows, lagging significantly behind telecommunications (44%) and electricity (28%) that accrued to the infrastructure sector. The reason for this dismal performance can be attributed to three causes such as, overly optimistic forecasts, lack of local financial capacity, and concession design problems.

According to the World Bank's PPI Database, from 1990 to 2002, private participation in transport projects took place in 66 developing countries, encompassing 704 projects and absorbing $120 bn in capital.[8] Thirty-five

---

7 rru.worldbank.org/PapersLinks/Open.aspx?id=539

8 rru.worldbank.org/PapersLinks/Open.aspx?id=3738

developing countries introduced private participation in airports in 1990-2002, granting 85 projects involving 224 airports. Private interest in the airport sector had been spurred by the growth in air transport and airport revenues—growth fueled by deregulation and the establishment of "open skies" agreement among countries. Concessions dominated private activity in airports, accounting for 76% of the investment and 49% of the projects in 1990-2002. The developing countries opted for concessions rather than for divestitures, to avoid political resistance to private participation, as airport assets tend to be seen as strategic for national security. Divestitures ranked second in investment, attracting 15% share over the period, followed by Greenfield projects which attracted 8% of the investment. Latin America and the Caribbean led the regions in private participation in airports, with 57% of the investment and 32 projects in 1999-2002.

Private participation in railways took place in 27 developing countries in 1990-2002. Concessions were the most common type of private participation in railways, accounting for 70% of the investment in the sub-sector in 1990-2002. Concessions were used to improve the management of loss making railways and rehabilitate deteriorating infrastructure. Greenfield projects ranked second in investment, capturing a share of 27%. The private participation focused on vertically integrated companies, which accounted for 73% of the investment and 64% of the projects during the period. In toll road projects, 28 developing economies introduced private activity during 1990-2002, awarding 343 projects.

In the transport sector, the highways segment dominated private activity in toll roads, accounting for 94% of the investments during 1990-2002. The Concessions category attracted the most investments in toll roads during the period, with a 51% share, followed by Greenfield projects (44%). (Table 3).

Seaports

During 1990-2002, 41 developing countries opened the seaport business to private participation. Among the transport sub-sectors, seaports ranked second in number of projects and third in terms of investment. Concessions, accounting for 53% of the investment and 46% of the projects were the most common type of private participation in seaports.

The Greenfield projects were the second most common type of private participation in seaports, with 44% of the investment and 33% of the projects[9]. These projects were undertaken mainly in East Asia and the Pacific, where rapid growth in trade and insufficient infrastructure created a need for new port facilities. Among the countries, China garnered the most investment ($3.1 bn), followed by Indonesia ($2.2 bn), Malaysia ($2.1 bn), Brazil ($1.7 bn), and India ($1.1 bn). When countries are ranked by number of projects, Brazil moves to the top (23 projects), followed by China (22), Mexico (18), Argentina (13), and the Russian Federation (9).

Private Sector Participation in Indian Transport Sector

In India, the delivery of infrastructure services has lagged behind the demand. The demand has been fueled by the tremendous increase in population, accelerating urbanization and by the success of India's industrial growth. Transport has been seen as the basic infrastructure, which is crucial for the success of a developmental plan. The Second Five Year Plan was more forthright in stressing the need for transport development by stating that, "An efficient and well-developed system of transport and communication is vital to the success of a plan of economic development which lays stress on rapid industrialization." Though in absolute terms, the expenditure on transport sector has increased during the Five Year Plan period, but in terms of percentage it has been reduced from 22.1% in the First Plan to 14% in the Ninth Plan.

Providing better facilities including infrastructure was the sole responsibility of the Government till the early 1990s. During the era of privatization and liberalization, the policies of the government have changed its role from a owner or sole provider to a facilitator. The planning exercise through Five-Year Plans set out objectives for creation of infrastructure. However, after 58 years of Independence and ten Five-Year plans, these targets were rarely achieved. The gap between demand and supply of infrastructure facilities progressively increased. The length of Indian national highways has grown by 70% in the last 50 years, while goods and passenger traffic has grown up by more than 5000% during the same period. Commercial vehicles in India travel an average of 200 km to 250 km in a single day compared to

9 ppi.worldbank.org/book/Chapter1.pdf

over 600 km in developed countries. The economy approximately loses Rs.200 to Rs.300 bn each year due to these inefficiencies.[10]

The road network in India is the main feeder to the rail system and ports and harbor, forming an integrated transport system. India has one of the largest road networks in the world measuring more than 3 million kms. However, the size does not commensurate the poor quality of the roads which affects the efficient and fast moving transportation.

To encourage private sector participation, a model concession agreement for major projects costing more than Rs.100 cr has been finalized under Build-Operate-Transport (BOT) scheme. Another model concession agreement for projects less than Rs.100 cr has also been finalized. Twenty projects involving an investment of around Rs.1707 cr have already been taken under BOT scheme. In addition to this, another six projects of 4-laning costing Rs.1760 cr have also been awarded by the National Highways Authority of India (NHAI) on annuity

Table 6: Expenditure on Transport Sub-sectors Under Plan Periods (in Rs. bn)

Sub-sector	1st Plan 1951-56	2nd Plan 1956-61	3rd Plan 1961-66	4th Plan 1969-74	5th Plan 1974-79	6th Plan 1980-85	7th Plan 1985-90	8th Plan 1992-97	9th Plan 1997-02
Railways	2.2	7.2	13.3	9.3	20.6	65.9	165.5	323.0	454.1
Roads	1.5	2.4	4.4	8.6	17.0	38.9	63.4	161.0	386.5
Road Transport	0.0	0.0	0.9	4.6	12.0	19.9	21.5	35.4	73.8
Ports	0.3	0.3	0.9	2.5	4.9	7.3	15.1	23.0	99.4
Shipping	0.2	0.5	1.4	4.5	7.6	8.3	7.2	30.3	63.1
IWT	0.0	0.0	0.1	0.3	0.7	2.3	1.9	1.5	5.3
Civil Aviation	0.2	0.5	0.5	1.8	2.9	9.6	19.5	72.5	113.7
Total Transport Sector	4.3	11.0	19.8	25.2	55.4	139.6	294.8	649.4	1202.5
Total Plan (All Sectors)	19.6	46.7	85.8	157.8	394.3	1092.9	2187.3	5332.5	8592.0

concept. The NHAI has set up its own Special Purpose Vehicles (SPVs) to commercialize and leverage the financial structure to the extent possible.

The railways have been performing the dual role of functioning as a commercial undertaking and a provider of public utility service. The railways have also taken

[10] www.adb.org/Documents/CSPs/IND/2003/appendix3_private_sector_assessment.pdf

Table 7: Sector-wise Expenditure as % of Transport Sector Total Under Plan Periods

Sub-sector	1st Plan 1951-56	2nd Plan 1956-61	3rd Plan 1961-66	4th Plan 1969-74	5th Plan 1974-79	6th Plan 1980-85	7th Plan 1985-90	8th Plan 1992-97	9th Plan 1997-02
Railways	50.0	65.7	66.9	37.0	37.2	47.2	56.1	49.7	37.8
Roads	33.9	22.0	22.2	34.2	30.7	27.8	21.5	24.8	32.1
Road Transport	0.0	0.0	4.6	18.3	21.6	14.3	7.3	5.4	6.1
Ports	6.5	3.0	4.7	9.9	8.8	5.2	5.1	3.5	8.3
Shipping	4.4	4.8	7.1	17.8	13.6	5.9	2.4	4.7	5.2
IWT	0.0	0.0	0.6	1.3	1.3	1.6	0.6	0.2	0.4
Civil Aviation	5.3	4.5	2.5	7.0	5.3	6.9	6.6	11.2	9.5
Transport Sector as % of Total Plan	22.1	23.5	23.1	16.0	14.1	12.8	13.5	12.2	14.0

Source: Indian Planning Experience – A Statistical Profile.

initiatives to attract private participation. It has set up a private terminal for providing rail connectivity to upcoming ports, e.g., Special Purpose Vehicle (SPV) on Pipavav Port. Joint ventures with some state governments, for executing projects have also been evolved.[11] The Expert Group on Indian Railways have recommended setting up of a tariff regulator—Indian Rail Regulatory Authority (IRRA) and corporatization of the Indian railways into Indian Railways Corporation (IRC). Recently, the Government of India approved the plan for expansion and modernization of the airports across the country with a proposal of investment of Rs.40,000 cr. The Government has also set plans for the development of 80 airports with public-private partnership in the next five years.

Need for Private Participation in Port Infrastructure

With the liberalized industrial and trade policies, India is striving to carve a niche market for itself in the global economy. Exports have become an essential plank for our policy of economic growth. As the cheapest mode of transport providing larger capacity and flexibility to carry heavy and bulky goods and facilitating international trade, the sea-mode of transport has acquired prominence and popularity throughout the world. Having a vast coastline of more than 6,000 kms., there are 12 major

[11] indiabudget.nic.in/es2001-02/chapt2002/chap98.pdf

ports and 160 minor ports in the country which handle about 90% in volume and 75% in value of India's foreign trade. In spite of tremendous potential for growth in the port sector, so far India has been able to exploit only 12.5% of its coastline. The productivity of Indian ports is also far below the international standards.

The average ship turnaround time, which is about 6 to 8 hours for Singapore, is about 6 to 8 days for Indian ports. Similarly, the number of containers handled per ship-hour for Colombo, Bangkok and Singapore is 35, 38 and 69 respectively; for Indian ports it is only 7 to 15 containers per ship-hour. The existing Indian port infrastructure suffers problems owing to operational constraints like breakdown of port equipment and use of obsolete cargo handling equipment, inadequate facilities for dredging of berths and channels, inefficient and non-optimal development of port equipment and excessive reliance on labor-intensive methods of bulk handling of cargo.

The reasons for the slowdown in Indian port development are many. One of the main reasons is the low plan investment in the transport sector as a whole, with only a very insignificant part of it devoted to ports over half century after Independence. By the end of Ninth Plan, the major ports handled traffic of about 424 million tonnes as against the assessed capacity of 377 million tonnes. Almost all the major ports are operating beyond their capacity, which proves the matching capacity inefficiency of the ports.

Some of the other factors that have led to inefficiencies in the Indian Ports are:

- Most of the major ports, which were originally designed to handle specific types of cargoes, have declined in time, while other types of cargoes gained importance. The ports have not been able to adjust to these categories of cargo, which grew the most. Thus, there are several berths for traditional cargo, which are underutilized, and only a few for new cargo, which are overutilized.[12]
- Equipment utilization is very poor, mainly because equipment is obsolete and poorly managed.

[12] www.teriin.org/division/regdiv/docs/ft22.pdf

- Over staffing at Indian ports remains rampant and productivity indicators in respect of cargo and equipment handling continues to be poor.
- Complicated documentary procedures relating to cargo handling, such as customs clearance requirements suffer from unnecessary delay in time. Electronic Document Processing is yet to be commissioned in all the ports.
- The facilities and arrangements of port access for moving the cargo, both inbound and outbound, are inadequate and not satisfactory.
- The inter-port and intra-port competition, which has been instrumental in increasing the port productivity in other countries, is absent in India. This is because of poor inland connectivity and the policy regime that protected domestic ports against competitive pressures.

The consequences of these shortcomings are severe for the Indian economy. Indian container cargo is transshipped to Colombo, Dubai or Singapore, resulting in additional costs and transit times[13]. As a result, the Indian exporter is not in a position to avail "fixed-day-of-the-week" services offered by the liner industry at a time when manufacturing and trading companies abroad are increasingly selling and buying on a "Just-in-time" basis. Indian exporters are therefore operating on the basis of substantial buffer stocks, which also make them less competitive[14]. It has been estimated that the annual incidence of these various factors such as demurrage charges, transshipment costs, pre-berthing delays and vessel turn-round time could be as high as US$1.5 bn per annum. These costs are ultimately to be borne by the end user, raising the costs of India's exports in international markets, and the prices of imports for the Indian economy. Thus, to overcome these shortcomings of the sector in general and to make ports more competitive, stay in the global competition and attain the economic objective in particular, private participation is highly essential for the sector.

Private Sector Participation in Indian Ports so Far

The post-liberalization period witnessed a sudden increase in port traffic, which brought to light the capacity constraints, inefficiencies and low productivity of

---

[13] www.teriin.org/division/regdiv/docs/ft22.pdf

[14] Ibid.

the Indian ports. To encourage private participation in port projects, the government issued a comprehensive guideline for private participation in major ports in 1996, in the areas of leasing out of assets, construction and operation of terminals, berths, warehousing, tank farms, container freight stations, and captive power plants; pilotage and captive facilities for port based industries. 100% FDI in ports has been allowed through automatic approval route by the RBI. Model bid documents, including license agreement, have been finalized to attract private sector investment and participation. The norms for private BOT projects in major ports have been relaxed in 2001-02 in the context of limited private participation in major ports. To give further fillip to this sector, the 10th Five Year Plan assigned high priority to modernization and the development of port infrastructure through private investment.

In response to the Government initiatives, the private sector participation in the major ports has been quite enthusiastic.

- Out of 24 projects identified for the private sector participation, 17 projects have already been approved, which will add capacity of 60.05 MT at various ports with an investment of Rs.45.26 bn.
- There are about four projects under bidding process, which will add to the capacity of 27.40 MT with an estimated investment of Rs.29.00 bn. Three more projects are ready for private sector participation, for which the bids are likely to be invited.
- Gujarat has been by far the most active state in attracting private players. Two private ports—Mundra and Pipavav have already become operational. Mundra is a bulk port being developed by Gujarat Adani Port Limited. Pipvav port is under public-private ownership, through a joint venture of Seaking Engineering and the Gujarat Maritime Board.
- Andhra Pradesh, Tamil Nadu and Orissa have also invited private participation to develop minor ports by offering leases upto 50 years for developing new port projects. On the West Coast, the Government of Karnataka and Kerala have identified a number of minor ports for creating commodity-specific facilities.

The Action Plan

Of late, the Government has realized that the involvement of private sector including foreign investment is essential to supplement the public sector efforts. Sequel to this effort, various reforms have been made in the infrastructure sector, and rules and procedures for investment have been liberalized in order to provide an enabling environment and augment the rapid growth of this sector. In the transport sector, several measures are proposed to be undertaken during the Tenth Plan period. The Tenth Plan aims at reducing heavy cross-subsidization in freight and passenger fares in railways. The plan also envisages setting up of a Rail Tariff Regulatory Authority for tariff fixation for railways on technical and commercial considerations.[15]

To make the railways more efficient, it is proposed to reduce the staff strength to 12 lakhs. Emphasis is also proposed to be laid on doubling the tracks, opening up of new lines, gauge conversion and increasing the high value traffic. In the field of road transportation, rationalization of road transport taxation structure, restraining overloading, promoting road safety, upgradation of national highways and encouraging private participation in road construction are some of the areas to receive attention. Indian Ports are projected to handle about 800 MT of traffic by the end of the Tenth Five Year Plan. This would require 300 to 400 additional berths to handle the increased cargo. The government is targeting private investment to the tune of Rs.24,000 cr to create additional port capacity during the Tenth Plan period. Again, the Ministry of Surface Transport (MOST) projects that the total traffic handled by the ports will reach 1373 million tonnes by the year 2021-22 which requires an investment of Rs.1,00,575 cr (Table 8). In order to enhance inter-port competition, port connectivity needs to be improved with inter-modal coordination between Railways, Container Corporation of India (CONCOR), Central Water Commission (CWC) and National Highway Authority of India (NHAI). For sustaining competition, both inter-port and intra-port, the key regulatory issues such as dispute resolution mechanism, entry of new players, issue of concession, and merger/de-merger in the ports sector need to be clearly enunciated.

---

[15] planningcommission.nic.in/plans/planrel/fiveyr/10th/volume2/v2_ch8_3.pdf

To bridge the gap between demand and supply, the development of minor ports is also necessary. The share of minor ports in traffic handling has increased from 10% to 25% during the period. Many maritime States, especially Gujarat and Maharashtra, have set up separate maritime boards for the development of minor ports including creation of new ports in Greenfield sites, through private participation.

Table 8: Investments Required for Creating Matching Port Facilities in the Next 20 Years

Year	Estimated Total Traffic in MTPA	Investment Required (in Rs. crores)
2001-02	394	5525
2006-07	653	34955
2011-12	860	17530
2016-17	1115	25600
2021-22	1373	16965
Total		**1,00,575**

Source: Government of India, Ministry of Surface Transport, New Delhi.

Conclusion

The major changes in world order in the last two decades can be attributed to two factors. The first is the retrenchment of the public sector since the mid-1980s, in most industrial and developing countries, from its dominant position in the provision of infrastructure, under the increasing pressure of fiscal adjustment and consolidation. Second, opening up of infrastructure industries to private participation, as part of a global drive towards increasing reliance on markets and private sector activity. According to the World Bank Report on Global Development and Finance-2004, the present economic environment in which the capital markets of the developing countries are not fully integrated with the global financial system, and where considerable administrative restrictions remain on capital flows, tapping the international capital markets to meet the high demand for infrastructure in developing countries requires solutions on five fronts. First, establishing transparent rules of the game, based on which investors can form expectations of future returns, assess risks, and have the assurance that contracts will be enforced with legal remedies in the case of default.[16] On the second front, the scope of local capital markets, as an instrument of hedging against currency risk as well as a fountainhead for long-term local currency finance needs to be strengthened. The third step would be to develop feasible public-private risk-mitigation and financing tools, which can address the risks on various fronts—political, currency, credit, contractual, and regulatory. Fourthly, the access of sub-sovereign public utilities, such as municipal utilities should be facilitated, to these capital markets. The fifth point stresses on supporting public providers of infrastructure services in attaining the commercial standards of creditworthiness over a long term to access capital markets on a sustainable basis. To meet the booming Indian trade, substantial new investment will be required along with modernization of existing infrastructure facilities. This will need significant organizational restructuring of existing port trusts, including the traditional, restrictive, labor practices. To attain the target growth rate of 8% in the Tenth Plan and 9.3% in the Eleventh Plan period, a revamping of the entire infrastructure sector is essential. When the country is planning to utilize a part of its forex reserve for the development of infrastructure, appropriate policy regulations keeping in view the world trend coupled with political and social interest can take the country to a new height of developed India by 2020.

(Pradeepta Kumar Samanta, Faculty Member, Academic Wing, The Icfai University, Hyderabad.)

References

1. 3i Network (2004), *"India Infrastructure Report 2004—Ensuring Value for Money"* Oxford University Press, New Delhi.
2. Antonio, E and Tomas, S (2004), "Where Do We Stand on Transport Infrastructure Deregulation and Public-Private Partnership?", World Bank Policy Research Working Paper 3356, Washington, D.C.
3. Bellier, M, Zhou, M Y (2002), "Private Participation in Infrastructure in China: Issues and Recommendations for the Road, Water and Power Sectors". The World Bank Working Paper No. 2. Washington, D.C.

[16] rru.worldbank.org/PapersLinks/Open.aspx?id=3738

4. Fay M and Yepes T (2003), "Investing in Infrastructure: What is Needed From 2000 to 2010?", World Bank Policy Research Working Paper 3102, Washington, D.C.

5. Government of India, (1996), "The India Infrastructure Report: Policy Imperatives for Growth and Welfare", (Rakesh Mohan Committee Report on Infrastructure), Government of India, New Delhi.

6. Government of India (2004), "Infrastructure", Economic Survey 2003-04, Ministry of Finance, New Delhi.

7. Government of India (2002), "Transport", Tenth Five Year Plan 2002-07, Planning Commission, New Delhi.

8. Gray, P (2001), "Private Participation in Infrastructure: A Review of the Evidence". A World Bank Research Paper.

9. Harris, C (2003), "Private Participation in Infrastructure in Developing Countries: Trends, Impacts, and Policy Lessons". A World Bank Research Paper.

10. India Port Report—"*Ten Years of Reforms and Challenges Ahead,*" i-maritime Consultancy Pvt. Ltd. Mumbai, September, 2003.

11. Mohan R; *"Infrastructure Development in India: Emerging Challenges"*.

12. Mukherjee, A and Sachdeva R (2003), *"Maritime and Air Transport Services: India's Approach to Privatization"*, Transport and Communications Bulletin for Asia and the Pacific, No. 2.

13. Mukherjee, A (2001), "India's Trade in Maritime Transport Services under the GATS Framework". ICRIER Working Paper No. 76, New Delhi.

14. Sahoo, S (2000), "Infrastructure and Economic Growth: An empirical Examination", *Reserve Bank of India Occasional Papers*, Vol. 21, Nos. 2 and 3, Monsoon and Winter, Mumbai.

15. Samanta, P K and Mohanty A K (2005), *Ports Infrastructure and Economic Development,* Kalpaz Publications, New Delhi.

16. World Bank (2002), "*Accounting for Poverty in Infrastructure Reform—Learning from Latin America's Experience,*" World Bank Institute, the world Bank, Washington, D.C.

17. World Bank (2002), "India's Transport Sector: The Challenges Ahead," Vol. I & II, *World Bank Policy Research Report,* Washington, D.C.

18. World Bank (2003), "Private Sector Development Strategy Implementation Progress Report," World Bank Policy Research Report, Washington, D.C.

19. World Bank (2004), "Highway Sector Financing in India: A Policy Note", Vol. I & II, *World Bank Policy Research Report,* Washington, D.C.

20. World Bank (2004), "Private Participation in Infrastructure: Trends in Developing Countries in 1990-2001," World Bank Policy Research Report on Private Provision of Public Services Group, Washington, DC.

21. World Bank (2004), "Public and Private Sector Roles in the Supply of Transport Infrastructure and Services," World Bank Report on Transport Sector, Washington, D.C.

22. World Bank (2004), "Reforming Infrastructure—Privatization, Regulation and Competition," World Bank Policy Research Report, Washington, D.C.

23. World Bank (2004), "Global Development Finance: Harnessing Cyclical Gains for Development", World Bank Policy Research Report, Washington, D.C.

Section III

Experiences

14

The Road from Mumbai to Pune

Jyoti Ahluwalia and Swapna Gopalan

The Expressway project is the country's first, with massive investment connecting two vibrant commercial hubs—Mumbai and Pune—covering 94 km, and was built according to global standards. It was started in January 1998 and completed well before the stipulated time, that too without cost overruns. Because of the Expressway, travel time between Mumbai and Pune has been reduced only to two hours as against five hours on NH4.

The 95-km long, six-lane Mumbai-Pune Expressway, extending from Kon near Panvel to Dehu road near Pune, is India's first infrastructure project built to global standards. It was built by the initiatives of the Maharashtra State Road Development Corporation Ltd. (MSRDC). The expressway linked the commercial capital of India, Mumbai, to the cultural capital of Maharashtra, Pune, which has also grown into a major industrial and commercial center.

The Government of Maharashtra (GoM) had decided to construct the Expressway, because the National Highway No. 4 (NH4), which was the only link between Mumbai and Pune earlier, was unable to cope with the high traffic density. The Rs.1630 cr Expressway project was planned with a 60:40 debt equity ratio;

Source: Projects and Profits, November 2005.

but after the change of government in 1998, the new government withheld the equity contribution forcing MSRDC to finance the project with debt alone.

The construction work, which started in January 1998, was completed in record time and without cost overrun. The full length of 95 km of the Expressway was opened to traffic by mid-February 2002. However, after the Expressway was fully operational, the revenue generated from the tolls failed to meet the estimates. The idea of paying tolls did not go down too well with the Indian public, especially the truck drivers, who continued to use the parallel non-tolled NH4. Revenues expected for the project from other non-tolled sources also did not materialize. The average annual toll collection was only Rs.75 cr, while the annual debt burden was Rs.250 cr. Consequently, as on March 31, 2003, MSRDC had accumulated debts totaling Rs.3,200 cr and annual interest liabilities of Rs.350 cr.

In such a worsening financial situation, MSRDC decided to sell the entire stretch of 95 kms of the Mumbai-Pune Expressway. To make the project viable for the private operator, it added the Mumbai-Pune section of NH4 to the offer. The sales deal, thus, gave the private party the right to toll both the highways for 15 years. This was to ensure that the selected private player participated in the entire road connectivity between Mumbai and Pune. During the same period, the private party is required to maintain the Expressway and also to strengthen, widen, operate and maintain the Mumbai-Pune section of NH4.

In December 2003, MSRDC advertised the sale and invited tenders. In April 2004, the bid was granted to Ideal Road Builders (IRB), the highest bidder for the project, at an upfront payment of Rs.918 cr. However, MSRDC retained the advertisement and land development rights.

The Mumbai-Pune Expressway has thrown up some interesting issues like the need for another highway when NH4 was already in existence, the selling of rights to toll and maintain the highways for 15 years to a private party, the changing role of MSRDC, etc. What remains to be seen is how profitable the venture turns out for IRB and how successful MSRDC will be in developing the land surrounding the Expressway and utilizing its advertisement rights.

Background

During the Seventh Five Year Plan[1], the Ministry of Surface Transport (MoST) identified the Mumbai-Pune Corridor—a part of the National Highway NH4—as one of the most congested national highway corridors and proposed to develop as part of the "National Expressway System". This congestion was the result of the growing traffic between the cities of Mumbai and Pune. Mumbai was already the commercial hub of India and Pune was fast growing into another industrial zone. This region contributed 86% of the total industrial output of the state and contained 72% of the factories. The potential of Pune to develop into a computer and Information Technology (IT) hub of India further emphasized the need for a better road link between the two cities.

The approximate travel time between the two cities under good traffic conditions was four to five hours. However, the narrow two lane winding curves of the Mumbai-Pune National Highway passed through the Western Ghats where landslides and floods occurred frequently. This resulted in blockages and accidents, increasing the travel time to more than ten hours, and made the journey unpleasant. The GoM was concerned that the lack of proper road infrastructure between the twin cities would hinder the industrial growth and prosperity of the region.

During 1990, the flow of traffic between Mumbai and Pune was 20,000 PCUs[2] a day. This wa projected to grow up to 100,000 PCUs by the year 2004, necessitating a ten-lane corridor between the two cities.

RITES Feasibility Study

As a long-term solution to the problem, in 1990, the GoM appointed RITES[3] and Scott Wilson Kirkpatrick (UK) to conduct a feasibility study for a new expressway between the two cities. In 1995, RITES submitted its report and recommended a new expressway to be constructed from Kon near Panvel to Dehu road near Pune and to be operated as an access-controlled tolled road. RITES

1 The Seventh Five Year Plan period in India was 1985-1990.

2 PCU (Passenger Car Unit) – Traffic is measured in terms of PCUs. The unit depends on the time a vehicle takes to move along a road. A bus is equivalent to 3.6 PCU while a bullock cart is 4.5 PCU. One lane is required for every 10,000 PCU.

3 An ISO 9001-2000 company established in 1974 by the Government of India, as a multi-disciplinary consultancy organization in the fields of transport, infrastructure and related technologies.

Exhibit 1: RITES Feasibility Report
1. The construction of a dual three-lane expressway taking off from Kon near Panvel and ending on the Westerly Bypass outside Pune at Dehu Road.
2. The total length of the proposed road is 85 km.
3. The estimated project cost at 1994 prices is Rs.11,464 mn.
4. Diversion of traffic to the new expressway is estimated to be between 40-45%.
5. The EIRR for the project is 17.81% as opposed to the Planning Commission's cut-off rate of 12%. Hence, the project is economically viable.
6. Property development on the land in the vicinity of the expressway is a possible source of subsidy for the project.
Source: The RITES-SWP Report, Volume 1.

recommended a wide road to avoid congestions, use of the latest technology for construction, and incorporation of speed monitoring systems to make it safer. Some of the other recommendations of the report are as specified in Exhibit 1.

Formation of MSRDC

Based on the recommendations of the RITES report, the GoM was keen on constructing the Expressway. Traditionally, the onus of financing and building roads in India was vested with the government. However, the government which did not have enough funds to even upgrade existing roads was not in a position to finance this huge investment needed for the Expressway. The government was, thus, left with no option but to involve the private sector in road construction and financing on a Build Operate and Transfer (BOT)[4] basis.

With the view to speed up the process of Project Investment, the GoM, in August 1996, established the Maharashtra State Road Development Corporation Ltd. (MSRDC) under the Companies Act. MSRDC's role was to expedite the development of State Transport infrastructure by managing new projects and completing existing ones through active private sector participation under time-bound programs.

[4] BOT (Build/Own/Transfer) projects are public infrastructure projects, wherein, the private sector designs and builds the infrastructure, finances its construction and owns, operates and maintains it over a period, often as long as 20 or 30 years. This period is sometimes referred to as the "concession" period. Traditionally, such projects provide infrastructure which is to be transferred to the government at the end of the concession period.

Though MSRDC was set up as a wholly government-owned company, it was given maximum operational freedom in terms of planning, execution, funding and day-to-day administration. All decision-making powers were vested with the company. Reputed professionals from various public and private institutions were appointed as directors of the company. The MD of MSRDC was also authorized to decide staff positions and commensurate pay scales to attract the best talent.

Invitation of Bids

When the Maharashtra Public Works Department (PWD) invited bids, only one bid was received from Reliance Industries.

Exhibit 2: Benefits

1. Reduction in accidents.	4. Fast crossing of Khandala Ghat.
2. Saving in travel time.	5. Economic development through speedy traffic.
3. Saving in fuel consumption by vehicles.	6. Reduction in pollution.

Source: Website of MSRDC

Reliance projected the total project cost to be approximately Rs.3,600 cr and bid accordingly, while the government's projections, which were based on the RITES report, projected costs at Rs.1,630 cr, after taking into account escalation, extra items and interest rates. The reason for the glaring variance between the two projected costs was not immediately clear. However, later studies and analysis conducted by various groups confirmed that the cost of the same project would be higher for a private party due to the non-availability of government subsidies, high construction costs, risk of cost overruns due to construction hold-ups for various reasons, and the uncertainty of toll revenue within the contract period.

After its efforts generating at a feasible response from the private sector had failed, the GoM, in March 1997, entrusted the Mumbai-Pune Expressway to MSRDC on BOT basis. MSRDC quickly started work on the project. It selected most of its workforce from the PWD and CIDCO,[5] apart from a few, who were taken on deputation from the revenue department to assist in the land acquisition works.

5 CIDCO—City and Industrial Development Corporation of Maharashtra Ltd., is responsible for development of new urban areas in the state of Maharashtra.

Political Support

With a view to hasten the project implementation process, the Chief Minister of Maharashtra held a meeting with the State Secretaries to emphasize the importance of the project and mobilize political support for the project. The GoM also constituted two high-powered committees with various responsibilities. One committee under the chairmanship of the Managing Director and Vice-Chairman of MSRDC was set up for proper coordination among the various government departments to obtain the requisite clearances. The other was a Steering Committee, under the chairmanship of a retired PWD Secretary, to recommend the necessary geometric and technical standards to be adopted for construction and to decide upon the various provisions of tender documents and related matters.

Based on the Steering Committee's proposal, it was decided to allot functions relating to designing, cost estimation and supervision of construction to a panel of Project Management Consultants (PMCs). Thus, while the PMCs took care of the technical details, MSRDC was left to concentrate on activities relating to coordination of administrative requirements like getting clearances and raising finances.

Appointment of Project Management Consultants

The Mumbai-Pune Expressway construction was a mega project, requiring huge investments and resources. The Steering Committee realized that one PMC could not handle all the work, so it was decided to divide the construction work into six sections and allocate one section to each PMC. To avoid inconsistency of work and ensure standardization between the different sections, committees were formed to handle various tasks, by drawing members from each of the PMC.

Bids were invited from prospective PMCs and evaluated on the basis of technical and financial criteria, giving weightage of 80% to technical skills. The whole selection process was completed within two months and in June 1997, six PMCs were fixed for the construction. (Refer to Annexure I for the details of the PMCs and contractors selected and the work allotted to them).

MSRDC also realized that the timely completion of the Expressway was important for its success. So, even before obtaining clearance from the environment and forest departments, technical consultants were appointed for each section of the road. This decision had the risk of the expenditures going defunct in the event of environmental clearances not being met. But with the initiatives of the State Chief Minister and even the Prime Minister at some stages, the Environment Clearance was obtained in October 1997, and the Forest Clearance in November 1997. However, clearance was not approved for the Ghats portion, which was home to rare species of animals. Therefore, in this portion of the Ghats (Adoshi to Kusgaon), it was proposed to widen and improve the existing NH4.

Concurrently, MSRDC officials made arrangements to provide the necessary resources so that the concerned PMCs could get to work as soon as they were awarded the contracts. These activities included acquiring land (646 ha for Right of Way, 455 ha for quarry and dumping area, and 1338 ha for real estate development), persuading the concerned utility service departments like power, telephone and sewer to divert the services wherever they crossed the alignment, seeking permission for cutting of trees, and other related work.

Appointment of Contractors

Meanwhile, tender documents for inviting contractors for all the sectors were made ready. Bids were invited on technical and financial basis in November 1997–133 tenders were sold and 55 were received in December 1997. Within a week, the bids were evaluated by a high power Steering Committee consisting of both officers from MSRDC and outside technical experts. The Board of Directors approved the proposal of this Committee and work orders granting only one section to any one contractor were issued on January 1, 1998.

Tenders for widening of Khandala Ghat and Lonavala-Khandala Bypass works were invited in July 1998 and work orders issued in September 1998. The tenders for the last section of the expressway, viz., Panvel Bypass, were invited in March 1999 and work orders were issued in April 1999.

Change of Government

An important development in 1998, during the construction of the expressway that had considerable impact on the project was the change of government. The Congress-NCP combine wrested power by defeating the ruling BJP-Shiv Sena government. Though the change of power at the helm did not have any effect on the construction work or support for the project, the decision of the new government to hold back its equity contribution resulted in long-standing financial consequences. The project, an initiative of the BJP-Shiv Sena government, was planned with a 60:40 debt equity ratio. But, with the withdrawal of the government's equity, the project was highly leveraged and funded by debt alone. MSRDC raised Rs.2,420 cr on an equity base of Rs.5 cr at 11-13% interest rates, on the basis of state government guarantee.

Financing the Expressway

In January 1998, MSRDC issued Rs.500 cr bonds with a proposal to raise a similar amount through the green-shoe[6] option and successfully raised Rs.1,300 cr through private placements. MSRDC offered 14% for taxable bonds and 11.5% for tax-free bonds for seven year resources. These bonds were guaranteed by the government and were rated AA (Structured Obligation) by CARE. Twelve arrangers were appointed for the issue, of which 11 were banks or financial institutions. The funds were raised to finance the Mumbai-Pune Expressway, for building 50 flyovers in Mumbai and for 29 rail overbridges all over the State.

A similar exercise of raising resources through bonds was done in January-July 1999 and an amount in excess of Rs.1,000 cr was raised. But as the credit rating and the government guarantee for the bond issue was only Rs.950 the excess amount had to be returned to the investors.

In effect, MSRDC was able to raise Rs.2,200 cr through private placements on the basis of government guarantee and project strength. The government guarantee was essential since MSRDC was a newly formed company with an equity base of only Rs.5 cr.

MSRDC as Facilitator and Coordinator

The construction work began in January/February 1998, following the issue of work orders. The contract stipulated the completion of construction work in 27 months, with a substantial completion in 24 months, with a view to open the Expressway in January 2000. This was a tough challenge for MSRDC as the

6 An option that allows the underwriting of an IPO to sell additional shares to the public if the demand is high. The Green Shoe Company was the first to issue this type of option; hence, the name.

construction involved building a length of 95 kms running through a hilly terrain constituting black regur soil[7]. Also, part of the work was the construction of bridges, underpasses, overpasses, pedestrian crossings, etc.

MSRDC made every possible effort to ensure support and assistance to the consultants and contractors and tried to remove all hindrances that could cause delay in the work. MSRDC's homework was complete in terms of facilitating construction activities by making arrangements for power, water for construction, drinking water, shifting of high tension power lines, explosives for blasting of rocks, acquiring for sites for metal and *murum*, locating petrol pumps adjacent to the alignment, etc.

Special provisions were included in the contract with the contractors. This was designed to ensure that the contractors tried to complete the project as early as possible. Some of these provisions were:

- Contractors to be paid bonus at the rate of Rs.20 lakh per week for early completion and levied a penalty of Rs.30 lakh per week for delay in completion.
- Delays in payment of certified bills beyond 10 days entitled contractors to an interest of 15% on the undisbursed amount.
- A simple dispute redressal mechanism was set up.

The construction work took place under the close scrutiny of the Managing Director (MD) of MSRDC. The consultants of each section were required to submit a cumulative daily report, which comprised detailed information relating to men, machines and progress on the site. The MD personally examined the daily reports and also conducted monthly onsite review meetings to remove any impediments in the progress of the project. These review meetings with the contractors and consultants were held in the presence of the District Collector and the Technical officers of MSRDC, and the decisions taken were binding.

---

7 Black soil, also called regur or black-cotton soil, is spread mostly across the Deccan Lava Plateau, the Malwa Plateau, and interior Gujarat, where there are both moderate rainfall and underlying basaltic rock.

Construction of Tunnels

The Expressway also included construction of four lane wide tunnels at five locations spanning a length of approximately 6000 meters. The Konkan Railway Corporation Ltd., was entrusted with this task, since the company had prior experience in dealing with such projects. The cost of construction of tunnels alone was estimated at about Rs.200 cr. Separate tunnels for traffic flowing both ways, modern facilities of lighting, ventilation and fire-fighting equipments were some of the unique features of this project. The details of the tunnels are as specified in Annexure 3.

Modern and Advanced Technology

Indian roads are prone to extremely high wear and tear due to heavy traffic and climatic conditions like heavy rains during the monsoon season (between June and October) and high temperatures during the rest of the year. MSRDC had decided to construct the Expressway using concrete technology keeping in view the longer lifespan of rigid concrete roads as against the cheaper, asphalt roads. Such construction necessitated the use of advanced technology and sophisticated equipments, some of which were new to the country. MSRDC provided the much needed financial assistance to small contractors, who could not afford the investments to purchase the required equipments. Around Rs.300 cr was spent on the purchase of machinery alone.

The use of modern technology enhanced the quality and speed of construction. Offices of all units involved in the project, viz., MSRDC, PMCs and contractors, were linked via networking. This improved coordination and flow of information, and at the same time increased speed of communication. Maintenance of data relating to inventory, financial accounts and work progress was also made easier and, hence, not much time was wasted in tracking resources. Further, wireless sets were provided for on-site communication and coordination. In short, the use of technology helped keep the project under control.

Environmental Issues and Litigation

Environmental issues were a major cause of concern for MSRDC, as the magnitude of the project itself was evidence of the significant impact it could have on the

Exhibit 3
Summary of the impacts predicted on biodiversity resources in the route of the Expressway: • Increased silt load would lead to degradation of the Lonavala Lake; • The proposed expressway would most probably bisect the proposed Father Santapau Sanctuary; • Deforestation and land-take would adversely affect wildlife; • Degradation of habitats and disruption of migratory routes of a variety of bird species; • Destruction of species of flora and fauna which are unique to the region; and • Hardship to the local people as resource areas on the opposite side of the carriage way would become inaccessible.
Source: Summarized from The Integration of Biodiversity into National Environmental Assessment Procedures, National Case Studies, India, September, 2001.

region's environment. An Environmental Impact Assessment (EIA) study was conducted by RITES. The RITES report identified the negative and positive impacts of this decision (Refer Exhibit 3).

An Environment Management Plan was formulated to mitigate the adverse impact on the environment, to protect and enhance the existing environmental resources wherever possible, and to monitor the success and failure of these measures. At an additional cost of nearly Rs.40 lakh, more than 1000 trees were transplanted. Also, all the rich fertile soil that was cleared for the expressway was dumped on farmlands in the interior areas to help the farmers in their agricultural activities.

Litigation was another issue MSRDC had to grapple with. Various legal issues had to be addressed:

- The Bombay Environmental Action Group (BEAG) filed a writ petition in the Bombay High Court against MoST, the NHAI, MoEF, GoM and the MSRDC, alleging violation of Expressway sanction conditions. The charges included improper EIA study, dumping of rubble in protected forest land for which MoEF sanction was not taken, felling of trees not within the right of way, construction of the Lonavala-Khandala bypass without obtaining clearance, and others.

- A private party filed a petition against the acquisition of his property, on the grounds that he was not given due notice and adequate hearing before the land was taken into possession. However, the objection was subsequently squashed, on the ground that the State Government proved that they had complied with all the conditions of acquisition of land, which fell in the path of the expressway.
- In yet another case, 18 tribal families displaced by the construction of the expressway, filed a case seeking higher compensation. The case was subsequently ruled in the claimants' favor and the Maharashtra State Government was asked to pay 20% more than the amount already offered. The government was also asked to draw up a rehabilitation plan.

The strong political support shown by the State Government and the proactive stand taken by MSRDC ensured that the progress of the construction was not hampered by these or other public interest litigations filed against the construction.

Construction Completed

The construction of the Expressway was completed in record time and within estimated costs. MSRDC's hard work in the form of evolving an effective process of selection of PMCs and contractors, formulation of incentive and penalty scheme for contractors, and prudent decision making like use of latest technology in construction paved the way for the success. Throughout the project, the staff had been highly motivated.

Thus, the Expressway built to international standards with all road amenities and beautiful landscaping along the roadway was touted to be one of the few showpieces of well-implemented infrastructure projects in the country. This smooth Expressway was a welcome change for the Indian public much used to pothole-ridden and chaotic road conditions.

As and when the construction of each section was completed, it was opened to traffic. The Sections 'A' and 'B' (Kon to Aadoshi), were opened to traffic on May 1, 2000, Section 'C' (Kusgaon to Ozarde) and Section 'D', in part (Ozarde to Somatnephata), were opened to traffic from July 27, 2000 and the remaining section (Somatnephata to Kiwale) was opened to traffic from June 10, 2000. The entire Expressway was ready and operational by mid-February 2002.

The success of the project raised the confidence levels of the engineers and contractors involved in the project. The project demonstrated that with modern technology and dedicated workers any project could be completed within the estimated cost and expected time.

Expressway Operational

The Expressway reduced the travel time between Mumbai and Pune to two hours as against five hours on NH4. Farmers, horticulturists and other exporters in the perishable goods business welcomed the expressway as it helped them to transport their goods faster to ports and, hence, reach newer markets abroad.

It facilitated safer and faster movement of traffic and saving of fuel, along with the provision of wayside amenities such as petrol pumps, food malls and repair facilities. These facilities appealed and attracted an ever increasing traffic of business travelers.

But, in spite of its inherent appeal, the Expressway did not attract the required traffic levels due to the existence of the alternative NH4 route and the reluctance of the users to pay the toll. The other users, especially trucks and trailers which formed a major chunk of the traffic, still preferred the old NH4 despite the longer time it required. The 95 km of the tolled expressway formed only a small portion of their thousand odd km long journey and they were unwilling to shell out Rs.680 extra for the saving of a few hours.

After one year of its operation, toll collections revenues started falling short of the target. Lower than expected revenues coupled with high interest payments threatened the sustainability of the project. But MSRDC was optimistic about the revenue streams as it expected the traffic to increase and it hoped to generate additional revenue by integrating and developing its landholdings along the Expressway.

In June 2002, MSRDC asked the National Highways Authority of India (NHAI) to share 40% of the costs of Rs.1,630 cr and make the Expressway a part of the Rs.54,000 cr Golden Quadrilateral Project[8]. Although MSRDC argued

8 Under the 'Golden Quadrilateral' project, 5,952 km of new roads were to be built to link national highways and connect the four metros of Delhi, Kolkata, Mumbai and Chennai under the Rs.54,000 cr National Highways Development Project (NHDP).

that NHAI would have to make the road if the Expressway was not made, NHAI was reluctant to finance the project as it was not part of its original plan of the Golden Quadrilateral.

The Expressway funded entirely by debt, at an average rate of 13%, was incurring an annual interest burden of Rs.250 cr and on March 31, 2003, MSRDC had debts totaling Rs.3,200 cr and annual interest liabilities of Rs.350 cr.

Landslides and Accidents

Though the Expressway was built as a better alternative to NH4, it continued to be plagued by the same problems faced by the latter, namely, landslides and accidents. These events slowed down the traffic and also caused traffic jams.

Another problem that cropped up after the Expressway was opened to traffic was the breach of fencing. The fence constructed at a cost of Rs.5 cr, breached at several places resulting in cattle straying onto the highway and thieves sauntering on to the road, leading to serious accidents.

Revenue Shortfall

According to projections, 50,000 Passenger Car Units (PCUs) were expected to ply the expressway every day by 2004. But only 16,000 vehicles were actually using the expressway with annual toll collections of Rs.75 cr only.

The viability of the project was based on plans to develop townships at both ends of the Expressway to generate revenues to the tune of Rs.750 cr. An Infotech Park outside Pune was also planned to generate additional revenue. But both these plans were not implemented. Although MSRDC generated some non-toll revenue from advertising rights, petrol pumps and motels, it was not substantial in comparison to the Rs.3,000 cr debt. So, the main revenue source continued to be tolls.

Efforts to Improve Income

In its efforts to promote the economic development of the region, MSRDC identified 11 potential areas along the 95-km expressway for commercial development in a profitable and environmentally sensitive manner.

The Maharashtra Industrial Development Corporation (MIDC) also contributed its might by conducting a sophisticated survey, with the help of satellite remote sensing, geographical remote sensing and Geographical Information System (GIS) technologies to identify an array of suitable sites along the expressway for the development of knowledge-based industries. This was done to project the Expressway as a knowledge corridor and to attract more companies from outside the state as well as abroad to set up base here.

Decision to Sell

In an unprecedented move, the NHAI handed over the NH4 to MSRDC with the permission to toll the highway. MSRDC decided to sell the Expressway along with NH4 to a private party to toll and maintain the roads for 15 years. The private party was required to widen NH4 from a two-lane to a four-lane highway and to maintain and toll it for 15 years along with the Expressway.

In December 2003, MSRDC advertised for the sale of Mumbai-Pune Expressway along with NH4. Both the roads connecting Mumbai and Pune were sold together to make the purchase financially viable for the private party.

On December 8, 2003, MSRDC invited tenders from private parties in response to which they received bids from seven national and international companies[9]. The bid was granted to Ideal Road Builders (IRB) in April 2004, since it turned out to be the highest bidder for the project at an upfront payment of Rs.918 cr. The total expenditure for IRB has been estimated at Rs.2,060 cr which includes Rs.360 cr towards construction cost of widening NH4, Rs.754 cr on Operating and Maintenance of the two routes over the concession period, and Rs.29.4 cr as various payments to MSRDC.

MSRDC's decision to sell its rights of the highways was criticized due to the fear of 'monopolization' of the important commercial route between Mumbai and Pune by a private party. Issues were also raised about the safety and maintenance of the highways. At the time of this sale, approximately 16,000 vehicles were plying on the Expressway every day, thereby, contributing Rs.75 cr annually as toll income.

---

9 The seven companies that submitted their bids were: L&T, Punj Lloyd, IL&FS, Gammon India in joint venture with Ashoka Buildcon, Viva Highways and Viva Infrastructure Private Limitd, Hindustan Construction Company, and Ideal Road Builders (IRB).

According to MSRDC officials, with the addition of toll income from the 9,000 vehicles plying on NH4 every day, the revenue was poised to grow approximately by Rs.110 cr annually with the further potential of 8% growth. This revenue stream for 15 years would lead to the Net Present Value (NPV) of Rs.2,500-3,500 cr, taking into account the traffic and toll rates and the rates at which the buyer is able to finance the cost. Another factor was that the construction risk was restricted only to the upgradation and maintenance of NH4.

Meanwhile, there were some areas of concern. The New Delhi-based Central Road Research Institute (CRRI) had detected design and structural flaws in the Expressway. In its draft report it pointed out errors like "improper curvatures, inadequate shoulder width, absence of crash barriers and flaws in the space between two traffic ways". CRRI suggested various corrective measures which IRB would be implementing. IRB would also be implementing the corrections suggested by the Maharashtra Institute of Technology, Pune, to correct distortions due to 'geopathic' locations.

Further, though it was claimed that the construction matched global standards, the MD and Chief Economist of Morgan Stanley, who visited India in 2004, rated the Expressway as a mere B-minus by Chinese standards.

Future Outlook

Will the long run story of the Mumbai-Pune Expressway be as beautiful and successful as it was predicted to be is yet to be seen. Presently, along with the upgradation of NH4, IRB is also in the process of implementing the recommendations of CRRI for correcting the faults on the Expressway. Heavy rains during monsoons have created cracks and potholes. Occasional landslides have also occurred at various places leaving commuters stranded for hours. The use of concrete for the construction of the highway has been criticized by experts who opine that it is unsuitable for roads exposed to high temperature fluctuations. Under the given climatic conditions, the road would have survived better, if it had been reinforced with steel.

IRB is expected to complete the upgradation of NH4 by March 2006 and begin tolling NH4 also by April 2006. The general public is yet to come to terms with the lack of a free passage between Mumbai and Pune. However, the traffic has increased steadily by 6-8% over the year. With the decline in interest rates, the cost of capital for MSRDC has also come down from 13% to 8-9%.

Meanwhile, MSRDC has identified its role as an incubator of projects. In 2003, it was looking for strategic partners to unlock its investments worth Rs.2,300 cr in seven[10] different infrastructure projects structured in the form of seven different companies. The money generated through this mechanism would be used for financing future projects.

MSRDC's aim is to tap its areas of strength in terms of easy access to funds and coordination with various government departments and political class to initiate new projects. It wants to carry this venture capitalist format till the completion of construction and leave management to other professional and private partners.

The dearth of funds with the government requires a paradigm shift in the perceptions towards 'the user pays concept' for providing funds for infrastructure. Thus, the users and the government have to find newer ways and formats to involve the private sector to finance the infrastructure projects. So far, BOT models have been the most popular method for public-private partnership in India. However, there has been rising skepticism among the private construction companies and engineering consultancy firms about this model due to the inherent risks and uncertainties involved. The public-private partnership in infrastructure projects in India is going through a transition and needs innovations in contractual designs. Also, financial viability might be a short-term hindrance, but the positive externalities associated with the road projects and their contribution to increased productivity for the economy could make projects viable.

(Jyoti Ahluwalia is an Adjunct Faculty Member at The Icfai Business School, Bangalore.

Swapna Gopalan is a Senior Research Associate at the Centre for Business Research, The Icfai Business School, Bangalore.)

---

[10] Rs.750 cr Satara-Kagal highway; Rs.410 Nagpur-Aurangabad-Sinner-Ghoti road; Rs.81 cr Thane-Ghodbunder Road; Rs.450 cr Nagpur Integrated Road Development project; Rs.280 cr Pune Integrated Road Development Project; Rs.143 cr Aurangabad IRDP and 19 rail overbridge projects aggregating Rs.195 cr in various parts of the state.

References

1. "MSRDC and the Mumbai-Pune Expressway: A Sustainable Model for Privatizing Construction of Physical Infrastructure?", Dr. Hemalata C Dandekar and Sulakshana Mahajan, paper submitted to the *Economic and Political Weekly of India*, 1/17/2001.
2. "The Mumbai Pune Expressway: A Case Study" dated September 5, 2000, submitted by Amrut Nashikkar, Nirav Shah, Siddharth Nautiyal, Vinayraj AK, Vivek Sahay, in partial fulfillment of the course, Infrastructure Development and Financing, to Prof. G Raghuram, Prof. Sebastian Morris and Prof. Rekha Jain, Indian Institute of Management, Ahmedabad.
3. "Effective Project Management: Mumbai-Pune Expressway", a Lecture by R C Sinha, former Addl. Chief Secretary and Vice-Chairman and Managing Director, Maharashtra State Road Development Corporation. Ltd., on March 25, 2000.
4. "NH 4 Privatisation, Punekars to Pay for MSRDC's Sins", Abhijit Atre, August 21, 2004, Times News Network.
5. "From Concept to Commissioning", by P L Bongirwar and S S Momin, *The Indian Concrete Journal*, June 2000.
6. "Buy One, Get One Free", *Businessworld*, January 26, 2004, online link: *http://www.business worldindia.com/Jan2604/indepth02.asp*
7. "MIDC's Market Gimmick Expressway is SmartWay" dated March 28, 2003, *The Times of India*, online link: *http://www.cdacindia.com/html/press/2q03/spot290.asp*
8. "The 'Untolled' Story of Mumbai-Pune Expressway", December 15, 2003, *The Indian Express*, online link: *http://web.mid-day.com/news/city/2005/february/103651.htm*
9. "Expressway ... to Where?", Pankaj Sekhsaria, *The Hindu*, dated March 14, 2004. Online link: *http://www.hindu.com/thehindu/mag/2004/03/14/stories/2004031400 310800.htm*
10. The Integration of Biodiversity into National Environmental Assessment Procedures, National Case Studies, India, September 2001, Page 5. online link: *http://www.unep.org/bpsp/EIA/Case%20Studies/India.pdf*
11. Online sources:

    http://www.msrdc.org

    http://www.businessworldindia.com

    http://www.expressindia.com

    http://timesofindia.indiatimes.com

    http://www.hindustantimes.com/news/181_771650,0006.htm

http://www.skalmadi.org/story/2004/5/21/55644/8563

http://www.expressindia.com/fe/daily/20000730/fec30031.html

http://www.roadtraffic-technology.com/projects/mumbai/

http://www.nriol.com/content/articles/article57.html

http://www.projectsmonitor.com/detailnews.asp?newsid=8647

http://www.civil.skanska.com/skanska/templates/page.asp?id=3363

http://www.indiantelevision.com/mam/headlines/y2k4/aug/augmam57.htm

http://www.frontlineonnet.com/fl1714/17140380.htm

http://in.news.yahoo.com/050618/48/5z0eu.html

http://www.projectsmonitor.com/detailnews.asp?newsid=7221

The country's first and only such project. Connecting two vibrant commercial hubs, Mumbai and Pune. 94 km of class and convenience. In operation for the last three years. Annual toll revenues of Rs.110 cr and growing. **The Mumbai-Pune Expressway is a project you could operate and maintain.**

The project

- To operate and maintain the Mumbai-Pune Expressway for a predefined period.
- To strengthen, widen (four-lane), operate and maintain about 111 km of the Mumbai-Pune section of NH4.
- Toll collection on both Mumbai-Pune Expressway and the Mumbai-Pune section of NH4.

This will ensure that the selected private sector player participates in the entire road connectivity between Mumbai and Pune. Put together, the toll income is sure to be more than Rs.110 cr per annum with a potential of 8% revenue growth, year after year.

This is it. Determine the future. Create history. The choice is yours.

Excerpts from MSRDC's advertisement inviting bids for the sale of the Mumbai-Pune Expressway along with the National Highway No. 4 (NH4), dated December 2003 (Refer Annexure 4 for the full advertisement).

Annexure 1

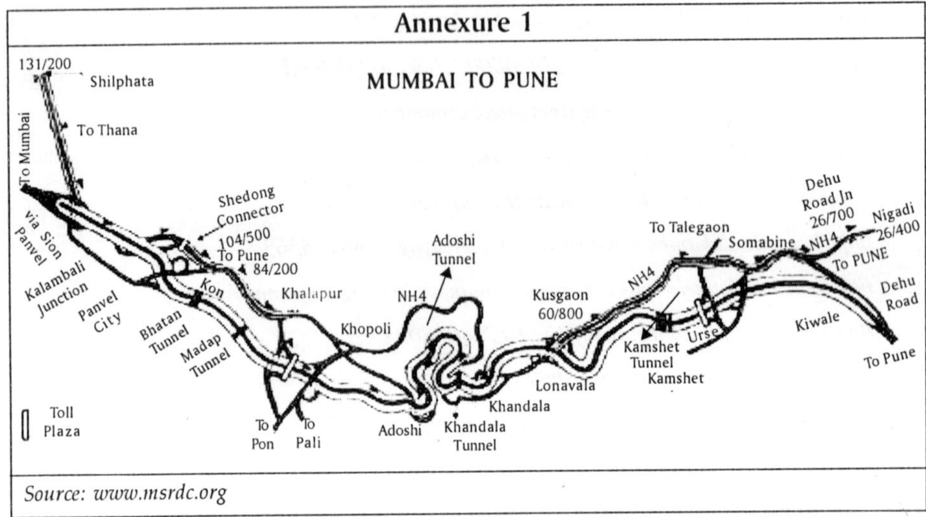

Source: www.msrdc.org

Annexure 2

Date/Year	Progress
1990	Decision by GOI to construct a new expressway. Appointment of RITES & Scott Wilson Kirkpatrick (UK) to conduct a techno-economic viability study.
1995	RITES submits its report. Recommends construction of new tolled expressway connecting Kon near Panvel to Dehu road near Pune.
1996 (July-August)	State Government established Maharashtra State Road Development Corporation Ltd. (MSRDC) under the Companies Act to channelize project investments.
1996 (July)	Maharashtra Government decides to construct the Mumbai Pune Expressway (MPE) on BOT basis.
1996	Invitation of bids for BOT project.
1996	One bid received (Reliance India Ltd.)—unacceptable to the government on financial grounds.
1997 (March)	The government of Maharashtra entrusted the MPE to MSRDC on BOT basis.
1997 (April)	Bids invited for appointing Project Management Consultants.
1997 (May)	Receipt of bids from prospective Project Management Consultants.
1997 (June)	The road divided into four sections and Technical Consultants appointed for each section.

Contd...

Contd...	
1997 (June)	Fixing of six Project Management Consultants—one each for Sections A, B, C and D; one for the Panvel Bypass; one for the Ghat section.
1997 (October 13)	Environment clearance obtained from Ministry of Environment and Forest.
1997 (November 11)	Forest clearance from Ministry of Environment and Forest.
1997 (November 11)	Tender documents ready.
1997 (November)	Tenders (technical and financial bids) invited.
1997 (December 18)	55 tenders received and evaluated within seven days.
1998 (January 1)	Board of Directors approves the evaluation of tenders. Work orders estimated for Rs.633 cr issued.
1998 (January/ February)	Construction work starts in right earnest with issue of orders to proceed.
1998 (April 8)	Groups in Pune oppose the project terming it as a waste.
1998 (July 6)	Objection raised by a private party squashed.
1998 (July 14)	Tenders invited for widening the Ghats.
1998 (August 4)	Tenders evaluated. Work orders estimated at Rs.197.50 cr issued.
1998 (December 9)	Mumbai High Court admits writ petition and restrains the MSRTDC from further acquisition of land and displacement of tribal and villagers.
1999 (January 4)	Stay on acquisition released.
2000 (May)	Certain sections of the newly constructed MPE opened to public.
2001 (March 1)	MPE opened for full length of 95 km. The average number of vehicles plying the expressway was 12,000.
2003 (Marrch 31)	The MSRDC has debts totaling Rs.3,200 cr and annual interest liabilities of Rs.350 cr.
2003 (December)	The MSRDC advertises for the sale of MPE along with NH4.
2004 (January 5)	MPE, along with NH4, put up for sale to the private players for 15 years.
2004 (February 12)	Last date for bids to buy the MPE and NH4.
2004 (April)	IRB wins the bid for Rs.2,060 cr.
Complied from various sources by the authors.	

Annexure 3: Section Details

Sections	Technical Consultants	Est. Cost in cr (Rs.)	Tender Amount in cr (Rs.)	Contractor	
Section 'A' (Kon to Chowk) 13.232 km. (Open for Traffic)	Stup Consultants with Hyder Consulting Ltd. UK	127.33	136.82	IJM/SCL Joint Venture	
Section 'B' (Chowk to Aadoshi) 16.629 km. (Open for Traffic)	Intercontinental Consultants & Technocrats Pvt. Ltd. India	183.73	194.00	Hindustan Construction Co. Mumbai	
Section 'C' (Kusgaon to Ozarde) 22.995 km. (Open for Traffic)	Frishmann Prabhu (India) Pvt. Ltd.	177.46	163.56	Larsen and Toubro Ltd. Mumbai	
Section 'D' (Ozarde to Dehu Road) 16.150 km. (Open for Traffic - In part)	Sir Owen Williams Innovestment	132.70	133.47	V.M. Jog Engineering Ltd. Pune	
Ghat Section Package - I Aadoshi to long tunnel 7.13 km.	Consulting Engg. Service (India) Ltd.	86.46	93.15	Shapoorji Pallonj & Co. Mumbai.	
Ghat Section Package - II Long tunnel to Lonavala bypass 8.28 km.	Consulting Engg. Service (India) Ltd.	108.96	104.35	Larsen & Toubro Ltd. Chennai	
Panvel Bypass Package - I 0/0 to 8/200, 8.20 km.	Technogem Consultants Thane	108.00	88.89	PBA - PCEC (JV) M Venkat Rao Visakhapatnam	
Panvel Bypass Package - II 8/200 to 9/750, 1.550 km.	Technogem Consultants Thane	64.50	49.99	PBA - PCEC (JV) M Venkat Rao Visakhapatnam	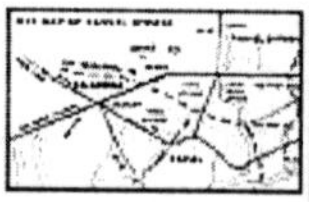
Tunnel Work 5 Twin Tunnel 5724 m. Tunnel Length		200.00	200.00	Konkan Railway Corp. Ltd.	
Other Exp. Tollplaza, Building, fencing sign boards, Technical consultants fees, etc.			324.00		
	Total...	1200.46	1488.00		

Source: www.msrdc.org

Annexure 4

It's not every day that we—as individuals, or society—are faced with the chance to alter the course of history.

MSRDC – Invitation for BIDS

Now this reality faces you in the form of the Mumbai-Pune Expressway: A golden opportunity that won't knock twice. Let's face it, the country's first and only expressway didn't take much time to enhance the lives of countless Mumbaikars and Puneites, leave alone the myriad industries it continues to enrich. And herein lies your opportunity—a dream 'untolled'—one that can translate into monetary gains in excess of Rs. 2000 cr. Interested? Read on...

The country's first and only such project. Connecting two vibrant commercial hubs, Mumbai & Pune. 94 kms of class and convenience. In operation for the last three years. Annual toll revenues of Rs.110 cr and growing. The Mumbai-pune Expressway. It's a project you could operate and maintain.

Mumbai, clearly the most vibrant and critical commercial hub of the country, is more often than not referred to as the commercial capital of the country. Pune, on the other hand, is a well-established manufacturing base, increasingly vying to be one of India's key IT and Education destinations.

Maharashtra State Road Development Corporation Ltd. (MSRDC) has developed, built and been operating and maintaining arguably the country's first and only expressway, and definitely the most talked about road sector project of the nation: The Mumbai-Pune Expressway. Having addressed the technical, construction and the initial tolling risk, MSRDC now proposes to invite Private Sector players to operate and maintain the Mumbai-Pune Expressway.

The Project

- To operate and maintain the Mumbai-Pune Expressway for a predefined period.
- To strengthen, widen (four-lane), operate and maintain about 111 km of the Mumbai-Pune section of NH4.
- Toll collection on both Mumbai-Pune Expressway and the Mumbai-Pune section of NH4.

This will ensure that the selected private sector player participates in the entire road connectivity between Mumbai and Pune. Put together, the toll income is sure to be more than Rs.110 cr per annum with a potential of 8% revenue growth, year after year.

This is it. Determine the future. Create history. The choice is yours.

Contd...

Contd...

Bidding Process

Prerequisites: The bidders or the lead member of the consortium (in case the bid is from a consortium of companies) should have a tangible Net Worth of Rs.40 cr, as per the audited financial results of the financial year ending March 31, 2003. The bidder or the lead member of the consortium should have completed at least one road project under BOT with a minimum cost of Rs.100 cr in the last three years. Should have experience of collecting toll for a minimum period of one year, on at least one road project during the last three years.

The Process: The bidder will be selected through a competitive bidding process. Bidders are invited to submit the following:

Technical Bid:

Part 1 – Information on the financial and technical parameters, outlined in the Prerequisites section above.

Part 2 – A letter of comfort signed by any of the:

i) Nationalized banks,

ii) State Bank of India or its group associate banks,

iii) All India Financial Institutions including HDFC,

iv) Banks promoted by any of the institutions mentioned in point iii, offering an 'in-principle' approval to fund the bidder or the consortium for undertaking the project.

Financial Bid:

The bidder would pay MSRDC net consideration for undertaking 'The Project' (as mentioned above). The Project activities will be contracted out for a period of 15 years. The details related to consideration and other matters are incorporated in the Project Information Memorandum and Bid Document.

Only the financial bids of bidders who qualify on the technical bid will be opened. The right to reject any or all bids, without assigning any reasons, is reserved.

The Project Information Memorandum detailing the information about the project may be obtained from the office of MSRDC at the address given below, from December 10, 2003 to January 30, 2004, on any working day, between 10.00 am and 5.00 pm, on payment of Rs. 10,000/-.

A complete set of Bid Document can be had on payment of any additional amount of Rs.40,000/-.

- **Bids:** Both technical and financial bids must reach MSRDC, at the address given below, by 5.00 pm on February 12, 2004.

  For details, contact: **Mr. Anil Kumar Lakhina,** Vice-Chairman and Managing Director.

- **Maharashtra State Road Development Corporation Limited, (MSRDC)** Priyadarshini Park, Nepean Sea Road, Mumbai - 400 036, Maharashtra, India. Tel: (91 22) 2368 5909, 2369 6109 Fax: (91 22) 2369 1031 E-mail: vcmd@msrdc.org

Source: www.msrdc.org

15

RESEARCH SUMMARY

Fair Payment for Infrastructure Use

A Phased Approach to a Common Transport Infrastructure Charging Framework in the EU†

Deepak Kumar

It is extremely important for the European transport sector to decide on the suitable user charges for transport sectors in order to provide new and consistent ways of financing, not only for maintaining the existing infrastructure but also for building new infrastructure so as to promote its economic growth. This case discusses how the user charges can influence the flow of investments from the private investors for infrastructure development taking the example of transport sector in the European Union. It also explains how user charges can be developed as a means of raising funds to finance new projects apart from the maintenance of the existing projects, illustrating the cases relating to various charging structures. The article points out that direct charging of the traffic may be the best means of promoting PPPs as this encourages private parties to invest more in the infrastructure projects.

† This is a white paper presented by the Commission of the European Communities. The complete white paper is available at http://europa.eu.int/comm/transport/infr-charging/library/lb98-en.pdf

Source: The Icfai Journal of Infrastructure, December 2005.

Introduction

In order to build economic growth, it is of utmost importance to the European transport sector to decide the suitable user charges for transport sectors so that it can provide new and consistent ways of financing, not only for maintaining existing infrastructure but also for building new infrastructure. Dependence on public financing of transport infrastructure increases the financial burden of government and the situation becomes worse when new infrastructure needs to be created. Increasing congestion and pollution have also created new challenges and the accord has come forward how to sustain the transport sector. On the other hand, users are now more knowledgeable and they can't be charged on differential basis, at least in developed countries. The demand for equity is a basic norm in the European Union. This white paper calls for a community system of user charges, which aims to provide a noncontroversial framework for the same. With this framework, it would be much easier to choose the tariff structure and above all, much easier to defend it.

The key issues discussed in the article are:

- The current existing problems of infrastructure user charges and the need for introducing more practical principles to enforce the same.
- Community wide principles for user charges are discussed. It has also discussed their implications in relation to the problems;
- A plan for the implementation of such principles in all modes is outlined;
- The implications for the proposed charging regime are examined.

Cases

In order to build up transport sector efficiently and competitively, it is very important to balance between fixed costs and variable costs. Both these costs are added in the user charges. In case of less user charges, the operators have to bear the losses, which make the whole transport system uncompetitive and unattractive enough to attract private investment. Sometimes, the charges levied to different Member States are not same and do not reflect the balance between the cost and modes of transport. This creates the problem of distortion of competition in road, port, rail freight, etc.

Table 1: Fuel Excise Duties in the EU, Across Modes, January 1997, ECU

Mode	Leaded Petrol Kiloliters (kl)	Unleaded Petrol kl	Diesel kl	LPG/tonnes	CNG/ Methane tonnes
Motor fuel, lowest	396	349	252	0	0
Motor fuel highest	617	576	501	776	776
Aviation fuel	0 for international flights				
Rail (mineral oil)	Varies across Member States*				
Shipping	0	0	0	0	0
Inland waterways	0 on the Rhine (where over 70% of European traffic takes place)				

* European Countries.

Source: DGXXI.

Case 1: Different Charging Structures

The Tables 1 and 2 show the differential fuel excise duties, which were charged in 1997 and 1998. It has been found that only one Member State levies registration taxes on heavy goods vehicles, five Member States levy road tolls, six others use a different scheme for heavy commercial vehicles, one State applies a different form of user charge and three others do not charge for road use at all. All Member States levy annual vehicle taxes, but these vary up to 3000 ECU. On the other hand, diesel fuel excise duties vary by as much as 330 ECU per 1000 litres. This has created the scenario, where the owners are helpless to choose alternative routes, where ownership taxes, fuel taxes and routes where road tolls are lowest. This called forth the issue of uncompetitive and unhealthy situation in transport sector.

- In the case of railways, there are two types of tariffs i.e., multi-part tariffs and social marginal cost-based. This complexity makes the system administratively difficult and discourages competition. In case of railways, the administrative cost is also more than other transport modes and thus creates unnecessary differential charges in transport sector.
- In case of ports, there are certain heavily subsidized ports, which charge lesser tariffs and make easier maritime access for

Table 2: Excise Duties on Diesel Fuel, as of January 1998, ECU

Member State	10001
EC Minimum	245
Lowest tax rate	248
Highest tax rate	585
Difference	333

international trade. Less traffic in a port also creates more congestion in these ports and other connecting roadways.

Case 2: Arranging Costs for New Infrastructure

The article points out that if we want to promote PPP, the direct charging of the traffic is the best solution. This direct charging encourages private parties to invest more. Even today, 10% of road infrastructure costs and less than 30% of rail infrastructure costs are obtained from direct charges. However, there is a timely need to harmonize the charging frameworks, which is not done even after full liberalization of the road haulage and market opening in inland waterways. These entire inefficient frameworks reduce mobility, economic activity, economic growth, and hampers peripheral areas of the EU.

A Community Approach to Infrastructure Charging

"A Community approach is the approach to address the weak points of above two cases and to find out the favorable approaches which may help to increase the overall efficiency of the provision and thus better use of European transport infrastructure." This aims to take exact user charges for infrastructure usage, which would provide greater efficiency in building and maintaining transport infrastructure.

A sound community based approach formulates following points:

- In order to make the road transport more efficient, the charging approach proposed for commercial vehicles should be same as it is in case of passenger cars. *This should be uniform for each Member State of the European Union.*
- It is also suggested that wherever there are restriction of weight carrying and the maintenance of standards, the user charges must be lesser than the usual charge, as this process reduces the infrastructure damage costs and accident costs.

A Community Approach is thus Expected to

- Improve the overall efficiency of the provision and use of European transport infrastructure,
- Promote fair competition, safeguard the single market and enhance the sustainability of the transport system,

- Safeguard transparent and non-discriminatory schemes from both public and private parties equally, and
- Improve the land use plannings, so that there will be better transport links between different locations.

The paper therefore has thus provided a phased approach to implement the community charging approach (see the Box):

Phases	Approaches
Phase I: 1998-2000	• Methods to estimate marginal costs including external costs have to be developed, proposed to set up a Committee of Governments experts on charging for the use of infrastructure. • Formulated-cost based charges to develop future infrastructure. • The modification of the existing directive on heavy goods vehicle charges to be permitted.
Phase II: 2001-2004	• Charges should be set at total social marginal costs (marginal infrastructure and external costs). • Committee should begin reviewing. • Charging practices with potentially significant cross border impacts. • Infrastructure should lead to a higher degree of cost recovery directly from users. It must levy supplementary charges. • Restructuring of the existing tax and charges structure in the transport sector.
Phase III: 2004 onwards	• Community wide charges for externalities should also be reviewed which would alleviate pressure on Member States to reduce local charges. • Marginal social cost charging implemented.

Implementation, Priority Actions and Modal Implications

Priority actions during the first two phases of the implementation process were as follows:

Development of consistent costing and accounting practices: This is possible by the proper coordination of the work between the Commission and the Member

States. To implement this practice successfully, it was recommended that the Committee of Government experts on charging for the use of transport should begin to work effectively. It was also suggested that following purposes must be identified:

- Development of Community guidelines on methods to estimate the marginal costs of transport.
- Development of practices to promote transparency of accounts and develop "transport accounts" at Member State level.
- Review charging practices.
- Advisory guidelines on statistical and research needs and priorities.
- Appointment of Independent experts and representatives from relevant organizations.

The implementation issues were specific to various modes of transport sectors.

For Roads

In the first phase, it was recommended:

- To take the user charges based on the cost of infrastructure and congestion costs.
- To develop common accounting and costing methodologies.
- Also to develop a proposal for the environmental classification of Heavy Goods Vehicles to facilitate the development of charges.
- To encourage Member States to develop urban road pricing schemes, and
- To deal with the external costs, including congestion costs.

In the second phase, it was decided that distance related charges should be extended to include external costs in addition to infrastructure costs. Such charges would be implemented to new road concessions, which will allow cost recovery.

In the third phase, it is decided that marginal-cost based charges for Heavy Goods Vehicles (HGVs) and commercial passenger transport should replace existing charging schemes. It should be based on the basis of a variety of instruments such as including tolls and user charges. The white paper has listed out following action points to be taken in this regard.

- Communication on interoperable electronic fee collection systems in Europe.
- Proposal on electronic fee collection convergence and standards.
- Further develop a proposal on charging for HGVs and commercial passenger transport.
- Set up groups of urban and regional authorities seriously considering implementation of road pricing.
- Set up an advisory group to develop a best practice on motor liability insurance schemes and internalization of road traffic accident risks.
- Revision of regulation 1107/70 on State aid in inland transport.

For Railways

The figures (Table 3: Indicative Railway Charges in Various Member States (ECU, 1997) show the annual charges and distance charges. It shows how there was a huge difference of charges between two member countries. Therefore, it was suggested to implement action points in phases.

- In Phase I: It was recommended that the charges should be based on actual cost of each journey. It may be based on marginal costs and addition charges may be taken for new infrastructure. It should be based on actual cost of each journey.
- In Phase II: As per the paper, it was suggested that "railway undertakings should pay differing amounts for different routes and times to reflect the scarcity of capacity and to ensure that allocation is more efficient."
- In phase III, allocation of rail infrastructure capacity would be given a priority.

Table 3: Indicative Railway Charges in Various Member States (ECU, 1997)				
Country	Annual Charge	Distance Charge	Weight Charge	Cost Coverage
Austria	9,700-18,900/km	0.73/train km	0.001/tkm	26%
Belgium		•		
Denmark	200-400/km[1]	2.7-3/train km		20-25%
Finland			0.0015-0.0017/gross tkm	15%
France	38-1,680/km	0.13-15/train km[2]		
Germany		2.5-12.6/train km[3]		
Sweden	•	0.0027-0.1/train km		
UK	•	•		

[1] From 1999; [2] Varying with time of travel; [3] Varying with route.
(In remaining Member States, railway infrastructure charges are not yet developed.)
Source: NERA 1998.

For Inland Waterways

The paper recommends that there should be a common accounting and costing methodology if one wants exactly how to determine the cost of infrastructure. As seen from Table 4, the marginal cost of inland navigation was very low in the year 1998 and it needs the reform of inland waterway navigation charges. The Table given at the end shows the action points and the implementation done in this regard.

Table 4: Inland Waterway Costs and Cost Recovery, 1998			
Country	Type of Charge	Recovery of Costs	Note
Belgium	Variable[1]	7.5% of investment	It should be borne in mind that only 20% of the use of inland water ways is thought to be attributable to navigation
France	Variable	10% of receipts	
Germany	Variable for 20% of traffic	13% of running costs	
UK	Variable	8.75% of maintenance costs	
Finland	Variable	21% of maintenance and development costs	

[1] Variable charges tend to change according to weight, distance, boat type, type of travel.
Source: DGVII Questionnaire.

This paper illustrates how the EU has been successful in implementing the charges used in a phased manner to improve the transport infrastructure. The paper is the long-term vision of the policy makers of Commission of the European Communities, in which it has been successful. One thing is clear that we can't impose user charges in one goal and must implement the policy in phases. Another important aspect is how to communicate the policy better, rather than just imposing the heavy tax. The third phase is yet to be completed but the future is bright, as phases I and II illustrate the success stories.

In case of India and other developing countries, it may be an eye-opener. It shows the ways to Indian policy makers how to implement policy and to generate the user charges. The circumstances are of course different, but the implementation methodology could essentially be the same. The model may be adopted both for maintaining the existing infrastructure and building new infrastructure. The EU had started this process in 1998 itself, and the actual results have been seen in recent years only. But there are still many aspects which the EU has to address. Countries like India and other developing countries can adopt the same model, against any political and economic opposition. Yet this is being gradually done. The summary of the report has been tabulated in the next two pages, which provides the past, current and future status of implementation.

(Deepak Kumar, Former Associate Consultant, The Icfai University Press, Hyderabad. He can be reached at bornwaldeepak_11@rediffmail.com).

Summary: Community Rules (and Actions) on Infrastructure Charging in Transport

	First (Current) Stage (1998-2000): Define and Establish Detailed Charging Approach	Second Stage: Consolidate Consistent Charging Basis for Road, Rail, Airports and Ports	Third Stage: Complete Transition. All Modes of Transport Subject to the Same Charging Principles
Air traffic services	Current charges are (roughly) cost based and use related. • Communication on air transport and environment. • Communication on air transport market. • Follow up to the study on taxation of aviation fuel. • Analyze possibilities to link en route charges to pollution levels rather than develop a separate scheme for the purpose. • Green Paper on Financing of air traffic management infrastructure.	Charging directive allowing charges for infr. Costs and externalities (although external costs also proxied by airport charges).	Update
Airports	Infrastructure charging Directive making charges cost related. • Adoption of Council Directive on airport charges. • Communication on air transport and environment. • Communication on air transport market. • Communication on airport capacity and airport cost developments in the EU (inc. policy options to relieve congestion).	Charging for external costs becomes mandatory (e.g., Swedish landing charges).	Update

Contd...

Contd...

Maritime shipping	• Examination of options for reducing fuel emissions.	• Improve international standards. • Community instrument to implement standards.	Update
Ports and maritime infrastructure	• Inventory of public funding and charging practices in ports.	Infrastructure charging Directive, making charges cost related, with marginal costs related to both Infrastructure and external costs. • Implement port infrastructure charging directive.	Update
State Aid	Clarify and update State aid rules permitting coordination of inland transport under Article 77. Exemptions, *inter alia*, for compensatory payments for uncovered external costs of competing modes. • Modification of Regulation 1107/70 State aid guidelines. • Voluntary investment co-ordination initiative. • Evaluation of need to clarify State aid guidelines.	Consider extension of structure to all modes of transport. • Develop state aid guidelines for ports and airports.	Update
Energy taxation/VAT	• Taxation should not distort transport decisions or inhibit development of efficient transport charges. Adoption of energy taxation proposal. • Consultation paper, possibly followed by a proposal for a Directive on VAT in transport.	Further harmonization.	Further harmonization.

16

SPEECH

Renewing Australia's Infrastructure*

Addressing the Australian Council for Infrastructure Development, Mr. Lindsay Tanner (Federal Member for Melbourne) discusses the impediments for infrastructure development and funding in Australia, its infrastructure investment climate besides referring to some of the avenues of infrastructure finance in Australia. Planning and funding infrastructure has always been a difficult task, because it relies on forecasting future use, and often involves very large financial commitments. The overall picture of the physical state of Australia's infrastructure is mixed, suggesting that there is no immediate crisis but that there is a fairly urgent needs to act to ensure no future crisis eventuates. Though the emergence of specific purpose vehicles like PPPs has changed infrastructure investment in Australia, the need for government borrowing is still substantial for the recent cycle of fiscal consolidation has reached a point where refusal to borrow for infrastructure investment is economically counter-productive.

* This is a speech by Lindsay Tanner M P to the Australian Council for Infrastructure Development.

Infrastructure is fashionable again. For the past six months or so, media and political attention has focussed on the state of Australia's infrastructure. An often neglected aspect of economic debate is back at centre stage.

Over the past year or two there have been numerous problems around Australia with services usually taken for granted, such as electricity in Queensland and Western Australia and rail services in New South Wales. The inevitable interest these problems have generated has been heightened by recent concerns about the capacity of Australia's transport infrastructure to hand our commodity exports.[1]

If we are to avoid descending into the glib slogans that so often dominate political debate, it is important to examine the issue in some detail. Is there an infrastructure crisis? Have State or Federal Governments neglected our infrastructure in times of prosperity? Do we need major reforms in the way we invest in and manage our nation's infrastructure?

Infrastructure is often divided into economic infrastructure such as transport, energy, communications and water infrastructure, and social infrastructure such as schools and hospitals. This division is a little artificial, as economic infrastructure fulfils profoundly important social functions, just as social infrastructure is crucial to economic well-being. The current debate focuses primarily on economic infrastructure, and whether Australia has neglected necessary investment in that infrastructure in recent years.

Economic infrastructure underpins the entire economic performance of the nation. There is compelling evidence that investment in public infrastructure is linked with productivity growth and economic prosperity.[2]

Governments have long played a direct role in the provision of economic infrastructure, because of its particular attributes, including externalities, natural monopoly, and public good characteristics.[3] In particular, the fact that infrastructure generates benefits for direct users, particular groups of indirect beneficiaries and the community at large often makes purely private provision problematic.[4]

There is no shortage of anecdotal evidence suggesting that Australia's infrastructure is crumbling, but the overall picture is more complex and harder to interpret. Reports by Engineers Australia on Australia's infrastructure (2001)[5] and New South Wales infrastructure (2003)[6] present a mixed picture.

These reports draw attention to particular problems, such as inadequate road and rail infrastructure, but also indicate that in some areas, such as New South Wales electricity generation and distribution, existing infrastructure is adequate.[7] This latter observation is confirmed by the Statement of Opportunities by the National Electricity Market Management Company (NEMMCO) in January 2004, which concluded that Australia has no current problem with electricity generating capacity.[8] In similar vein the Australasian Railway Association states that Queensland has invested heavily in rail recently, and the outcome is high quality infrastructure.[9] Nevertheless, in its report to the Property Council of Australia on urban infrastructure, the Allen Consulting Group concluded that "there is increasing evidence of an emerging infrastructure deficit in Australia".[10] Yet locating and quantifying that deficit is not easy. Particular examples, such as electricity problems in Queensland and Western Australia, rail problems in Sydney, and capacity constraints at the Dalrymple Bay coal terminal, do not necessarily add up to a systemic problem, even though there may be specific crises emerging.

The common thread running through the numerous recent studies is that although Australia does not have a generic infrastructure crisis, we are quickly approaching the point, where if appropriate decisions are not taken, such a crisis will become unavoidable. There are numerous signs of economic infrastructure reaching capacity or approaching the end of its useful life. Australia's stormwater infrastructure will need to be renewed over the next twenty years, and much of it is already too old, inadequately maintained and no longer suitable for its purpose.[11] A number of major ports require deepening.[12] Major rail investment is required to cope with the anticipated increase in freight movements over the next twenty years, particularly upgrading the existing Melbourne-Sydney-Brisbane line and building an inland Melbourne-Brisbane line.[13] The Victorian Infrastructure Planning Council identifies the need to spend between $100 and $300 million upgrading existing dams to the required safety level, and the need to fix major weaknesses in transport infrastructure such as access to the Dynon rail terminals.[14] It also highlights the need for around $300 million investment in the Wimmera-Mallee pipeline project, to replace a one hundred years-old system that loses between 70 and 90 percent of water distributed, through evaporation and leakage.[15] The Howard Government's *Auslink* land transport strategy acknowledges that the current framework for planning and funding is too fragmented and short-term, and unable to cope with the major increase in investment that is now required.[16] Australia is lagging well behind most of the developed world in the rollout of broadband. As at mid-2003 we were 20th in the OECD, well behind comparable nations like the USA and Canada, and based on a very generous definition of broadband which tends to favour Australia.[17] Even where existing infrastructure is working well, the need for upgrading arises periodically, such as additional runways at major airports.

Planning and funding infrastructure is a difficult task, because it relies on forecasting future use, and often involves very large financial commitments.[18] The overall picture of the physical state of Australia's infrastructure is mixed, suggesting that there is no immediate crisis but that there is a fairly urgent need to act to ensure no future crisis eventuates. As the Allen Consulting Group observes, "there is compelling evidence that public infrastructure operational risks … are rising".[19]

There is also some evidence that governments are aware of the emerging threat, and are treating it seriously. Various State Governments have established infrastructure councils and published strategic infrastructure plans in recent years.[20] The Federal Government's *Auslink* strategy is a long overdue attempt to build an integrated approach to investment in land transport in Australia.

The debate on infrastructure investment often revolves around comparisons of total spending over a number of years. As infrastructure investment as a proportion of Gross Domestic Product (GDP), has declined over a long period, such figures are often cited as evidence of inadequate infrastructure spending. The OECD noted recently that total government spending on infrastructure fell from 2.6 percent of GDP for the 1991-97 period to 2.2 percent in 1997-03.[21] Government capital formation as a percentage of GDP has fallen from 7.5 percent to 3.9 percent between 1984 and 2002.[22]

Such figures need to be treated with some caution. Privatisation and Public-Private Partnerships (PPPs) have moved a significant amount of previously public investment in infrastructure into the private sector. The changing structure of the Australian economy, and in particular the increasing dominance of services, has reduced the level of reliance on infrastructure[23], in the same way that oil consumption is now a significantly smaller proportion of GDP than it once was.

There is evidence to suggest that greater efficiency in infrastructure construction and operation has contributed to the proportionate reduction in infrastructure investment. The Productivity Commission estimates that infrastructure sector reforms have increased Australia's GDP by 2.5 percent, or $20 billion over the 1990s.[24] Engineers Australia estimates that construction costs for gas pipelines and related infrastructure declined by 40 percent between 1985 and 2000.[25]

State governments have been accused of stripping dividends out of government business enterprises, thereby denying them the funds required for investment.[26] However, it is reasonable to expect that some maintenance and upgrading costs would be accounted for as pre-profit items and therefore notionally unaffected.[27] Data on dividend income for State Governments in recent years indicates that only New South Wales has increased significantly (from $717 million in 2000-01 to $1,086 million for 2004-05) whereas other States have remained steady or fallen.[28]

Recent Australian Bureau of Statistics data also casts doubt on the claims of infrastructure neglect by State Governments. Figures for gross fixed capital formation, as a percentage of Gross State Product since the early 1990s show New South Wales, Queensland and Western Australia fairly steady over the period, Victoria and South Australia slightly higher after a slump in the mid-90s, and Tasmania slightly higher after a slump around the turn of the century. Equivalent figures for the Commonwealth show a significant decline at the end of the 90s, followed by increased activity which is nonetheless still below typical levels in the early 90s.[29] Much of the decline in direct government investment is in fact accounted for by privatisation and PPPs, and it is difficult to discern unequivocal evidence of neglect by governments, State or Federal.

Similarly, ABS data on government engineering construction activity shows only modest signs of reductions in infrastructure investment. From 1989-90 to 1999-00, this fluctuated between 1.9 percent and 2.2 percent of Gross State Product (GSP) in New South Wales, falling slightly to 1.7 percent by 2003-04. Most States show a similar trend, with a fairly stable pattern of government investment in engineering construction activity, softening in the last four to five years. However, total activity across public and private sectors remained stable, or even increased, over this later period. Western Australian investment peaked in 2002-04. Queensland's, South Australia's and Tasmania's recent activity was higher than throughout the 1990's. These data suggest that the apparent reduction in State Government investment in infrastructure is predominantly a product of privatisation and PPPs, rather than a reduction in actual investment.[30]

Funding for infrastructure investment and operation comes from a variety of sources, including taxation, government debt, user charges, producer levies, and special purpose vehicles like PPPs.[31] Across all forms of economic infrastructure, and all sources of investment capital, it is difficult to obtain an accurate picture of investment trends. It is particularly hard to quantify the level of need for future infrastructure investment, as cost estimates will inevitably be rubbery.

The overall picture, then, for economic infrastructure in Australia is a mixed one. There clearly are major problems, but these are not necessarily generic, and vary from sector to sector. Regardless of whether recent investment has been adequate, there is a need for significant increases in investment, at least in some sectors, to deal with problems of declining capacity and utility.[32] It is by no means clear that any particular government or governments should be blamed for neglecting our economic infrastructure, but all governments need to face up to the major task which now confronts them. Rather than allocating blame for recent mistakes or omissions, we need to focus on the task at hand. That means identifying the obstacles to increased infrastructure investment, and dealing with them.

The most common popular explanation for recent infrastructure problems is the heavy emphasis on reducing government debt in recent years. Indebtedness of Federal and State governments is at an extremely low level. By 2002-03, borrowings for the various States had reached very low, even negligible levels.[33] Australian Government debt is almost the lowest in the OECD.[34]

However, available evidence does not indicate a pattern of shrinking government borrowing coupled with shrinking investment in infrastructure. Between 1996-97 and 2004-05, net debt of State public non-financial corporations has remained relatively stable, according to Parliamentary library analysis of the relevant budget papers.[35]

The primary rationale for government debt as a means of financing infrastructure is intergenerational equity. As future generations enjoy the benefits of infrastructure constructed now, it is appropriate that they contribute to the cost.[36]

Moreover, economic modelling by the Allen Consulting Group indicates that of all the available methods of financing infrastructure, government debt is the most economically beneficial, followed by special purpose vehicles like PPPs[37] Allen Consulting concludes that "the objective of zero debt does not make economic sense", and by restricting infrastructure development in the name of fiscal conservatism, the approach of Australian governments has undermined our future economic potential.[38]

In spite of respected economists making this argument, politicians have studiously avoided advocating government borrowing as an avenue to better infrastructure. Liberal MPs Tony Smith and Greg Hunt recently published an article attacking State Governments for under-investing in infrastructure, arguing that they should either reduce recurrent expenditure or increase private involvement as the solution.[39] The state of State Government balance sheets and scope for increased borrowing was not mentioned.

The use of PPPs for infrastructure financing is now well-entrenched in Australia, particularly in New South Wales and Victoria, although it is much more established in some sectors than others. Rating agency Fitch notes that in spite of some failures, this method of financing is "perhaps more advanced and more successful than in any other country".[40]

A vigorous debate has emerged around the appropriateness of PPPs, which are sometimes portrayed as an expensive mechanism for beautifying government balance sheets. The higher cost of capital involved supposedly reflects the assumption of risk by the private developers, which would previously have been hidden in government finances.[41] However defining and measuring such risk is not easy, and may be complicated by the existence of ancillary anti-competitive measures such as road closures adjacent to a private toll road.[42] State Governments typically employ a Public Sector Comparator mechanism to assess the overall value of a PPP project. [43]

Private investment in infrastructure has long been complicated by the existence of S.51AD and Division 16D of the Income Tax Assessment Act. These provisions prevent private developers from claiming interest deductions on borrowings used to invest in infrastructure where they do not exert sufficient control to be deemed the genuine owners. Originally designed to prevent State Governments circumventing Loan Council restrictions, these provisions make private investment in public infrastructure significantly less attractive. They are intended to protect the Commonwealth from State Governments using the interest deductibility available to private providers (but not State Governments) as an effective subsidy at Commonwealth expense.

Both Labor and Liberal Governments have sought to ameliorate the impact of these provisions, through Infrastructure Bonds and the Infrastructure Borrowing Tax Offset Scheme respectively, by means of a rebate equivalent to interest that would otherwise be deductible[44]. In doing so they have sought to keep control of the amounts involved, by limiting access to the arrangement. Private investors in infrastructure have campaigned for reform of these tax arrangements for many years. The Howard Government has drafted a proposed new Division 250 of the Income Tax Assessment Act to replace the existing legislation on July 1, 2004.[45] Dissatisfaction with the detail of the Government's proposals has led to them being shelved, with further discussions due to occur. The issue therefore remains unresolved. Infrastructure investors have also not benefited from the recently lowered company tax rate as much as others, because they are often consortia with limited access to accumulated tax losses.

Regulation is also becoming a major influence in private investment in infrastructure. The Howard Government has made much of the recent congestion at the Dalrymple Bay coal terminal, blaming the Queensland Government for inadequate capacity. In fact, the barrier to further investment lies in a draft decision by the Queensland competition regulator regarding the regulated rate of return applicable to access arrangements for new terminal capacity. The long-term lessees of the terminal contend that the level required is too low to justify investing. The break up of Epic Energy is alleged to have been triggered by a regulatory decision regarding the company's Dampier-Bunbury gas pipeline.[46] The Victorian Infrastructure Planning Council argues that regulatory arrangements unduly diminish the incentive to invest in baseload electricity capacity.[47]

Competition regulatory issues are prominent in many infrastructure debates because of the widespread move away from monopoly public sector provision. Telecommunications policy is dominated by the complex task of regulating access by competitors to Telstra's fixed line network. The issues involved invariably boil down to an unavoidable tension between investment and competition. Unduly favourable treatment of one may diminish the other. Productivity Commission Chairman Gary Banks has described this new regulatory framework as "experimental", and points out that price increases leading to more investment without excessive returns can be positive.[48] The Productivity Commission has proposed substantial reforms to the national access regime for declared infrastructure, to remove inappropriate disincentives to investment. The Howard Government is yet to respond.[49]

The Productivity Commission's recent review of National Competition Policy focused heavily on infrastructure. It concluded that in spite of improvements arising from competition reforms, "significant impediments to competition and efficiency remain evident in several infrastructure areas." The Commission argues that existing regulatory arrangements may distort investment in sectors such as gas and electricity, and that further structural separation may be required in energy and telecommunications.[50]

Other regulatory issues also affect investment in infrastructure. The absence of a uniform national regulatory regime on issues like safety and communications is often cited as a problem for investment in the rail industry.[51]

Australia has a lengthy history of inappropriate infrastructure investment, driven by short-term political considerations. Although this is perhaps less of a problem than it was in the past, there are still instances of poorly directed investment more designed to build political support than economic development.

The Howard Government's Auslink strategy has commendable features, such as integrating road and rail investment, but it is carefully designed to enable political considerations to prevail in decision-making. The strategy is built around the concept of a National Network and the notion of long-term transport corridor investment strategies, but it does not commit the Federal Government to funding any particular part of the network.[52] The Federal Government has abandoned its obligation to fully fund the National Highway, and all future funding of road and rail will be based on one-off deals with the States.[53] The pork-barrelling and misdirection of scarce investment funds long apparent in the Roads of National Importance program will now dominate Federal involvement in transport infrastructure investment across the board.

Auslink renews funding for Roads to Recovery,[54] a program of regional road funding which has funded roads overwhelmingly in Liberal and National electorates.[55] It also dedicates $400 million over four years for strategic regional investments by local councils[56]. The blatant pork-barrelling nature of this program is indicated by the statement that "the Government will give preference to funding applications that are supported by relevant stakeholders", and the acknowledgment that in some cases benefit-cost ratios will be adjusted "to give greater weight to factors other than economic efficiency".[57]

The Liberal Opposition's commitment at the 2005 Western Australian election to build a canal from the Kimberley region to Perth is a reminder of how easily politics can override rationality in infrastructure investment decisions. Hopefully the outcome of the election will ensure that no future oppositions make such enormous unfunded commitments without any feasibility study or cost-benefit analysis. Political pork-barrelling, including the use of funds which might otherwise have financed infrastructure investment, for programs like the Howard Government's Regional Partnerships, is a significant obstacle to better infrastructure outcomes.

Other difficulties for infrastructure investment include planning regulation, mixed public and private ownership across different jurisdictions, the uncertainty surrounding Australia's approach to climate change, and the need to keep infrastructure operating while it is being upgraded.[58] None of these problems is critical, but they all act to inhibit the process of renewing Australia's economic infrastructure.

The overall picture, therefore, is by no means clear-cut. The available evidence suggests that claims of chronic neglect of infrastructure by governments are exaggerated. There are, nevertheless, serious problems which need to be dealt with. Moreover, although recent investment levels may have been reasonably adequate, there are clear signs that higher levels of investment will be required in the near future. Pursuing the politics of blame may be attractive but the real challenges of improving Australia's infrastructure must be the key priority. Aside from simply spending more money, there are four related initiatives which Federal and State Governments should pursue:

1. Increased government borrowing to help finance the renewal of Australia's infrastructure.
2. Completion of taxation reform to make infrastructure investment more attractive to private investors.
3. Further reform of the national access regime.
4. A national Infrastructure Commission, independent of governments, to scrutinise and report on infrastructure projects and financing.

Australian infrastructure has always been funded by private investors, predominantly though government borrowing.[59] The emergence of specific purpose vehicles like PPPs has changed infrastructure investment, but the need for government borrowing is still substantial. The recent cycle of fiscal consolidation has reached a point where refusal to borrow for infrastructure investment is economically counter-productive. Allen Consulting argues that there is ample room for increased government borrowing without adverse effects on interest rates or AAA credit ratings,[60] stating that "the case for the greater use of government debt is strong".[61] Since the Financial Agreement Act 1994, the Loan Council has played a much lesser role. Individual States can borrow on their own behalf, without Loan Council approval. The Loan Council is now little more than an annual reporting mechanism. If government borrowing for infrastructure investment is to increase, revitalising the Loan Council is one option for ensuring national scrutiny and co-ordination, and minimising the risk of excessive and wasteful borrowing. In particular it is crucial to ensure that borrowing only funds productive investment, not current consumption.

The case for finishing the reform of infrastructure taxation arrangements is very strong. Direct private investment in infrastructure is now a reality, and if we are not to return to the past level of reliance upon government debt, taxation impediments to private investment need to be removed. This may have an impact on Federal Government revenue because of deductions created which are not available to governments, but the equivalent reduction in government debt levels effectively diminishes state government expenditure on interest. The process of reforming S.51AD and Division 16D of the Income Tax Assessment Act has been slow and meandering. It should be completed as soon as possible.

The regulation of access to monopoly infrastructure is complex and challenging, and involves different considerations in different sectors. Nevertheless, the reform agenda set out by the Productivity Commission provides an appropriate starting point for action. In particular, the Commission identifies a number of administrative and process deficiencies in the existing regime, reform of which would not significantly alter the effective balance between the needs of investment and the needs of competition. It also suggests that the existing regime does contain aspects which unduly deter investment. [62]

The most important initiative which should be undertaken is the creation of a national Infrastructure Commission. Australia has been well-served by bodies like the Grants Commission, Australian Competition and Consumer Commission, Reserve Bank, Australian Bureau of Statistics and Productivity Commission. The role of such expert, non-partisan bodies in economic policy is steadily increasing. Although in many cases the ultimate decisions properly remain in the hands of elected governments, such bodies play a vital filtering role. They elevate public debate on economic issues, and provide benchmarks against which the actions and promises of governments can be measured.

At the 2004 Federal election, Labor promised to establish a National Infrastructure Advisory Council to conduct "rigorous analysis on who should build infrastructure, how it should be funded, and who should own it".[63] This proposal is now being embraced by Howard Government backbenchers.[64] The Victorian Infrastructure Planning Council has called for an independent statutory body to assess the quality and performance of Victorian infrastructure and implementation of government strategies.[65]

We should take such proposals one step further, and establish an Infrastructure Commission on the same basis as the ACCC, with joint Federal and State Government control. This Commission would:

- Undertake indicative planning and analysis with respect to Australia's long-term infrastructure needs, such as that conducted by NEMMCO
- Scrutinise the viability and financing arrangements of infrastructure projects
- Establish model regulatory codes for all sectors, to facilitate the emergence of uniform national regulatory approaches
- Monitor the quality and performance of existing infrastructure, and gather data on infrastructure issues.

Increasing government borrowing without appropriate external scrutiny and restraint would be dangerous, as the Western Australian canal proposal indicates. An independent expert body charged with evaluating infrastructure financing proposals would provide a critical safeguard against the excesses of the past. Governments which pursued proposals in spite if the Commission's disapproval, would take a very substantial political risk.

An advisory council would tend to reflect sectoral interests, and therefore may not be seen as truly independent. A statutory commission, properly appointed and run, would add rigour and depth to national debate on infrastructure. It would not be able to instruct governments, but it would exercise a powerful discipline over governments. The blame-shifting and finger-pointing between Federal and State governments which currently characterises our national infrastructure debate would be much harder to sustain.[66]

Australia is at a turning-point on infrastructure, but not for the reasons currently supposed. Serious challenges are looming. Rather than adjudicating a debate about responsibility for emerging deficiencies, we should be preparing to tackle the challenges of the future. There are weaknesses in our recent performance, but they are not egregious. Without serious reform, however, we may face future problems of a much more serious nature.

(Lindsay Tanner M P is Federal Member for Melbourne.)

Endnotes

1 See for example "Rundown rail crisis to last for years" *Australian* November 13, 2004, p.4; "Push to clear freight bottlenecks", *Australian Financial Review* February 15, 2005 p.1; "Miners demand big spend on ports", *Australian Financial Review*, February 22, 2005 p.1

2 Allen Consulting Group: *Funding Urban Public Infrastructure*, (Melbourne, 2003), p.vii et seq. See also Econtech Pty Ltd: *Modelling the Economic Effects of Overcoming Underinvestment in Australian Infrastructure* (Sydney), 2004, p.5

3 Allen Consulting, op.cit., p.5

4 Mundy,W., and Tanner, L: *Building Australia: Governments and Infrastructure* (Canberra, 1997) p.22.

5 Engineers Australia*: 2001 Australian Infrastructure Report Card* (Canberra 2001)

6 Engineers Australia*: 2001 Australian Infrastructure Report Card* (Canberra 2003)

7 ibid. pp.34, 76

8 Econtech, op,cit., p.10.

9 Australasian Railway Association: *Investing for the Future* (Canberra 2004) p.3

10 Allen Consulting op. cit., p.94

11 Engineers Australia (2003), op. cit. pp 71-2

12 Engineers Australia (2001), op.cit., p. 37

13 Econtech , op. cit., p.15

14 Infrastructure Planning Council: *Final Report* (Melbourne 2002) pp 31, 14.

15 ibid, p. 33

16 Department of Transport and Regional Services: *Auslink White Paper* (Canberra, 2004) p. 12.

17 OECD: *Science, Technology and Industry Scoreboard*, (Paris), 2003.

18 Infrastructure Planning Council, op. cit, p.9.

19 Allen Consulting op. cit., p. xiii.

20 Infrastructure Planning Council, op.cit., p.16; Allen Consulting, op. cit., p.22.

21 "Economy needs more reform: OECD", *The Age*, March 4, 2005 p.4.

22 Allen Consulting, op.cit., p. 14. However, figures calculated by the ANZ Bank from ABS data suggest that overall infrastructure investment in the Australian economy has increased strongly after a slump in 2001-02: "The Australian Economy: A delicate point in the business cycle" (ANZ Bank, Melbourne, 2005) p.17.

23 Makin, T: "The Changing Public Private Infrastructure Mix: Economy-Wide Implications", *Australian Journal of Public Administration* vol 62(3), September 2003, pp. 32-39

24 Productivity Commission*: Review of National Competition Policy Reforms Discussion Draft:* (Melbourne 2004) p. xxvii

25 Engineers Australia, 2001, op. cit. p. 83. Although it is also worth noting that technological change is also adding to infrastructure costs, such as the advent of electronic tolling technology.

26 For example, Engineers Australia (2001) contends that in some cases the entire profits of water utilities have been taken as dividends by State Governments: op. cit., p. 45.

27 "It's worth spending time to find facts", *The Australian*, November 13-14, p. 4.

28 Webb, R: *Infrastructure* (Parliamentary Library, Canberra, 2005).

29 ABS State Accounts, Cat. No. 5220.0: National Accounts Cat No 5204.0

30 ABS Cat. No. 8762.0 ABS State Accounts, Cat. No. 5220.0. The ABS definition of engineering construction activity is quite complicated, but seems to be a good proxy for infrastructure investment.

31 Allen Consulting, op. cit., p. viii

32 A recent Boston Consulting Group report to the Business Council of Australia suggests that Australia faces a $90 billion shortfall in investment in road, rail, water and electricity infrastructure over the next twenty years: "Push for infrastructure summit", *Australian Financial Review*, March 7, 2005, p. 1.

33 Webb, op.cit, p.15

34 Allen Consulting, op.cit, p.39

35 Webb, op.cit, p. 3

36 Allen Consulting, op.cit, p. 56

37 ibid, p. x

38 ibid, p. 40

39 "States failure will hit us further down the track" *Australian Financial Review*, March 7, 2005 p. 55

40 Fitch Ratings: *Asia-Pacific 2004. A year of Innovations in Public and Infrastructure Finance* p.4

41 Allen Consulting, op.cit., p. 58

42 ibid, p. 70

43 Infrastructure Planning Council, op-cit, p.21

44 Allen Consulting, op.cit., p. 44

45 Department of Transport and Regional Services: *Auslink White Paper* (Canberra, 2004) p. 27

46 "Regulator denies blame in Epic failure", *Australian*, June 1, 2004, p. 21

47 Infrastructure Planning Council, op. cit., p. 43.

48 Banks, G: "Regulating Australia's Infrastructure: Looking Forward": (Financial Review/ AusCID National Infrastructure Summit, Melbourne 2002) pp.2, 10. See also recent debates regarding the impact of access regulation on investment: "Regulators hinder power spend", *Australian Financial Review*, March 14, 2005, p. 63.

49 Productivity Commission: *Review of the National Access Regime* (Melbourne, 2001) p.xii

50 Productivity Commission, op.cit, pp xxviii, xxxviii, 24, 164, 238 and 292

51 *Auslink*, op. cit., p. 114.; Australasian Railways Association, op.cit., p. 7.

52 *Auslink*, op. cit., pp. 16, 22

53 ibid., p. 63

54 ibid., p. 81

55 "Recovery' scheme is a one-way street," *Australian Financial Review,* March 7, 2005, p. 5.

56 *Auslink*, op. cit., p. 83

57 ibid., pp 84, 98

58 For example, the Australian Rail Track Corporation has indicated that although more is needed, it is unable to do any more track upgrading than is already scheduled because of the need to keep the system operating: Auslink, op. cit., p. 30

59 Mundy and Tanner op. cit., p. 28

60 Allen Consulting, op. cit., pp. 40, 91

61 ibid., p xii

62 Productivity Commission, Review of the National Access Regime, op. cit., p. xxi.

63 Ferguson, M: *Labor's Integrated National Land Transport Plan* (Canberra, 2004)

64 Smith and Hunt op. cit..

65 Infrastructure Planning Council, op. cit., p. 22

66 See Alan Mitchell's perceptive column. "Infrastructure needs review", *Australian Financial Review,* March 9, 2005 p. 62.

17

Funding Innovations for California Infrastructure: Promises and Pitfalls*

Ellen Hanak and Kim Rueben

Sustained, rapid population growth and a variety of fiscal constraints have challenged the ability of California's state and local governments to provide and maintain adequate levels of civil infrastructure. The Governor has proposed a ten-year program to revitalize the state's infrastructure. We examine the current state of infrastructure spending and the extent to which new public and private sources can be mobilized to build for the future. With a focus on two main areas of public infrastructure needs—transportation and water resources—we point out the pitfalls of relying too heavily on additional bond financing or general-source revenues and focus on the potential for strategies that align the benefits of new infrastructure with the costs of provision. By aligning costs and benefits, California can help satisfy its current and future infrastructure needs while protecting the ability of future generations to make their own spending choices.

* Study prepared with a grant from the Keston Institute for Infrastructure, University of Southern California and with financial support from the Public Policy Institute of California. The views expressed herein reflect those of the authors and do not necessarily reflect the views of the staff, officers or Boards of the Keston Institute for Infrastructure, the Public Policy Institute of California, or the Urban Institute. The authors wish to thank David Haskel and Stephen Ciccarella for excellent research assistance and numerous experts in the transportation and water sectors who kindly granted us interviews on infrastructure financing issues. We also thank Len Burman, Sonya Hoo, Richard Little, and Martin Wachs for helpful comments on an earlier draft.

1. Introduction

In his January 2006 State of the State address, California's Governor Schwarzenegger unveiled an ambitious ten-year plan to rebuild the state's infrastructure (Schwarzenegger, 2006). In doing so, he evoked the legacy of his predecessors from the 1950s and 1960s, who oversaw a major public investment program in roads, schools, and water supply to accommodate the post-war population boom. The infrastructure challenges facing California today rival those of that earlier period, often considered a "golden era" of public investment. Although the population growth rate has slowed, the absolute increases are still substantial—on the order of 400,000 to 500,000 new residents per year—and this pace is expected to persist well into this century (Johnson, 2005). Meanwhile, it has become more difficult to build, as Californians have become more ambivalent about the consequences of growth on the environment and the quality of life (Barbour and Lewis, 2005). They have also become more reluctant to tax themselves for public works. In the years since the 1978 passage of Proposition 13, California's legendary property tax revolt, the state's voters have passed additional restrictions on local taxing and fee-raising authority, making California arguably one of the most difficult places in the nation for increasing local public revenues.

The public's reluctance to raise taxes is a consistent message emerging from opinion polls,[1] and it is a message that the state's elected officials have chosen to heed. State infrastructure investments in the late 1990s and early 2000s were largely funded by floating general obligation (GO) bonds (de Alth and Rueben, 2005). Governor Schwarzenegger came into office in late 2003 on a "no new taxes" platform, and his infrastructure plan maintains that promise (Office of the Governor, 2006). The plan relies instead on various forms of debt financing, earmarking of existing revenues, and increased federal contributions. It does call for new user fees, some of which would back new private equity investments in transportation. It also aims to save costs through reforms in transportation project management and contracting.

Many of these proposals are drawn from the toolkit of "innovative financing" that has been gaining popularity with governments nationwide as they aim to stretch the infrastructure dollar. Particularly in the transportation sector, there has been growing interest in the potential for public-private partnerships, new types of user fees, and new debt-financing instruments to enable faster completion of projects, increase cost-effectiveness, and mobilize new capital resources.[2] Such innovations often require changes in legislation and in the way public agencies oversee or operate projects. The successful introduction of new user fees, which can help manage demand growth while generating revenues, can also require changes in public perceptions.

In this paper, we examine the potential for funding innovations to enhance California's ability to meet its civil infrastructure needs. We compare elements of the "innovative finance" toolkit with some of the more traditional taxing instruments available to state and local governments, and we examine the trade-offs between bond and pay-as-you-go financing. This broad perspective is important, because ultimately, all civil infrastructure must be paid for by user fees or taxes. Although various debt-financing tools make it possible to augment today's investment resources, they place a claim on future revenue streams, thereby reducing funds available for future investments as well as future current expenditures.

The analysis focuses on two sectors that have been singled out as particularly suited to innovation—transportation and water. In both cases, user fees have historically been an important source of revenue, in contrast to sectors funded primarily by general taxes, such as public education. Both sectors also present opportunities for increased private sector participation in operations, management, and investment. And both face funding challenges. For transportation, a central issue has been the erosion of the primary user-fee based revenue source—per gallon fuel taxes—through inflation and improved fuel efficiency. For water, the core challenge is to develop appropriate mechanisms to fund programs outside of the traditional purview of utilities, such as flood control and environmental mitigation.

The paper is organized as follows. Section two provides some background on infrastructure financing in California, including spending patterns and sources and the nature of existing funding constraints, both overall and for the two sectors of interest. Sections three and four assess the experience to date with funding innovations in transportation and water, respectively, and highlight the opportunities and potential drawbacks of new approaches. A concluding section summarizes the main findings.

2. Infrastructure Financing in California: Spending, Needs, and Constraints

In 2002, California spent $931 on infrastructure per capita, about the same level as the rest of the country.[3] This figure reflects a recent increase in capital expenditures, which are now comparable to the levels of the 1950s and 1960s. California invests relatively more than the national average in water supply, natural resources, and community development projects and relatively less in highways and roads. Since the late 1970s, California has also been spending substantially less on education facilities, but from 1997 to 2002, this spending rose by 70 percent in real per capita terms.

The Local Role

California's local governments face a number of revenue-raising constraints. Proposition 13, passed in 1978, capped property tax increases at 2 percent per annum for existing homeowners, limited assessments to one percent of assessed value and authorized reassessments only upon resale. It also mandated supermajority (two-thirds) voter approval for the passage of special taxes. In 1986, state voters passed Proposition 62, a statutory law that mandated that a majority of voters within a locality approve any new general local taxes. In 1996, the courts declared Proposition 62 constitutional and applicable to all (charter and non-charter[4]) localities. In that same year, voters passed Proposition 218, a constitutional amendment that mandated majority votes for general taxes and extended Proposition 13's supermajority requirement to local assessments and non-specific fees.[5] California is also one of only eight states with supermajority voter requirements on the passage of local bonds.[6]

Judging by the recent experience with local school bonds, these supermajority hurdles appear to be a significant constraint. After the supermajority threshold on local school bonds was lowered to 55 percent in November 2000, there was a substantial increase in local capital support to K-12 and community college facilities. Between 2001 and 2004, nearly half of the $20 billion raised for K-12 was passed with margins below the two-thirds threshold, as was over three-quarters of the $9.1 billion for community colleges.

The State Role

On a real per capita basis, state spending on infrastructure is also roughly the same in recent years as it was during the "golden era" of the 1950's and 60's, accounting for about 30 percent of the total (in 2003 dollars, $307 in 1965-66 versus $299 in 2002-03).[7] However, the state's spending priorities and revenue sources have shifted, creating pressures on civil infrastructure. In the mid-1960s, transportation accounted for a little over half of total capital expenditures (52%); resources (mainly water) was the next largest slice (24%); and spending on higher education and K-12 facilities constituted only 9 percent each. In the more recent period, spending on K-12 facilities shot up to 69 percent of the total—reflecting not only the recent increase in education spending, but also a longer term shift in state and local responsibilities in this sector after Proposition 13. Transportation spending, meanwhile, dropped to 22 percent, resources to 5 percent and higher education to just 4 percent of state capital expenditures.[8]

The drop in state transportation spending reflects substantial declines in two "pay-as-you-go" funding sources—the state highway account (funded by gas and weight fees) and federal highway trust fund transfers (which declined during the 1970s, with the end of the freeway expansion era). Since the mid-1960s, the state has allocated very little general fund revenue to infrastructure projects. Instead, state capital projects are now largely financed with bonds.

Whereas local GO bonds are tied to specific new revenue streams (for instance, new parcel taxes or property tax rate increases), state GO bonds are repaid with general fund revenues. State GO bonds are relatively easy to pass, requiring only a simple majority approval by the state's voters. Unlike local bonds, moreover, ballot materials for state GO bonds do not include any explicit revenue source.[9] These factors help explain the fact that by 2002-2003, bond funds made up over three-quarters of state capital outlay sources, up from 42 percent in the mid-1960s. A majority of the recent GO bonds were used to finance school facilities ($25.4 billion between 2000 and 2004, of which $4 billion went to higher education), with others going toward natural resources ($5.7 billion for water quality and supply and $2.3 billion for parks and open space) and affordable housing ($2.1 billion). Compared to local bonds, state bonds are relatively easy to pass, requiring a simple majority approval by the state's voters.

Over the next several years, the state's ability to issue large additional volumes of GO bonds has been severely curtailed by its debt service ratio, projected to exceed 6 percent between 2007 and 2011.[10] The high debt service level is partly a result of the substantial GO bond activity for infrastructure noted above. But it also reflects the recent state budget crisis. The state refinanced much of its outstanding debt to avoid current payment obligations, and in 2004 voters authorized $15 billion for Economic Recovery Bonds to pay off short-term debt to balance the state budget.

Although there is no absolute standard for what constitutes "too much" state debt, a 6 percent ratio is a commonly used warning post.[11] High debt ratios can lower a government's bond ratings, leading to higher cost of capital. High debt financing obligations also encumber state revenues, forcing society to make trade-offs with other spending priorities. These factors need to be borne in mind when considering the state's capacity to float the new GO bonds proposed under the Governor's Strategic Growth Plan. Of the $68 billion proposed over the 10-year program, the $25 billion slated to appear on the ballot in 2006 would in all likelihood push the overall debt ratio well above 6 percent.[12] One legislative counterproposal would have lowered the 10-year total to $49 billion but frontloaded it—with $40 billion on the ballot in the first year—putting even greater pressure on the general fund in the short term (Furillo, 2006).

The recent experience in education facilities, finance also gives ground for caution. The boom in school construction projects, made possible by massive increases in state and local bond issues, has contributed to rapid cost inflation, given the limited supply of contractors with the requisite skills (de Alth and Rueben, 2005). As a result, many school districts find themselves facing much higher bills than anticipated. This problem is a consequence of the boom and bust spending cycles commonly associated with bond funding. Alternative funding mechanisms, such as the annual per pupil allocation for facilities proposed by the Legislative Analyst (2001), could provide a more predictable revenue stream.

Transportation: The Broken Wheel?

Among major infrastructure sectors in California, transportation has the least functional financing system.[13] Historically, the primary funding source, introduced in the 1920s, has been a per gallon gas tax—a simple type of user fee that charges vehicles in rough proportionality to their road use. Since 1994, California's state gas tax has stood at $0.18 per gallon, slightly below the national average.[14] Although fuel taxes continue to fund a large share of transportation spending in California and elsewhere in the nation, they have declined considerably in importance since the 1960s as a result of inflation and gains in fuel efficiency (Wachs, 2003a; Puentes and Prince, 2003). In real terms, the California fuel tax per vehicle mile traveled today costs approximately one third of what drivers paid in 1970. Raising the gas tax is politically unpalatable; during the recent spike in fuel prices, some state legislators actually suggested removing it to provide motorists with relief.[15]

The gap has been filled with a variety of other taxes and fees (Wachs, 2003b). Local transportation agencies in California have relied heavily on the introduction of optional sales taxes ranging from 1/4 to 1 percent. These taxes are levied in 20 so-called "self-help" counties. They generate roughly as much revenue as the state gasoline excise tax—about $2.5 billion per year (Crabbe et al., 2005). Some counties have also introduced transportation developer fees for new homes, either to fund specific projects or to generate local matches for general county programs.[16]

Meanwhile, the state has turned to ballot initiatives to draw on general fund revenues. In 1990 and 1996, voters approved GO bonds for rail transit ($3 billion) and seismic upgrades of bridges and highways ($2 billion). In 2002, they approved Proposition 42, which earmarks 80 percent of the 6 percent general sales tax on gas to be spent on transportation. (That revenue, previously allocated to the general fund, was expected to raise about $1.2 billion per year). Over the past few years, most Proposition 42 revenues were borrowed to help close the state's budget gap; the Governor's plan proposes a constitutional amendment to eliminate this possibility in the future.

Relative to the gas tax, these new sources all have drawbacks because they do not create incentives to economize on transportation infrastructure. Only the developer fees are even remotely linked to use of the transportation system, and even they do not create ongoing user incentives to manage demand. Moreover, measures such as Proposition 42, which simply earmark existing general fund revenues for transportation, take funds away from other public programs.[17] County sales taxes are particularly regressive, and the political process for gaining their passage limits flexibility in the use of funding and results in project mixes that are often not the most cost-effective (Taylor, et al., 2001; Wachs, 2003b). Since 1996, these sales taxes have also become more difficult to pass.[18]

On a real per capita basis, California spent as much on transportation in the 1990s as it did in the mid-1960s (roughly $375 for combined capital and current expenditures).[19] Transportation spending actually increased significantly by the early 2000s, reaching $525 per person in 2002. However, the composition of spending has shifted significantly, with considerable sums now going to transit (now over one-third of total transportation spending, versus 10 to 20% in the 1960s), and significantly smaller shares for capital investments (now less than 40%, versus more than 70% in the 1960s).

These shifts in composition may help explain the widely held view that California is not spending enough on transportation. The costs of building new lane miles have risen much faster than inflation, and road maintenance needs have increased with the age of the freeway system (Hanak and Barbour, 2005). Both factors have contributed to a relatively slow pace of highway construction since the mid-1970s, in the face of rapidly growing vehicle use. Meanwhile, transit investments in most urban areas have not yet been matched by significant shifts in ridership. The net result has been increasing congestion on roadways. Rapid increases in goods traffic compound this problem in some Southern California corridors (Haveman and Hummels, 2004).

This state of affairs implies several challenges for transportation finance: (i) raising funds more closely tied to user incentives, to help encourage more efficient use of transportation facilities; (ii) improving the effectiveness of transportation spending; and (iii) finding ways to increase total revenues.

Water Management: Let It (Over)flow?

In contrast to transportation, where state and local agencies share responsibility for an integrated network, many water-related services are primarily the responsibility of distinct local entities, with different degrees of state and federal involvement. Local water utilities secure supplies for their customers and build and operate distribution networks and treatment facilities. Wastewater utilities operate similar networks for the safe disposal of sewage. Flood control and reclamation districts maintain levees and invest in other flood management activities. A growing number of municipal governments are responsible for controlling polluted run-off. The financing challenges vary considerably across these activities, depending on the mechanisms available to local entities and the expectations regarding the state and federal role.

The situation is healthiest for the two biggest ticket items—investments by water and wastewater utilities. In the late 1990s and early 2000s, their combined capital spending was in the range of $4 to $5 billion annually, at the high end of estimated needs.[20] The vast majority of these funds were generated through user fees—monthly bills and connection fees for new homes. Raising utility fees is generally a straightforward process, requiring approval by elected or appointed boards. Moreover, because current fee levels are not especially high as a share of income, there is ample scope for increases to meet new regulatory standards and increasing costs of new water supplies. On average, water and wastewater bills in 2002-03 accounted for 0.8 percent and 0.5 percent of median household incomes, and fewer than ten percent of all communities had combined rates exceeding 2 percent. (The US Environmental Protection Agency considers rates of 4 percent or less to be affordable.)

The picture is quite different for local flood control and run-off programs, charges for which have been interpreted to fall under Proposition 218's strict voter approval requirements (Department of Water Resources, 2005a). No good statewide estimates are available for the costs of run-off management, but there is little doubt that new regulatory programs are straining the coffers of municipal governments. Without new revenue sources, cities will either need to cut back on existing services or fall into noncompliance due to a lack of funds.[21] Although Los Angeles County successfully passed a $500 million storm water bond in late 2004 by popular vote, meeting the high public approval hurdle is not a foregone conclusion in other locations.

For flood control, in which state and federal authorities share responsibilities with local entities, there has been a growing recognition that the current programs are woefully inadequate. Total state and local capital spending in recent years has been in the range of $40 to $55 million.[22] In January 2005, a preliminary assessment by the Department of Water Resources (2005a) put investment needs at three to four times that amount. The Governor's Strategic Growth Plan, coming in the wake of Hurricane Katrina flooding, ups the ante considerably, calling for $6 billion in spending over ten years, with half provided by the federal government, 42 percent by the state, and 8 percent by local agencies. The administration subsequently argued that the state should cover the entire program and seek federal reimbursement subsequently. Part of the justification for substantial state involvement is to maintain the levee system within the Sacramento-San Joaquin Delta, which is the conduit for freshwater exports to Southern California.

Another area with expectations of large state and federal contributions is ecosystem restoration—notably in the Delta and the wider estuary system encompassing the San Pedro and San Francisco Bays. Since 2000, over $1 billion in state bond funds have been made available for such activities under CALFED, a joint federal-state program with environmental and water supply reliability objectives (California Bay Delta Authority, 2005). Meanwhile, relatively few funds were provided by either federal or local sources. Since 2005, the CALFED program has faced a crisis of confidence both in its ability to deliver on its objectives and in its financing plan (Little Hoover Commission, 2005). Similar questions are looming for the proposed restoration of the Salton Sea in Southern California.

Finally, there have been calls for increased state spending on water supply projects.[23] Recent water bonds did provide some support to local water agencies for some types of supply increases—including conservation programs, recycling, desalination, and underground storage. However, many water agencies would like to see state investments in new surface reservoirs, both to augment supplies and increase reliability.

3. Financing Innovations in Transportation

Given the funding constraints facing US transportation agencies more generally, it is perhaps not surprising that some of the greatest push for innovation over the past decade has occurred in this sector. Many reforms have focused on the use of federal dollars, which remain a major component of state and local transportation budgets. Here we provide an overview of changes in federal legislation and assess how well California has fared in the adoption of some key innovations—toll roads and private equity investments, design-build contracting, and debt-financing. The section concludes with a discussion of a potential revenue source for the longer term, mileage-based fees.

The Federal Role

Financing innovations have been a major theme of federal transportation funding legislation since 1991, with the passage of the Intermodal Surface Transportation Efficiency Act (ISTEA). The reforms have been of two broad types (Congressional Budget Office, 1998). The first is a set of cash flow tools to allow more flexibility in the timing of the use of federal funds. The second type of reform was designed to make more investment funds available through leveraging. Tools include "flexible match" (allowing public or private donations to meet state's matching share), "toll investment credits" (allowing states to use anticipated toll revenues towards their matching share), "section 1012 loans" (allowing states to lend their federal aid funds to toll projects), "state infrastructure banks" (allowing states to use federal funds to establish revolving loan funds),[24] and more flexible rules regarding the use of federal aid to repay bond costs. By encouraging states to move from the traditional pay-as-you-go funding of transportation projects toward debt financing of projects capable of generating revenue streams, these tools opened up opportunities for more toll-based projects and for drawing in private investors.

Subsequent transportation legislation has continued in this tradition. In 1998, the Transportation Infrastructure Finance and Innovation Act (TIFIA) authorized the use of federal credit to leverage private co-investment in nationally or regionally significant projects.[25] The most recent transportation funding authorization, SAFETEA-LU (Safe, Accountable, Flexible, Efficient Transportation Equity Act: A Legacy for Users), passed in the summer of 2005, expands opportunities to charge tolls on interstate highways and authorizes a large ($15 billion) volume of tax-exempt private activity bonds to fund public-private partnerships (Legislative Analyst's Office, 2006b; Hedlund and Smith, 2005). It also further relaxes the restrictions on the use of "design-build" contracting—a streamlined bidding process that can speed up implementation and lower costs.

Throughout this reform process, the Federal Highway Administration has served as a clearinghouse for information on funding innovations, including public-private partnerships and experiments in "value pricing"—a term encompassing various forms of mileage-based and congestion-based fees for use of transportation infrastructure.[26]

How has California Done?

California was an early leader in certain areas, with some of the country's first modern toll roads involving private capital and some of the first high-occupancy toll (HOT) lanes and toll roads using congestion pricing. But California has been a laggard in others—notably in the use of design-build contracting and the revolving fund mechanism. And while other states—including Texas, Arizona, Florida, and South Carolina[27]—have continued to expand their efforts to mobilize private capital and introduce user fees to fund new highway capacity, California seems, at least until very recently, to have lost its momentum. Bills authorizing further toll roads and private equity participation stalled in last year's legislative session, as did bills authorizing the use of design-build for transportation projects.[28] The Governor's Strategic Growth Plan places considerable weight on moving forward in both areas; it envisages $2 billion in private equity for toll lanes and HOT lanes, $14 billion in private equity for goods movement and port mitigation, and $0.9 billion dollars in cost savings from the use of design-build.

Toll lanes and private equity participation. California's experiments with toll lanes and the use of public-private partnerships for highway projects have had teething pains, but on balance they demonstrate the potential for this model to expand capacity while generating new funding sources. To date, all of the experiments in capacity expansion have occurred in Southern California. Several projects drew on private equity investments, while others relied on a combination of user fees and public funds. Projects include:

- a section of I-15 in San Diego (publicly funded HOT lanes in median strip with congestion pricing, fees used for road improvements), in operation since 1988, with a planned expansion of "managed lanes";[29]
- a section of SR-91 in Orange County (initial private funding and ownership, HOT lanes in median strip with congestion pricing), in operation since 1995;[30]

- three new toll roads in Orange County (San Joaquin Hills (1996), Foothill (first segment 1993, second segment 1999), and Eastern (1998))—all managed by a Joint Powers Authority and partially funded by user fee-backed revenue bonds;[31]
- a new 11-mile toll road, SR-125, in San Diego County, due to open in 2006 (private equity funding of the toll road segment; local and federal funds for a freeway connector segment);[32]
- the Alameda Corridor, a grade-separated freight rail line to the Ports of Los Angeles and Long Beach (partial funding by user-fee backed revenue bonds), in operation since 2002.[33]
- in addition, seismic retrofitting of several Bay Area toll bridges has been partially funded by toll increases.

Only one of the new projects in which tolls were part of the funding package—the San Joaquin Hills toll road—has run into financial difficulties because of lower-than-anticipated traffic (Weikel, 2005). Although ridership has been strong on the other toll roads, SR-91—initially privately-owned—faced a controversy over the terms of a non-compete clause with the Orange County Transportation Authority (OCTA).[34] Deeming the restrictions on other road construction to be onerous to its congestion relief program, OCTA purchased the road in 2003.[35]

The Alameda Corridor project was also controversial, as it occurred in the midst of rising public concerns over the environmental consequences of rapidly expanding port traffic. There has been some public debate over whether the project is being underutilized, but it has repaid state loans ahead of schedule.[36]

A more general source of debate—and a likely explanation for the legislature's reluctance to authorize more toll road projects in recent years—has been the equity consequences of HOT lanes, which critics have dubbed "Lexus lanes." However, surveys of actual toll roads suggest this may be less of a concern in practice. Ridership studies of SR-91 and I-15, for instance, found that a broad cross-section of the population uses the toll facilities.[37]

In our view, the overall message emerging from California's experiments in this area is a positive one, albeit with caveats. If the project is to be paid for by a toll revenue stream, care must be taken to assess ridership potential. If it is not possible to develop terms for non-compete clauses that allow for other road improvements within a geographic area, private ownership may not be a politically viable option.[38] But in places where the expanded capacity provides options to drivers seeking congestion relief, they appear willing and able to pay the price. In this respect, California's experience has been generally more positive than the experience in some other parts of the country, where toll roads have run into financial difficulties because of low ridership.[39] The extreme congestion on many highway passages in both Southern California and the Bay Area creates targeted opportunities for success.

These same conditions increase the likelihood that user-fee-backed investments in goods movement, such as dedicated goods lanes, can be financially viable in places like the congested Los Angeles-area shipping corridors. Such projects are likely to be extremely controversial unless they provide adequately for pollution mitigation, given the public concerns with pollution generated by the expansion of port activities and goods traffic (Schoch, 2005).

As the example of the Bay Area bridge toll increases demonstrates, tolls can also be used to help fund maintenance on existing capacity. Here, a toll system was already in place, and the program simply involved rate increases. Conversion of existing facilities to tolls may be more difficult politically. A federal pilot program introduced in 1998 authorized states to convert interstate highways to toll roads, but only one state (Virginia) had used the pilot authorization as of 2004 (General Accounting Office, 2004). Analysts from the Reason Foundation have suggested that there is considerable potential for simultaneously improving traffic flows and generating maintenance dollars in California by converting existing, underutilized HOV lanes to HOT lanes (Poole and Orski, 2003). Although this approach might be more contentious than introducing tolls on new capacity, it certainly merits investigation.

Design-build. "Design-build" (DB) refers to a procurement process in which the public agency awards a single, fixed-fee contract for the majority of architectural and engineering services as well as construction of the project.[40] It represents a break with the traditional "design-bid-build" (DBB) process, which separates the design and construction phases, and in which the design phase is sometimes conducted by in-house engineers. "Design-build-operate-maintain" (DBOM) is a variant involving further integration within a single contract; the contractor also undertakes to operate and maintain the facility once built. In both DB and DBOM, the public agency continues to finance and own the project. Variants also exist in which the project is financed and owned by the contracting firm for a specified period (e.g., "design-build-finance-operate" or DBFO). These latter forms fall more strictly into the realm of private-public partnerships.

In recent years, there has been considerable interest in the use of DB and DBOM-type contracts to speed up implementation and reduce costs of transportation projects. The basic idea is that DB can reduce miscommunication, encourage the design team to provide a plan tailored to the strengths of its construction team, and shift responsibility for many cost overruns from the public agency to the contractor, who may have a greater incentive to minimize them. Contracts including operation or maintenance functions also offer the prospect of lowering a project's life-cycle costs.

As of late 2004, 28 states had authorized their Departments of Transportation to engage in design-build, at least on a pilot basis (US Department of Transportation, 2004). California was not among them. The privately financed toll road projects noted above were able to use DB, and transit operators in the state have been authorized to do so since 2000.[41] However, bills authorizing state and regional transportation authorities to use this tool have been stalled in the legislature. The reticence stems not only from parties who might stand to lose from the switch (notably Caltrans engineers, represented by the Professional Engineers in California Government),[42] but also from neutral observers such as the Legislative Analyst's Office (2005, 2006b), which has expressed concerns over public accountability in transportation projects using this bidding method.

The emerging evidence on design-build implementation suggests that although it provides clear advantages in terms of speeding up project delivery, it does not necessarily lower costs.[43] Drawing on a detailed review of experience in five states, Whittington (2005) argues that although California can benefit from the flexibility design-build affords, it should expect to make gains through a "long stretch of learning by trial and error" and should seek productivity gains where they will be greatest, often in smaller projects. Steps to ensure accountability, performance incentives, and staffing continuity are among the measures to facilitate a successful transition.

Signs that California may be moving down the path of design-build in transportation are reflected in the recent passage of a bill authorizing its use for a specific carpool lane project in Southern California (Liu, 2006). The impetus was to speed up the implementation of this half-million-dollar project, so as not to lose earmarked federal matching funds. This time, the engineers' union did not oppose the bill, which contains provisions requiring competitive bidding and various safety inspections and tests to be performed by Caltrans engineers. Passing more general authorizing legislation is a goal of the Governor's Strategic Growth Plan. Such a step should help speed up project delivery, especially if it receives buy-in from Caltrans personnel. There are greater questions over whether the Plan's anticipated cost savings from DB of nearly $1 billion over ten years are realistic.

Debt finance. Many of the tools in the federal reform package encouraged more debt financing, both to leverage new funding sources and to get projects done quicker. California's record has been mixed in the use of these instruments, but it is not clear that a state California's size would always benefit from using them.

Debt financing is a natural method for projects backed by specific user fees, such as tolls, because the project cannot generate the stream of revenues unless it is built. Debt financing is optional for projects funded by general revenues or even earmarked taxes. When there is a choice between pay-as-you-go and debt financing, one key question is whether there are clear advantages to building the project sooner, which debt financing makes possible. If so, the fact that debt financing entails higher interest costs is offset by the earlier availability of funds to build the project.[44] Debt financing may actually be advantageous in periods when interest rates are very low and construction costs are expected to rise significantly. However, debt financing poses drawbacks if it relies on repayment from revenue sources that would have been used for other purposes. Moreover, as California's recent experience with school bonds illustrates, flooding the market with bond-financed projects can, in and of itself, generate cost inflation.

With these considerations in mind, what does the record suggest for California? Most of the toll projects noted above used some form of revenue bond, backed by tolls. Many of California's self-help counties also use revenue bonds to leverage the stream of revenues from the optional sales tax to get projects started more quickly. California has generally used pay-as-you-go financing for projects funded out of general transportation revenue sources. Although it created a State Transportation Infrastructure Bank, it has not actively used this mechanism.[45]

California has made use of some tools authorizing the leveraging of federal dollars. The SR-125 and Alameda Corridor projects drew on TIFIA loan guarantees,[46] and California is one of ten states to make use of "Grant Anticipation Revenue Vehicles (GARVEES)—a provision allowing for bonding against future federal transportation revenues". California's first GARVEE issue, totaling $615 million, was floated in 2004, and will help finance a number of projects in Southern California and the Bay Area.[47]

The Governor's Strategic Growth Plan calls for additional GARVEE bonds of $3.1 billion in the later years of the 10-year program. This tool can provide valuable flexibility in the use of federal funds. The Governor's Strategic Growth Plan also calls for some major departures from the pay-as-you-go financing tradition for the state's share of transportation projects, with $12 billion in GO bonds, backed by general tax revenues, and $14 billion in revenue bonds, backed by future gas tax and weight fees. In our view, there are real questions about the desirability of this type and volume of bonding for state transportation projects, given the implications not only for current levels of debt service (an issue for GO debt), but also for the constraints it imposes on future spending (an issue for both types of debt). Using GO bonds for transportation projects decouples payment from use of the service and makes claims on future streams of general revenues. Bonding against gas tax revenues makes claims on funds that are largely relied on for maintenance expenditures. If there is a considerable excess demand for such projects relative to the steady stream of revenues generated by transportation sources, it would be more appropriate to raise additional revenues.

A final issue in debt finance concerns measures geared to make private sector debt more competitive with public debt, by giving it tax-exempt status. This tax disadvantage is considered a significant hurdle to private investment, conferring an effective interest rate premium on the order of 20 to 40 percent relative to publicly held debt (National Research Council, 2002). One of the new tools, known as a "63-20" corporation (named after its section in the federal tax code), creates a public-private governing structure that can leverage tax-exempt debt (Nossaman et al., 2001). The SR-125 toll road project made use of this structure. SAFETEA-LU provides additional opportunities through tax-exempt private activity bonds, which investors had long sought (Hedlund and Smith, 2005). Although such tools provide clear advantages to the projects themselves, tax exempt financing represents trade-offs from the economy's standpoint. At the federal level, in particular, the question is whether the benefits of facilitating the project outweigh the cost of the corresponding loss of tax revenues.[48] The caps on the total amount of debt that can be issued with these bonds are intended to limit the quantity of forgone tax payments.[49]

The Longer-Term Option: From the Gas Tax to Road-Use Metering?

Although some of the innovations discussed here can improve the efficiency of transportation spending, many were introduced with the primary aim of augmenting the pie in the face of declining fuel tax revenues. New tolls and private equity enable transportation agencies to add capacity at the margin, but they do not resolve the bread-and-butter issue of core funding for transportation.

As we have seen, the sector's main response to declining fuel tax revenues has been to augment the core budget with other taxes and fees. These measures have progressively decoupled investments from the user-fee base upon which transportation finance was founded in the 1920s.[50]

Rather than continuing on this path, some transportation experts see the potential to restore, and indeed improve upon, the core user-fee based finance system by taking advantage of new electronic toll collection technology (ETC). In principle, this technology—increasingly used for collection at bridges, tunnels and toll roads—could be used comprehensively to charge drivers for miles traveled, thereby replacing the gas tax. It can actually improve upon the gas tax, because fees can be varied according to the types of road and the level of congestion, two elements which affect the costs of road use.

ETC makes mileage-based fees possible, because it is both less costly and less cumbersome than traditional tollbooths. The system relies on global positioning system (GPS) receiver, which uses satellite signals to determine location. An onboard set of digital maps, an odometer feed, a rate table for computing distance charges, and some form of wireless communication technology are used to calculate and report billing data.

A comprehensive study of road-use metering recently found that this method is gaining considerable ground, especially in Europe (Sorensen and Taylor, 2005a and 2005b). Austria, Switzerland, and Germany have all launched automated weight-distance truck tolls across their national highway networks, and the United Kingdom is in the process of developing a similar system. In the US, a number of pilot projects and studies are underway. Oregon's Department of Transportation's pilot system of road user fees and congestion tolls, designed to replace the fuel tax, will be completed in the spring of 2007. In Washington State, the Puget Sound Regional Council is testing a network-wide congestion charge system. California's Department of Transportation participated in a multi-state study, conducted by researchers at the University of Iowa, to develop a multi-jurisdictional (state-to-state) mileage fee proposal.

When the aim is to replace the fuel tax, distance-based fees do not raise the same types of equity concerns as regular toll roads. Projects have also been able to alleviate one of the key objections—invasion of privacy—by decoupling the billing function from collection of vehicle-based information on road use. Solutions to another key objection—that flat mileage-based fees do not encourage drivers to use more fuel-efficient vehicles—are possible if fees are adjusted according to vehicle class.

The potential advantages of this type of transportation funding system are considerable—it can align user incentives with investments, enhancing both efficiency (by encouraging reduced road use) and equity (especially compared with sources like sales taxes). Relative to the gas tax, it can also better align the incentives of transportation agencies (who require stable funds to provide new and maintain existing roads) with the environmental goals of reducing fossil fuel use (Wachs and Taylor, 2005). With mileage-based fees, improved fuel efficiency and alternative technologies such as hybrids need not drain the transportation coffers. These many advantages lead us to conclude that California should aim to move towards a core funding system based on road-use charges. The transition is not likely to be easy—as recently as 2004, the state's new head of the Department of Motor Vehicles was widely criticized for making such a suggestion, on both privacy and environmental grounds (Sorenson and Taylor, 2005b). Nor there is a guarantee that the system would yield all of the potential benefits. In particular, there are likely to be political pressures against introducing differentiated vehicle charges that more accurately reflect usage costs, and the same forces that make it difficult to raise the gas tax may prevent a mileage based system from increasing net transportation revenues. Nevertheless, California has the opportunity to make progress while expanding capacity through more limited toll-based projects. As drivers become more familiar with ETC systems and congestion pricing, this should increase the public's overall comfort level with the principle of modern road-use fees.

4. Financing Innovations for Water Management

There are some similarities in the innovation toolkits for transportation and water management, but also some important differences. As in transportation, there has been a push to consider more private sector involvement. Because the water sector has long relied on debt finance, however, there has been no reason to encourage a shift from pay-as-you-go financing. Utilities commonly float revenue bonds to finance their facilities projects, and major statewide investments have also relied on bond funding, backed either by user fees or general tax dollars. Although the Governor's Plan relies heavily on new GO bonds ($9 billion) for its water projects, it also aims to provide the state with a source of pay-as-you-go financing through a new water fee.

As in transportation, some of the core debates in water center on the appropriate role of user fees versus general tax dollars in the investment portfolio. Proposals from various quarters suggest a greater role for user fees and regulations to help limit the need for new investments in water supply and flood control, but these are not always politically palatable.

Private Sector Participation

Because water and wastewater utilities have a straightforward user-fee-based financing mechanism, the push toward a greater private sector role is less about raising new funds than it is about taking advantage of new technologies and benefiting from potential cost efficiencies. A National Research Council (2002) panel on the role of privatization in this sector concluded that private firms could especially help smaller water utilities reap scale economies in various types of operations, including billing, lab work, and facilities management, even when their physical networks are separate.

Private ownership of wastewater utilities is rare in the US, but private firms currently own roughly one-sixth of municipal water utilities in California, comparable to the national percentage. Although some opportunities may exist for additional public utility acquisitions, many of the gains envisaged by private sector involvement could occur without a transfer of ownership, through management and operations contracts and design-build arrangements for specific facilities.

California is home to the country's first private management contract for a wastewater utility (Burlingame, 1972).[51] Since then, numerous utilities in the state have formed partnerships for facilities operations and service contracts with some of the large multinational firms operating in this sector such as Veolia (formerly US Filter) and United Water (an affiliate of Suez), as well as smaller firms (Parsons, Eco Resources).[52] California's regulations have been relatively liberal regarding private participation in this sector—it is among the handful of states allowing DB and DBO within a single contract and authorizing privately-owned utilities to gain access to low-interest loans (National Research Council, 2002). Federal regulatory changes, including a 1997 law lengthening the time permitted for long-term private operating contracts and the introduction of tax-exempt private activity bonds, have facilitated such partnerships (National Research Council, 2002; Johnson et al., 2002; Deane et al, 2005).

In general, these partnerships have been relatively uncontroversial, although this is not always the case. Issues that can raise public concern include employment conditions for utility staff, rate increases (even if they may be necessary), and any other potentially unfavorable changes occurring in the wake of the hand-over.

In Atlanta, for instance, a private operating contract for the municipal water utility generated public outcry when discolored water started coming out of the taps. Afterwards, the city was pressured into canceling the contract.[53]

In recent years, there has also been some interest in private investments in the development of new supply sources. The picture that emerges is quite different from that in transportation, where public partners are increasingly encouraged to provide greater support during the environmental approval phase, given the potentially long and costly delays (see, for instance, James, 2003). Because public water agencies have access to relatively inexpensive capital and can raise rates relatively easily, opportunities for private investment are only likely to occur under risky circumstances, such as projects facing substantial environmental and technical uncertainties. These same conditions mean that success is far from guaranteed.

Several firms with hopes of brokering water transfers in California have left the business,[54] and a privately owned project to sell water stored on flooded islands in the Delta has met with considerable political and legal opposition.[55] Similar problems faced a privately owned groundwater storage project in the Mojave Desert.[56] After numerous fits and starts, it appears that one privately developed groundwater banking project in Madera County has been successful. Here, the developers essentially transferred a ready-to-go project, complete with environmental permits, to a public agency. A similar project is under development in the Antelope Valley, with venture capital backing. The jury is still out on whether a private firm will succeed in its bid to build desalination plants in Carlsbad and Huntington Beach. These deals require the firm to obtain all environmental approvals; the facilities would remain privately owned and operated, with local water agencies' responsibility limited to guaranteed purchases through long-term contracts.[57]

User Fees and Regulatory Incentives

The current debates over the appropriate split between user and taxpayer responsibility reflect California's jumbled history of paying for water investments. Wastewater utilities now rely principally on user fees, but in the decade following the 1972 passage of the Clean Water Act, the federal government heavily subsidized the investments to upgrade treatment facilities. Contracting water agencies pay for the largely urban-oriented State Water Project, whereas the largely agricultural Central Valley Project relies on generous federal subsidies. Since the adoption of the CALFED Record of Decision in 2000, there has been a broad agreement that a "beneficiary pays" principle would apply for future water investments. But water agencies have been inclined to argue that many investments—ranging from water conservation to new surface storage—primarily benefit the environment, rather than their customers, thereby meriting taxpayer support. The distinction between user fees and taxpayer sources is most important for farmers, who account for a relatively small share of the tax base but use roughly 80 percent of the water. The profit margins in most farming activities are not high enough to support the investments in new surface storage that farm groups are advocating.

As in transportation, user fee-based finance has the built-in advantage of encouraging more efficient use of the resource, and recent studies suggest considerable scope for water savings.[58] It would be unfortunate if California were to rely on GO bonds to build new water supply infrastructure over the coming decades, rather than service contracts with users.

In principle, a statewide water fee could provide an incentive-compatible source of stable revenues to fund projects of regional or statewide significance, in the same way that water rates support local projects. However, the Water Resources Investment Fee proposed by the Governor's Plan does not meet this criterion. It would impose a flat monthly charge on each household, business and farm, unrelated either to the current volume of water use or the direct water benefits of future investments. We estimate that farms would only pay roughly 2 percent of the total, even though proposed investments in water supply reliability, such as improved levees or new storage, would benefit agricultural as well as urban users.[59]

By the same token, user incentives can play an important role in flood control. As the Department of Water Resource's (2005a) recent White Paper on Flood Management noted, there are numerous shortcomings with the current set of incentives. Local governments can approve development in flood plains, but they are not legally liable for damage caused to these properties. (Indeed, a recent court ruling held the state liable for flood-related damages caused by the failure of a privately-built levee.) Only a fraction of homeowners who face flood risks are required to hold flood insurance. Flood control and reclamation districts are hamstrung in their ability to raise fees by supermajority vote requirements. Meanwhile, floodplain development continues unabated in the Central Valley.

Without changes in this incentive structure, it is difficult to justify major taxpayer support to fund flood works. The Governor's Plan proposes a constitutional amendment to exempt local flood control agencies from Proposition 218, making it easier for them to raise fees. It also takes a step toward shifting primary liability from the state to the local land use authorities, as recommended by the White Paper.[60] That report also proposed a specific regional fee to help fund flood control in the Central Valley and mandatory flood insurance for homes at risk. As evidenced by the legislative history, such steps are bound to be controversial, precisely because they impose more of the costs of flood management on communities and households making decisions to locate in floodplains.[61]

5. Where can California go from Here?

California faces important decisions about how to provide the infrastructure to meet the needs of a growing population and economy. In planning for the future, it should weigh the costs and benefits of different funding options and consider both the short and long-term implications of new investment strategies. We believe the following criteria should be kept in mind as decisions are made.

(1) *Innovations that can raise funds while aligning the incentives of infrastructure customers with efficient use of the system should be encouraged.*

In some sectors, this means going back to some of the original principles of infrastructure finance. For example, funding transportation through sales tax revenues rather than through user fees is a move in the wrong direction. Although gasoline taxes are imperfect measures, they better align usage and payment than general taxes. Indeed, movement towards alternative, toll-based roads should be encouraged. Similarly, in water provision, using general obligation debt to provide new water supply, rather than revenue bonds paid for with service contracts, decouples cost from use. The State Water Project—a pillar of the "golden era"—was developed on the principle of service contracts.

In other sectors, this means breaking with tradition. In the area of flood control, for instance, the old way of doing business did not properly align incentives with future liabilities, and new laws and policies will be needed to encourage sounder development decisions. Developer fees or other taxes for new development in the Central Valley should take into account the need for flood control, and homeowners in at-risk areas should be required to take on flood insurance.

In general, this strategy implies reserving general funding sources to invest in areas where the benefits are diffuse or where there are clear social goals that make user fees inappropriate, such as public education. Public subsidies may also be warranted for some sectors where the provision of the service generates positive externalities, such as transit and some environmental programs.

(2) *Financing tools matter.*

California needs to assess the proper role for debt financing versus pay-as-you-go activities, recognizing that borrowing ultimately must be paid back. Current proposals fund a large portion of new infrastructure by earmarking existing and future revenues rather than by raising new revenue sources. It is one thing to engage in debt financing when there is a new revenue stream such as a toll to pay for it; it is another to expect to pay for increased spending with existing and future revenue streams. In determining how much debt financing is desirable, it is important to acknowledge the explicit tradeoffs between future repayments and other spending priorities, recognizing that there is no free lunch.

These considerations favor the adoption of an infrastructure plan that relies on new funds, tied where possible to the services provided. We do not believe that the long-term earmarking of gasoline revenues, the bulk of which now provide maintenance, is prudent. The state should especially be concerned with any large investment programs that might lead to increases in the cost of providing new capacity.

(3) *Fee-raising authority should be aligned with the regulatory responsibilities of local agencies.*

When local governments are required to provide services, for example the cleanup of non-point source pollution or flood control, they need to be able to raise fees to provide for this service, even in cases where benefits are not directly tied to the fees incurred. This might entail changing limitations introduced by Proposition 218.

(4) *Responsibilities and costs should be tied to those making planning decisions.*

At present, the state faces liability for flood control, yet local governments make the land-use decisions putting residents and businesses at risk. Legislative or constitutional changes that shift the primary liability to local governments and that require full disclosure of flood risks could help to rectify this imbalance.

(5) *There is a role for increased public-private collaboration, but private projects won't replace government planning and action.*

Private equity financing has potential at the margin, but is not a widespread solution, except perhaps for investments in dedicated goods movement. The opportunities to leverage projects using private resources are greatest when the benefits can be used to repay the costs and the return on investment is well defined.

Similarly, there is room for more flexible contracting arrangements with private entities using design-build or design-build-operate contracts. These contracting agreements can help the public sector take advantage of new technology. They also can help coordinate incentives in contracts and may lead to cost savings and limit contract overruns. Even if these cost savings do not materialize, they can speed up job completion. However, these relationships are relatively untried in California in the key area of transportation. To be successful, they need to be integrated into the Caltrans system and get the support of current employees.

Finally, while increasing the role of the private sector in providing for future infrastructure, it will be important to understand the contracting risk/return tradeoff and who is ultimately liable to pay for unsuccessful projects.

There may be a silver lining in California infrastructure funding politics. If the public is averse to raising general taxes, this can open up opportunities for more use of specific fees, where people can see the direct benefits of the services they are paying for. At the same time, this movement toward fees for service can improve the incentive structure. Explaining the need for fees or increased revenues to pay for services offers a different path than relying on statewide GO bonds.

In contrast to local bond issues, statewide GO bond proposals typically involve little, if any, discussion of the need to pay for additional services, and they inevitably entail regional jockeying to ensure a "share of the pie." This shift could open up more opportunities for regional fees to fund regional projects, more closely tied to the beneficiaries.

(Ellen Hanak, Research Fellow, Public Policy Institute of California; 500 Washington St., San Francisco, CA 94111; hanak@ppic.org

Kim Rueben, Senior Research Associate, Tax Policy Center, Urban Institute, 2100 M Street NW, Washington, DC 20009; krueben@ui.urban.org).

Endnotes

1 Surveys show the public equally divided between increasing taxes to provide more government services and decreasing spending. This impasse has contributed to the state's fiscal troubles and structural deficit in the aftermath of the bursting of the stock-market bubble. The only taxes for which there is broad public support are "vice" taxes (cigarettes and alcohol) and taxes for the wealthy. See Baldassare, 2004a, 2004b, 2005, and 2006.

2 See, for instance, Congressional Budget Office, 1998; US Department of Transportation, 2004; General Accounting Office, 2004.

3 Much of the information covered in this section is from work undertaken as part of the Public Policy Institute of California's *California 2025* project and can be found in de Alth and Rueben, 2005 and Hanak and Barbour, 2005.

4 As compared with "general law" jurisdictions, charter cities and counties have a charter that lays out the rules governing that area. The charter acts almost like a constitution for the local government adopting it. It can only be adopted, amended or repealed by a local majority vote. One advantage of a charter is that it allows a local government to tailor its organization and elective offices, taking into account unique local conditions and needs. Another advantage is that the charter transfers the power to adopt legislation affecting municipal affairs from the state legislature to the local government.

5 An alternative is passage by a simple majority of property owners. For more information on local vote requirements and the effect on local budgets see Rueben and Cerdán, 2003.

6 Missouri and North Dakota also require a two-thirds majority to pass local debt, and Idaho, Iowa, Oklahoma, Washington and West Virginia require a three-fifths vote.

7 For more information on the level and composition of state infrastructure spending from state general and special funds see de Alth and Rueben, 2005, Appendix Table A4.

8 We have included state funds for K-12 capital expenditures in our state capital spending estimates because there is explicit budget information on K-12 transfers for capital vs. current outlays. To the extent that state transfers to other local governments go for capital expenditures, we may be understating the state's role in these areas.

9 Local bond ballot materials include an estimate of how much property taxes are expected to increase over the bond's duration or include a new parcel tax assessment. In contrast, most state bonds are paid for out of future general fund revenues and do not include any explicit revenue source.

10 The debt service ratio is the ratio of anticipated debt payments to general fund revenues for a given year. We are basing our discussion on February 2006 estimates provided by the Legislative Analyst's Office.

11 For a general discussion, see Legislative Analyst's Office, 2006c. California's ability to pay back existing debt could be higher, given higher income levels and the economic health of the state. However, political considerations, including earmarking of general funds revenues and supermajority requirements to raise new taxes, can limit the states ability to take advantage of this capacity.

12 The Governor's plan actually calls for a debt cap at 6 percent, but it projects a lower debt ratio, and it does not include the Economic Recovery Bond debt in the calculations (Office of the Governor, 2006). Technically, the Economic Recovery Bonds are backed by sales tax revenues that would otherwise be part of the general fund.

13 Unless otherwise noted, information presented in this section draws from de Alth and Rueben, 2005 and Hanak and Barbour, 2005.

14 The average total gasoline tax for the 50 states is $0.21 (Hoo and Rueben, 2005).

15 Assembly Speaker Fabian Nuñez put forth a proposal in April 2005 to eliminate the state gasoline tax (http://www.samtrans.org/bodminutes050413.html).

16 Contra Costa, Riverside, San Bernardino, and Santa Clara all have general-purpose transportation developer fees. Orange County has used them to help finance specific toll road projects. According to data from the State Controller's Office, these fees raised roughly $40 million in 2002 and 2003.

17 Although one might argue that the sales tax on gasoline tapped by Proposition 42 does affect user incentives, it is important to recognize that this is simply a general state sales tax applied to most goods and services.

18 In 1996, with the passage of Proposition 218 and the court decisions upholding Proposition 62, sales tax increases imposed for a specific purpose (such as transportation facilities), or by a single-purpose authority (such as a county transportation authority) were determined to be

special taxes requiring approval by two-thirds of the electorate. See http://ceres.ca.gov/planning/financing/chap1.html under "County Sales Tax Legislation".

19 Data in this paragraph are from the Census of Governments, as reported in de Alth and Rueben, 2005, Appendix Table A.1.

20 Hanak and Barbour, 2005. These figures exclude capital spending by private water utilities, which serve roughly one-sixth of the state's population.

21 See Hanak and Barbour, 2005 for some cost estimates.

22 Data for the years 2001 to 2003, drawn from State Controller's Office Reports and Governor's Budgets.

23 See, for instance, Association of California Water Agencies, 2005.

24 These banks were authorized under the National Highway System Act of 1995. See http://www.innovativefinance.org/topics/finance_mechanisms/state_credit/statecredit.asp.

25 See http://tifia.fhwa.dot.gov.

26 See http://www.fhwa.dot.gov/innovativefinance/index.htm; http://www.fhwa.dot.gov/ppp/; http://www.fhwa.dot.gov/policy/vppp.htm. See also www.InnovativeFinance.org, a website sponsored by the American Association of State Highway and Transportation Officials (AASHTO), with additional financial support provided by the Federal Highway Administration (FHWA).

27 See US Department of Transportation, 2004. Other sources describing state actions include General Accounting Office, 2004 and http://www.fhwa.dot.gov/ppp/.

28 In the 2005 session, SB 371, SB 705, and AB 508 each proposed to authorize Caltrans to use design-build. AB 850 would have granted Caltrans the authority to conclude franchise agreements for toll roads and to build and operate its own HOV toll roads.

29 The initial project was for a 2-lane, 8-mile stretch, at a cost of $31.5 million. The toll revenue pays for operating costs, highway enforcement, and improvements in transit service along the I-15 corridor (http://fastrak.sandag.org/fundrev.html). The new "managed lanes" expansion would allow flexible use of HOT lanes in either direction, to adapt to rush hour flows.

30 This 10-mile, four-lane stretch, at a cost of $130 million, was privately funded (US Department of Transportation, 2004).

31 San Joaquin Hills: 15 miles, 6 lanes, $1.1 billion; Foothill: 6.4 miles, 4 lanes, $185 million; Eastern: 24 miles, four lanes, $780 million (US Department of Transportation, 2004 and (http://www.thetollroads.com/home/about_news_common.htm) Cost for Foothill is approximate (total cost minus cost of Eastern).

32 The project includes 9.5 miles operated as toll road, at a cost of $642 million, and 1.5 miles of connector and interchange, at a cost of $132 million, to be operated as a freeway (US Department of Transportation, 2004 and http://www.fhwa.dot.gov/ppp/sr125.htm).

33 This 20-mile stretch cost $2.4 billion (US Department of Transportation, 2004).

34 US Department of Transportation, 2004; Boarnet , DiMento, and Macey, 2002; Boarnet and DiMento, 2004.

35 The County Transportation Authority paid $207 million to purchase the lanes (Gordon et al., 2003).

36 On May 6, 2004, the Alameda Corridor Transportation Authority paid off the balance of a US Department of Transportation loan with interest 28 years early (Federal Highway Administration, 2004).

37 For I-15, a study by SANDAG, the metropolitan transportation authority, found no significant differences in ethnicities or income levels among users (University of California Transportation Center, 2003). A study of SR-91 ridership found similar results (Sullivan, 1998).

38 Indeed, drawing on the experience of the SR-91, possibly a "best-case" option for wholly-owned private franchising, Boarnet and DiMento, 2004 suggest that public-private partnerships are a more viable option than purely private projects.

39 For instance, Virginia's Dulles Greenway toll-road extension and Pocahontas Parkway and South Carolina's Southern Connector (General Accounting Office, 2004; US Department of Transportation, 2004). Performance of the Dulles Greenway extension apparently has improved more recently in response to housing growth in the area.

40 See http://www.fhwa.dot.gov/ppp/options.htm, last consulted on Jan. 8, 2006.

41 The privately funded SR 91 and SR 125 both used design-build, as did the locally funded Eastern and San Joaquin Hills projects. Making use of a loophole in the law authorizing transit operators to use DB, the Orange County Transportation Authority (which is also a transit operator) also used this method to build SR-22. This loophole was closed with SB1130 in 2004.

42 This group opposed DB legislation for transportation in 2005.

43 In a report prepared for the California Design Build Coalition, Tom Warne and Associates, 2005 argue that DB projects cost only 4 percent more than the original bid amount, whereas DBB projects typically cost 5 to 10 percent more. However, a recent review by the US Department of Transportation, 2004 argues that cost comparisons are difficult across projects. Drawing on preliminary findings from an extensive literature review on DB projects, Whittington, 2005 argues that DB can shave roughly 30 percent off delivery schedules, enabling transportation

authorities to temporarily augment their workforce with specialized personnel and more easily manage peak workloads. However, DB can also increase hourly costs of engineering and scope changes and precipitate substantial cost increases for unforeseen problems that the contractor finds unbearable, especially for large projects. Although DB may help access private investment (because investors prefer private engineers and constructors to bear schedule and cost risks), it may also limit the information available for environmental approvals.

44 In economic terms, the net present value of a debt-financed project is the same as that of project financed through pay-as-you-go methods, as long as the interest rate on the debt is equal to the social rate of discount.

45 The program, recently taken over by Caltrans, is only capitalized at $3 million (Federal Highway Administration, 2003-2004). Some smaller states have used this program aggressively. Notably, South Carolina has put most of its state transportation revenues into the fund, in addition to the federal contribution (US Department ofTransportation, 2002).

46 TIFIA loan guarantees were originally slated to support the Bay Bridge retrofit, but the project's funding package was altered when project management changed hands in 2004.

47 See (http://www.treasurer.ca.gov/bonds/garvee.pdf) for a list of all of the GARVEE projects in California.

48 See Congressional Budget Office, 1998 for a discussion of this issue. Individual states may gain if they use these tools more aggressively than other states.

49 Prior to the 1960s, there were very few limits on the use of tax-exempt debt. Limits were introduced in response to increasing use of municipal debt to finance private businesses or as loans for individuals. The federal government's ability to limit private use tax-exempt debt was further strengthened in 1988, when the Supreme Court ruled that federal taxation of municipal debt is constitutional. This ruling made federal tax-exempt status voluntary. Currently there are fairly strict guidelines restricting municipal debt to public uses with a limited amount of private activity debt for specific uses. See Zimmerman,1991and 2005 for a description of the tax-exempt bond market.

50 For a recent discussion of this issue in the nation context for the Transportation Research Board, see Committee for the Study of the Long-Term Viability of Fuel Taxes for Transportation Finance, 2006.

51 National Council for Public-Private Partnerships, n.d.

52 In addition to Burlingame, Veolia's California clients include wastewater utilities in Arvin, Atwater, Diablo Grande, Lathrop, Palm Springs, Petalunam Rialto, Richmond, and the facility of the International Boundary and Water Commission (http://www.veoliawaterna.com). United Water clients include municipal utilities in Avalon, Banning, Burbank, and Western

Riverside and the West Basin Municipal Water District in El Segundo (http://www.unitedwater.com/clients/htm). Parsons has partnered with San Diego's Water and Wastewater Departments (http://www.parsons.com). Eco-Resources, a division of the Southwest Water Company Services Group, operates the wastewater facilities in Corning (National Council for Public-Private Partnerships, n.d.). See Johnson, et al., 2002 and Segal and Moore, 2003 for a general discussion of contracting issues and data on national trends.

53 Segal, 2004 argues that some of the problems experienced by United Water in Atlanta were a result of long-term neglect by the municipal water department, too much focus on cost-cutting by the city, and insufficient communication between the city and United on performance goals.

54 The Western Water Company, a brokerage firm based in Richmond, California, declared bankruptcy in 2005. The Vidler Water Company, which also had hopes of brokering water sales, has been divesting itself of holdings in California groundwater banks.

55 The Delta Wetlands Project, which aimed to store and transfer water from flooded Delta islands, was approved by the State Water Resources Control Board (SWRCB), but met with considerable resistance in San Joaquin County. A judge recently ruled that the SWRCB's permit was invalid, because it did not specify who would be purchasing the water (Nichols, 2005).

56 The Cadiz project would have made available stored surplus Colorado River water and native groundwater to the Metropolitan Water District of Southern California (MWDSC) service area. Environmental opposition to the potential effects of groundwater withdrawals and uncertainties over the availability of Colorado River water for storage led MWDSC to drop the project from consideration in 2002 (Kasler, 2003).

57 As of this writing, the environmental impact report (EIR) for the Huntington Beach project had been certified and the project had been approved by the city, but it still awaited approval by the state's Coastal Commission. The EIR in Carlsbad was still under review, and the project faced competition from an alternative proposal for a desalination facility by the San Diego County Water Agency.

58 California Department of Water Resources, 2005b provides estimates of agricultural and urban conservation potential from recent studies. The Pacific Institute, 2005 argues that there is a potential for considerably greater savings.

59 Authors' estimation, using data from the 2004 American Community Survey (households), the 2003 County Business Patterns survey (firms), and the 2002 Agricultural Census (farms) and the proposed monthly fees of $3 per single family household, $10 per multi-family structure, $5 for commercial establishments, $10 for industries, and $10 for farms over 180 acres. Within the urban sector, households would pay the lion's share (roughly 85% of the total).

60 The proposed legislation (SB 1166) would make transferring of primary liability a condition of state support for flood control works.

61 For instance, the proposal to launch a regional flood assessment (AB 1665, introduced in the spring of 2005) has been stalled by stakeholder opposition. Other proposals to increase local government's responsibility (e.g., AB 802, introduced in 2005) and to require flood insurance (AB 1898, introduced in 2006) have also been controversial. See www.leginfo.ca.gov.

References

Association of California Water Agencies, *No Time to Waste: A Blueprint for California Water*, Sacramento, California, May 2005.

Baldassare, Mark, "PPIC Statewide Survey: Special Survey on the California State Budget" Public Policy Institute of California, San Francisco, California, January 2004 (2004a).

Baldassare, Mark, "PPIC Statewide Survey: Special Survey on Californians and the Future," Public Policy Institute of California, San Francisco, California, August 2004 (2004b).

Baldassare, Mark, "PPIC Statewide Survey: Special Survey on the California State Budget" Public Policy Institute of California, San Francisco, California, January 2005.

Baldassare, Mark, "PPIC Statewide Survey: Special Survey on the California State Budget" Public Policy Institute of California, San Francisco, California, January 2006.

Barbour, Elisa and Paul G. Lewis, "California Comes of Age: Governing Institutions, Planning, and Public Investment," in Ellen Hanak and Mark Baldassare, eds., *California 2025: Taking on the Future*, Public Policy Institute of California, San Francisco, California, June 2005.

Boarnet, Marlon G., Joseph F. DiMento, and Gregg P. Macey, *Toll-Highway Finance in California: Lessons from Orange County*, California Policy Research Center of the University of California, Berkeley, California, 2002.

Boarnet, Marlon G. and Joseph F. DiMento, "The Private Sector's Role in Highway Finance: Lessons from SR 91," *Access*, Number 25, Fall 2004.

California Bay Delta Authority, *CALFED Bay-Delta Program Finance Plan*, Sacramento, California, January 2005.

Congressional Budget Office, *Innovative Financing of Highways: An Analysis of Proposals*, Washington, DC, January 1998.

Crabbe, Amber E., Rachel Hiatt, Susan D. Poliwka, and Martin Wachs, "Local Transportation Sales Taxes: California's Experiment in Transportation Finance," *Public Budgeting and Finance*, Fall, 2005, pp. 91–121.

California Department of Water Resources, *Flood Warnings: Responding to California's Flood Crisis*, Sacramento, California, January 2005 (2005a).

California Department of Water Resources, *California Water Plan Update, Bulletin 160-05*, Sacramento, California, December 2005 (2005b).

de Alth, Shelley and Kim Rueben, *Understanding Infrastructure Finance for California*, Occasional Paper, Public Policy Institute of California, San Francisco, California, June 2005.

Deane, Michael, Karen F. Hedlund, and Andrew L. Shea, "Creating Additional Tools in the financial Toolbox: A New Look at Water Private Activity Bonds," *Underground Infrastructure Management*, November-December, 2005.

Federal Highway Administration, "Caltrans Administers Transportation Finance Bank," *Innovative Finance Quarterly*, Vol. 9 (4), Fall 2003/Winter 2004. Available at http://www.fhwa.dot.gov/innovativefinance/ifqwintr93.htm.

Federal Highway Administration, "Landmark Loan for Alameda Corridor Repaid," *Innovative Finance Quarterly*, Vol. 10 (1), March 2004. Available at http://www.fhwa.dot.gov/innovativefinance/ifq101.htm.

Furillo, Andy, "Nunez: No Sign of Bond Deal," *Sacramento Bee*, March 14, 2006.

Gordon, Peter, James E. Moore II, Harry Richardson, and Christopher Williamson, "The Economic Effects of Highway Widening: Tolled Lanes vs. General-Purpose Lanes – Using an Integrated Impact Model," Metrans report #01-14, University of Southern California, Los Angeles, California, June 2003.

Hanak, Ellen and Elisa Barbour, *Sizing Up the Challenge: California's Infrastructure Needs and Trade-Offs*, Occasional Paper, Public Policy Institute of California, San Francisco, California, June 2005.

Haveman, Jon D. and David Hummels, *California's Global Gateways: Trends and Issues*, Public Policy Institute of California, San Francisco, California, 2004.

Hedlund, Karen and Nancy Smith, "'SAFETEA-LU' Promotes Private Investment in Transportation," Nossaman, Gunther, Know and Elliot, LLP, August 1, 2005.

Hoo, Sonya and Kim Rueben, "Gasoline Taxes and Rising Fuel Prices," *Tax Notes*, Tax Policy Center, Urban Institute and Brookings Institution, July 18, 2005.

James, Nicholas, "Private Equity and Debt Poised to Help Build US Transportation Infrastructure," *Public Works Financing*, Vol. 199, December 2003.

Johnson, Hans P., "California's Population in 2025," in Ellen Hanak and Mark Baldassare, eds., *California 2025: Taking on the Future*, Public Policy Institute of California, San Francisco, California, June 2005.

Johnson, Robin A., John Mc Cormally, and Adrian T. Moore, *Long-term Contracting for Water and Wastewater Services*, How-To Guide No. 19, Reason Public Policy Institute, Los Angeles, California, May 2002.

Kasler, Dale, "Cadiz Strikes Back at District: The Would-Be Water Tycoon is suing MWD for Breach of Contract," *Sacramento Bee*, April 9, 2003.

Legislative Analyst's Office, *A New Blueprint for California School Facility Finance*, Sacramento, California, May, 2001.

Legislative Analyst's Office, *Design-Build: An Alternative Construction System*, Sacramento, California, February 3, 2005.

Legislative Analyst's Office, *Overview of the Governor's Budget*, January 12, 2006 (2006a).

Legislative Analyst's Office, *Funding for Transportation: What the New Federal Act Means for California*, Sacramento, California, January 19, 2006 (2006b).

Legislative Analyst's Office, *A Primer: The State's Infrastructure and the Use of Bonds*, Sacramento, California, January 2006 (2006c).

Little Hoover Commission, *Still Imperiled, Still Important: The Little Hoover Commission's Review of the CALFED Bay-Delta Program*, Sacramento, California, November 2005.

Liu, Caitlin, "405 Carpool Lane Bill Speeds Toward Approval," *Los Angeles Times*, January 11, 2006.

National Council for Public-Private Partnerships, "Case Studies: City of Burlingame Wastewater Treatment Facility," http://www.ncppp.org/cases/burlinghame.html,(stet) n.d.; last consulted on December 19, 2005.

National Council for Public-Private Partnerships, "Case Studies: Wastewater Operations, Maintenance and Management Program," http://www.ncppp.org/cases/corning.html, n.d.; last consulted on December 19, 2005.

National Research Council, Committee on the Privatization of Water Services in the United States, *Privatization of Water Services in the United States: An Assessment of Issues and Experiences*, National Academy Press, Washington, DC, 2002.

Nichols, Dana, "Water Board Asking for Court's Support," *San Joaquin Record*, January 19, 2005. Nossaman, Guthner, Know and Elliot, LLP, "The Use of "63-20"

Nonprofit Corporations in Infrastructure Facility Development", Los Angeles, California, May 2001.

Office of the Governor, "Strategic Growth Plan Briefing Packet," Sacramento, California, January 6, 2006.

Pacific Institute, *California Water 2030: An Efficient Vision*, Oakland, California, September 2005.

Poole, Robert W. Jr. and C. Kennet Orski, "HOT Networks: A New Plan for Congestion Relief and Better Transit," Reason Public Policy Institute, Los Angeles, California, 2003.

Puentes, Robert and Ryan Prince, "Fueling Transportation Finance: A Primer on the Gas Tax," The Brookings Institution Series on Transportation Reform, March 2003.

Rueben, Kim and Pedro Cerdán, *Fiscal Effects of Voter Approval Requirements on Local Governments*, Public Policy Institute of California, San Francisco, California, January 2003.

Rueben, Kim and de Alth, Shelley, "Infrastructure Financing in California," in Ellen Hanak and Mark Baldassare, eds., *California 2025: Taking on the Future*, Public Policy Institute of California, San Francisco, California, June 2005.

Schoch, Deborah, "Panel to Target Air Pollution at Southland Ports," *Los Angeles Times*, November 5, 2005.

Schwarzenegger, Arnold, "2006 State of the State Address," Sacramento, California, January 6, 2006 (www.governor.ca.gov/state/govsite).

Segal, Geoffrey F. and Adrian T. Moore, *Frequently Asked Questions About Water/Wastewater Privatization*, Policy Brief No. 26, Reason Public Policy Institute, Los Angeles, California, September 2003.

Segal, Geoffrey F., "Water Privatization: Learning from Atlanta," *Privatization Watch*, Vol. 28, No. 2, Reason Public Policy Institute, Los Angeles, California, 2004.

Sorensen, Paul and Brian Taylor, "Review and Synthesis of Road-Use Metering and Charging Systems," submitted to the Committee for the Study of the Long-Term Viability of Fuel Taxes for Transportation Finance, Transportation Research Board, The National Academies, Washington, DC 2005 (2005a).

Sorensen, Paul and Brian Taylor, "Paying for Roads: New Technology for an Old Dilemma," *Access*, No. 26, Spring 2005 (2005b).

Sullivan, Edward, *Evaluating the Impacts of the SR-91 Variable-Toll Express Lane Facility. Final Report,* Department of Civil and Environmental Engineering, California Polytechnic University at San Luis Obispo, 1998.

Tom Warne and Associates, LLC, *Design-Build Contracting for Highway Projects: A Performance Assessment, A report prepared for the California Design Build Coalition*, May 2005.

Taylor, Brian D., Asha Weinstein, and Martin Wachs, "Reforming Highway Finance: California's Policy Options," in *California Policy Options 2001*, School of Public Policy and Social Research, University of California, Los Angeles, and UCLA Anderson Forecast, 2001.

Committee for the Study of the Long-Term Viability of Fuel Taxes for Transportation Finance, *The Fuel Tax and Alternatives for Transportation Funding*, Special report 285, Transportation Research Board of the National Academies, Washington, DC, January 2006.

United States Department of Transportation, Federal Highway Administration, *State Infrastructure Bank Review*, Washington, DC, February 2002.

United States Department of Transportation, *Report to Congress on Public-Private Partnerships*, Washington, DC, December 2004.

United States General Accounting Office, *Highways and Transit: Private Sector Sponsorship of and Investment in Major Projects Has Been Limited*, GAO-04-419, Washington, DC, March 2004.

University of California Transportation Center, *Intelligent Transportation Systems: A Compendium of Technological Summaries*, Berkeley, California, 2003.

Wachs, Martin, "Improving Efficiency and Equity in Transportation Finance," The Brookings Institution Series on Transportation Reform, April 2003 (2003a).

Wachs, Martin, "Local-Option Transportation Taxes: Devolution as Revolution," State Tax Notes, September 22, 2003 (2003b).

Wachs, Martin and Brian D. Taylor, "White Paper on Transportation Finance," written for the American Automobile Association, September 6, 2005.

Weikel, Dan, "O.C. Tollway May Take the Junk-Bond Route," *Los Angeles Times*, November 3, 2005.

Whittington, Jan, "Design-Build for Transportation," Letter to California Secretary of Business, Transportation and Housing Sunne Wright McPeak, July 7, 2005.

Zimmerman, Dennis, *The Private Use of Tax-Exempt Bonds: Controlling Public Subsidy for Private Activity*, The Urban Institute Press, Washington, DC, 1991.

Zimmerman, Dennis. "Tax-Exempt Bonds," in Joseph J. Cordes, Robert D. Ebel and Jane G. Gravelle, eds., *The Encyclopedia of Taxation and Tax Policy*, The Urban Institute Press, Washington, DC, 2005.

18

RESEARCH SUMMARY

Financing Strategy of the Urban Wastewater Sector in Selected Municipalities of the Sichuan Province in China

Sadhu Ramakrishna

The article describes the steps taken by the OECD (Organization for Economic and Cooperative Development) and the Chinese government for treatment and usage of wastewater in the urban areas of China. It discusses at length the environmental condition of the Sichuan province in China and presents an overview of various financial strategies to improve the wastewater treatment, sewage facilities and water supply networks.

Introduction

The wastewater management in most of Chinese cities was neglected until 1980s. This caused a significant risk to human health and environment. During 1980-1990, it was also found that the newly built wastewater treatment plants were not being used efficiently, and there was a shortage of fund for regular operations and maintenance of these plants. By the early 1990s, the Chinese government realized the importance of improving sewage connections, drainage

Source: The Icfai Journal of Infrastructure, March 2006.

system and wastewater treatment services. Consequently, some selected municipalities were installed with wastewater treatment plants. This marked the change in the government's approach towards environmental protection. Gradually, there was an increase in the number of wastewater treatment plants and the situation began to change. The article here discusses three strategies (mentioned later) to build up urban wasterwater amenities in selected municipalities of the Sichuan province in China.

To improve the quality of environmental infrastructure, the Chinese government collaborated with OECD (Organization for Economic and Cooperative Development) and decided upon implementing the FEASIBLE approach[1] for investment in that sector. The approach was first tested on a small scale in 14 cities in Sichuan province. The Chinese government planned to implement it across all the other states on the basis of its outcome.

Infrastructure Development

There were only 20 wastewater treatment plants in China in 1980. By 2000, this increased to 400 plants and the total treatment capacity of those plants amounted to 40% by 2003. The Chinese government had set a target of treating 45% of the wastewater generated in the Sichuan by 2005. It was decided that cities with a population of above 500,000 should treat 60% of the wastewater effluents. However, the conditions did not improve, in spite of installing a number of treatment plants. Most of the urban population had to face pollution problem due to inefficient use of the wastewater treatment plants. The reason for inefficient use of the plants was lack of proper funds to administer the work, and the condition in the Sichuan province was even worse.

All the 14 cities studied are located in the Yangtzee river basin, which is the source of fresh water for the inhabitants. By 2000, 72% of the population in those cities was connected to water supply and this was expected to reach 84% in 2010 and 91% in 2015. The average water consumption in the area studied was 55-220 liters per capita per day. Revenues of wastewater treatment plants were

1 This approach was developed by the OECD Secretariat and Denmark to meet the needs of the countries undergoing transition to market economies, places particularly strong emphasis on realism and affordability of infrastructure development programs.

linked to water supply fees. In 2000, 65% of the population was connected with proper sewerage systems. But it was observed that by 2010, 71% of the sewerage ditches were to be renovated and equipped with modern pipelines, in order to meet the requirements of wastewater treatment. Table 1 presents an overview of the facilities available in the 14 cities. Until 2000, none of these cities had wastewater treatment plants. All the wastewater was discharged to surface waters without treatment. Of these 14 cities, the construction of wastewater treatment plants had begun in seven cities and was expected to be completed by 2004.

The state government observed the need to invest in the wastewater collection and treatment projects. The government and its project partners determined the targets for developing the wastewater collection and treatment facilities. By 2010, sewerage systems and services would be extended to a population of 4.7 million in 14 municipalities. It was decided that by 2010, seven of the remaining

Table 1: Overview of the Study Area in Sichuan Province

City/County	No. of Inhabitants (Thousands)			Urban Zone (ha)			Connection Rate in 2000 (%)		WWTP under Construction
	2000	2010	2015	2000	2010	2015	Water Supply	Sewerage	
Luzhou City	303	550	702	2,500	3,500	4,258	69%	80%	Yes
Leshan City	390	800	1021	2,200	2,200	2,677	80%	50%	Yes
Meishan City	128	170	217	1,500	1,650	2,007	71%	70%	Yes
Yibin City	356	500	638	2,950	6,195	7,537	58%	40%	Yes
Changing County	42	50	64	335	685	833	61%	50%	–
Gao County	52	100	128	500	1,050	1,277	48%	70%	–
Zigong City	472	600	766	2,400	2,700	3,285	90%	78%	Yes
Fushun County	92	200	255	1,200	1,332	1,621	97%	78%	–
Neijiang City	325	650	830	1,200	2,520	3,066	50%	66%	Yes
Weiyuan County	129	224	286	1,111	1,444	1,757	96%	65%	–
Zizhong County	145	200	255	650	657	800	58%	80%	–
Ziyanh City	162	250	319	1,566	2,336	2,842	70%	75%	Yes
Jianyang City	173	200	255	630	1,330	1,618	71%	60%	–
Linshui County	105	250	319	987	1,984	2,414	88%	58%	–

Source: Data and forecasts provided by the Sichuan expert team and checked by the OECD consultants.

municipalities would be provided with wastewater treatment plants, and the collected wastewater would be treated biologically. Estimates for the wastewater produced and collected (up to the year 2015) were made on the basis of factors like amount of water supplied to households, industry and budgetary organizations, patterns of water usage, amount of rainfall collected by the sewerage system and various other factors. Table 2 provides information pertaining to the status of wastewater production and treatment in 2005 in the area studied.

Table 2: Assessment of Wastewater Production and Treatment in the Study Area in 2005

City/County	Capacity of WWT Plants		Completion Date	Wastewater Collected (m3/y) 2005	Percentage of Wastewater Collected that can be Treated 2005
	l/d	m3/y			
Luzhou City	50,000	18,250	2004	26,650	68%
Leshan City	50,000	18,250	2004	20,454	89%
Meishan City	40,000	14,600	2004	6,202	235%
Yibin City	50,000	18,250	2004	25,963	70%
Changing County	–	–	–	1,591	–
Gao County	–	–	–	3,207	–
Zigong City	50,000	18,250	2004	21,669	84%
Fushun County	–	–	–	5,592	–
Neijiang City	50,000	18,250	2004	17,530	104%
Weiyuan County	–	–	–	8,262	–
Zizhong County	–	–		7,137	–
Ziyanh City	50,000	18,250	2004	11,670	156%
Jianyang City	–	–	–	5,182	–
Linshui County	–	–	–	5,528	–
Total	**340,000**	**124,100**	–	**166,637**	**69%**

Source: Data provided by Sichuan local experts. Estimates conducted by international consultants.

Issues in Financing Wastewater Collection and Treatment

Earlier, the sewerage systems and wastewater treatment plants were operated and maintained by the government. Similarly urban water supply and wastewater utilities relied on government financing. Later there were increasing financing

Figure 1: Present Structure of Sources of Financing Wastewater Infrastructure in 14 Cities in Sichuan Province

(Total for the Years 2000-2004 in Millions Yuans in Constant 2000 Prices)

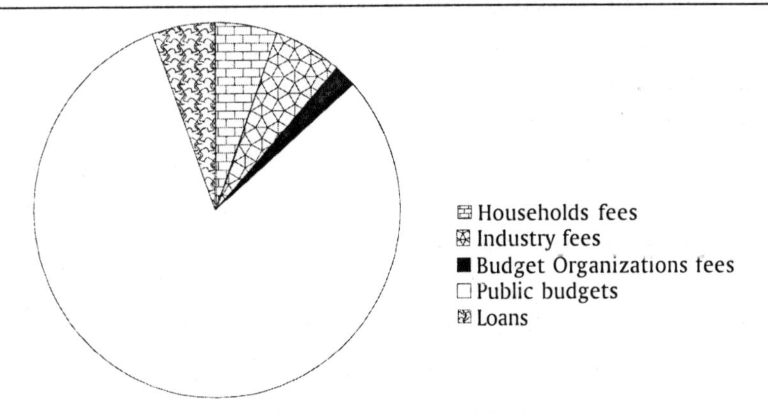

Source: Data provided by municipal governments and estimates made by local experts.

options from foreign government loans and institute financing for the development of urban wastewater infrastructure. But it was observed that collection of user fees was inevitable to enable construction and proper functioning of wastewater treatment plants. Construction of wastewater treatment plants was not the end. Operation and maintenance of those treatment plants was of utmost importance to provide continuous service to the public. The government was under the illusion that financing the investment program for this project would be done through bank loans. But after knowing that loans would not just be sufficient, it was proposed to collect money from public budgets apart from user fees (see Figure 1 to get an idea of the sources of financing wastewater projects in municipalities of Sichuan province selected for the study).

Financing Strategies and Affordability

The Chinese government identified three alternative strategies for financing the wastewater infrastructure in cities of Sichuan Province. These were:

- Taxpayers' pay strategy
- Users' pay strategy
- Creditors' pay strategy

Various sources of financing that constituted the above mentioned strategies were: User charges, public budgets, private financing etc. According to the "Taxpayers' pay strategy", much of the financing for the wastewater infrastructure was dependent on the increase of allocations from public budgets both at the regional and central level. It was assumed that a modest increase in the user fees and decrease in the borrowings would take place. Under "Users' pay strategy", the user fees would go for a steep increase so as to obtain full cost recovery of the infrastructure expenditure. It might also include an increase in allocation of local budget and borrowings. The "Creditors' pay strategy" was based on aggressive and rapid borrowing from both domestic and foreign credit markets in the form of loans or bonds and also an increase in private direct investments. User fees would go up to ensure all debt obligations were met with. Figure 2 represents the increase in wastewater tariffs under various strategies.

Figure 2: Schedules of Increase of Household Wastewater Tariffs in Different Financing Strategies (2000 Yuan/m3)

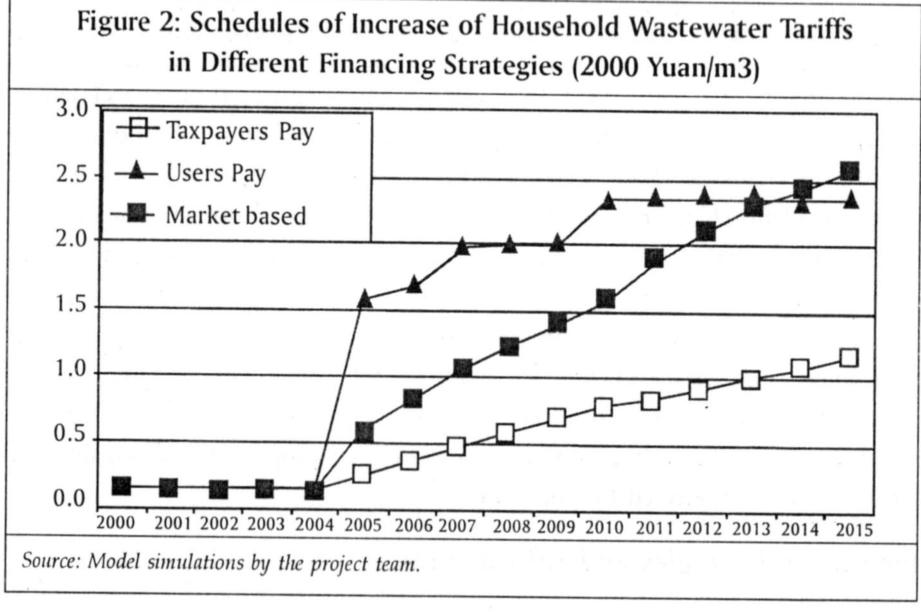

Source: Model simulations by the project team.

Implementing the investment programs in the wastewater sector in China required a proper study of affordability and feasibility of the strategies. The Chinese government authorities and the OECD team experts studied the affordability and feasibility of each of the above mentioned strategies. There were some assumptions for each of those strategies:

- Increase in user fees should result in efficient infrastructure development programs.
- Increase in user fees would have to be accompanied by appropriate measures to protect the poor and vulnerable households from uneven practices.
- Increase in user fees might lead to social and political opposition.
- Social issues if not addressed might result in non-payment of tariffs or excessive poverty.

Conclusion

The article discusses three possible broad strategies to increase financing to the urban wastewater in selected municipalities of the Sichuan province in China. These three strategies are: "Taxpayers' pay", "Users' pay" and "Creditors' pay". These strategies may help the province to meet the capital, maintenance and operational expenditure. OECD estimates that this expenditure would increase by about four to five times by the year 2010. This is because the network of modern sewerage expands in proportion to its population; and the wastewater resulting from the increased population has to be treated biologically. Therefore, a mere dependence on these three strategies is not enough to meet the target, because of some key obstacles as pointed out by OECD:

- "Taxpayers' pay" strategy is not at all feasible since it banks on the increase in expenditures from local budgets which might result in liquidity problems.
- The feasibility and success of "Users' pay" strategy and "Creditors' pay" strategy would depend on a number of issues like implementation of legal and institutional reforms. Both the strategies are restricted due to the limited ability of the poor households to pay, and the constraints of the local budgets.
- Huge borrowings by the wastewater utilities for the implementation of those programs would not be wise since it might end up in a heap of non-performing loans in the sector. This would only contribute to damaging the fiscal position of the government.

After analyzing various strategies, it was found that issues like affordability were likely to occur at some point in the execution process of all the three strategies. So for the above strategies to be both socially and politically feasible, it was important to allocate some social protection budgets (which were financially viable) in order to compensate the poor families and households for the payments they made towards water and sanitation bills.

(Sadhu Ramakrishna, Research Associate, The Icfai University Press.)

INDEX